SKETCHES OF INTRIGUING PEOPLE
and the Curious Events They Suffered
While Living in the Wilderness
of the Northwest Territory

SKETCHES

OF

INTRIGUING PEOPLE

AND THE

CURIOUS EVENTS THEY SUFFERED

WHILE LIVING
IN THE WILDERNESS

OF THE

NORTHWEST TERRITORY.

BY

FRANK E. KURON

TOLEDO, OHIO
KURON PUBLISHING
2020

Kuron Publishing
Copyright © 2020 by Frank E. Kuron

All rights reserved, including the right of reproduction
in whole or in part in any form.

Designed by Frank E. Kuron

Manufactured in the United States of America

ISBN 978-0-578-65635-9

For My Grandchildren
That they may be inspired to be bold and fearless.

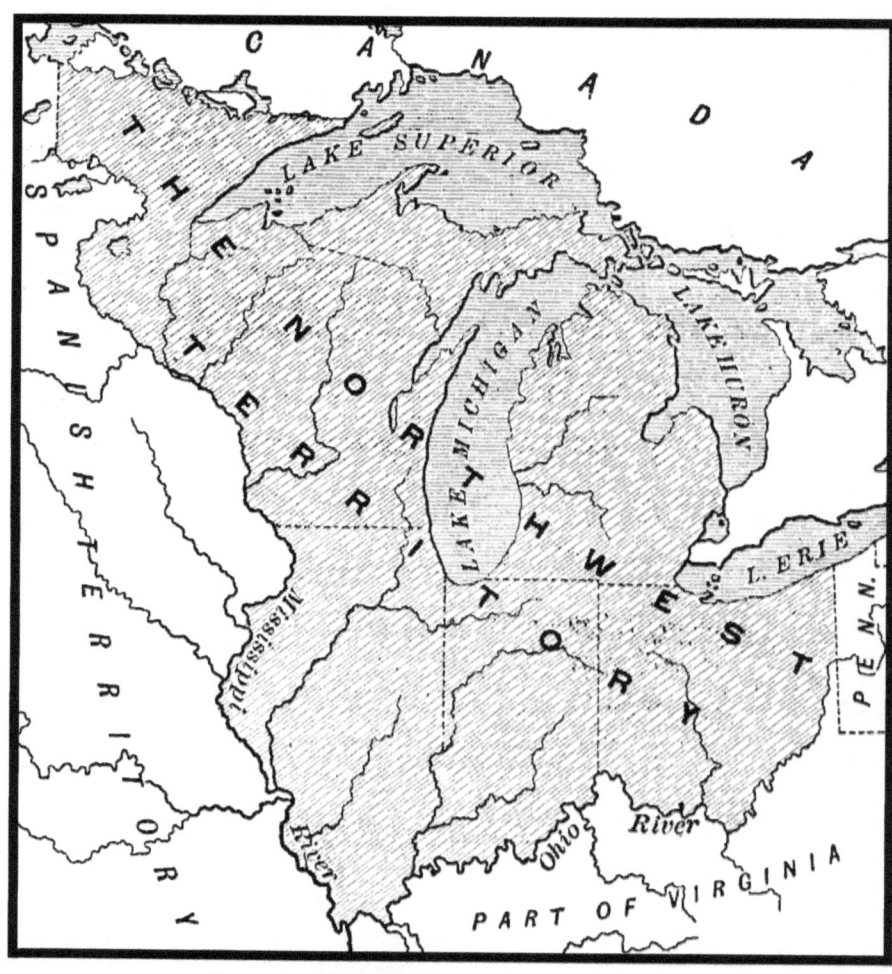

By means of *An Ordinance for the Government of the Territory of the United States, North-west of the River Ohio,* the Northwest Territory was established by the Congress of the Confederation of the United States on July 13, 1787.

This map appeared in *The Household History of the United States and Its People,* by esteemed historian and antiquarian Edward Eggleston in 1888.

CONTENTS.

ILLUSTRATIONS		viii
PREFACE		ix
ACKNOWLEDGEMENTS		xiii
INTRODUCTION		1
SKETCH I	An American in Canada	13
SKETCH II	The Melmore Man	35
SKETCH III	And This Little Piggy Went to War	45
SKETCH IV	The Jersey Boys	51
SKETCH V	Jane the Pious	83
SKETCH VI	O Lard! O Lard!	101
SKETCH VII	Camels That Got Over the Hump	111
SKETCH VIII	Wildcat McKinney	125
SKETCH IX	Oliver Swift	129
SKETCH X	The Brothers Clairvoyant	149
SKETCH XI	The Race to Paris—Harmar's Victory	179
SKETCH XII	The Forgotten Colony of Clark	201
SKETCH XIII	Reserved for Connecticut	223
SKETCH XIV	The Mud Duck	253
SKETCH XV	My Husband Went to War	257
SKETCH XVI	A Lytle Indian Influence	279
SKETCH XVII	Keen Indian Insight	299
ANECDOTES	.... 11, 34, 44, 49, 81, 99, 110, 124, 128, 148, 177, 199, 221, 252, 256, 277, 297, 301	
SKETCH NOTES		303
INDEX		313

ILLUSTRATIONS.

Map (Northwest Territory) vi	Wildcat McKinney Episode 128
Treaty of Paris 3	Fort Wayne (circa 1812) 135
Proclamation of 1763 and Map 6	Toledo Strip Map 142
John Graves Simcoe 18	Sunrise Court Illustration 145
Map (Upper Canada, circa 1812) 23	The Oliver House 147
Isaac Hamblin 26	Tecumseh 152
Henry Proctor 29	The Prophet 153
Raised British Vessel (circa 1813) 32	William Henry Harrison 162
Ezra Brown 37	Darkness at Noon/Nautical Almanac 167
Masonic Meeting House (circa 1820s) 40	New Madrid Earthquake 172
North San Juan, California 43	Treaty of Paris 181
Wild Pig 47	Josiah Harmar 184
John Cleves Symmes 57	Packet Ship (circa 1780s) 193
Pioneer Flatboat 61	Map of Harmar's Defeat 196
Fort Washington 62	George Rogers Clark 205
Centinel of the Northwest Territory 67	Map (Western Frontier circa 1780) 208
Cincinnati (circa 1800) 70	H.Dodge/L.Linn/A.Dodge 219
Map of Ohio Valley (circa 1790s) 75	Map of Connecticut Reserve 225
Exploits of Daniel Boone Comic 78	Map of New London/Groton 228
Jane Allen Trimble 85	Family Emigrating to CT Reserve 232
Allen Trimble 90	John Young 235
Cane Ridge 95	Henry Ellsworth 236
Eliza Jane Trimble Thompson 98	Joseph Badger 249
Map (Salt Licks) 104	American Coot 255
Wild Buffalo 107	Frontier Womens' Chores 261
Old Kettle Furnace 109	Battle of Tippecanoe 268
Daniel Dobbins 113	Map of Fort Detroit 273
Presque Isle Bay 116	Fort Dearborn/Kinzie Mansion 288
Sawpit 119	Fort Dearborn Massacre 293
Camel Application 122	Juliette Gordon Low 296

PREFACE.

In the course of doing research for my first book titled, "Thus Fell Tecumseh," I discovered a good deal of dusty history. By that I mean that it was material that had been lying dormant for decades, sometimes for centuries, upon library shelves, unread. Much of it was relevant to my research into the mystery surrounding Tecumseh's death, but there was so much more. I found diaries, newspaper reports, letters, and all sorts of documentation of people who lived in what was called the Northwest Territory. Fascinating people. Some are souls that few have ever heard of, or if they did, only knew of them for one historic footnote to their lives. In the most unexpected places, I found intrigue, suspense, and resolve of the human spirit. I gained a new appreciation for these distant ancestors known as frontiersmen, and my hope is that you'll feel the same.

With the utmost respect, I would like to make an observation. The frontier did not belong exclusively to the likes of Daniel Boone, Simon Kenton, Anthony Wayne, or even Tecumseh; as profound and impactful as their lives were. The fact is that many, many ordinary people who settled this region proved to be extra-ordinary at certain times in their lives.

The U.S. Census Bureau recently reported that the average American will move a dozen times in his lifetime. That alone is incredible, but these moves are generally from one community to another. What the people of the Northwest Territory did was move from a community to a wilderness. A wilderness that today remains only in a few scarce pockets across the Midwest.

They were not sent over the Appalachians and into these lands by force; they chose to go there. Skilled or not in construction, they built cabins for themselves in the middle of nowhere, often with only their own two hands and an axe or a saw. They had to defend themselves from wild animals, Indians, and sometimes their devious neighbors. Can you imagine what was it like to get to the frontier by sailing the river systems or by hiking over the mountains? What was the daily, nitty-gritty frontier life like? Was it lonely? What happened if you got sick or injured? Was church-going a priority? What was the Native American perspective on the influx of white men? Did any of them befriend the Americans? Were frontier families really that emotionally and morally different from us ? Was there anything to laugh about out there? If these are the types of questions that run through your mind when thinking about early American history, then maybe the stories ahead will at least in part help to answer them.

Much of this book is in the form of quotes. Many are lengthy. This is deliberate, as I hope once again to present these stories in a broad context. This is not a book of "sound bites" as the world of journalism subjects us to in each day's news. No one-sentence snippet will be used to summarize and often skew the story. This is a compilation of details because that is where the nuances of these people's lives are found.

People spoke differently back then. Some were uneducated and hard to understand, but others had a wit and romanticism in their words. Either way, it is fascinating to hear centuries old stories in the first person. This is why most of the quotes used in this book are from primary sources or at least from those in closest contact to the individual or situation discussed.

As a matter of practicality, it should be noted that an ellipsis (…) has been added to any text where a word was indiscernible or where a portion of the original quote was omitted at the author's discretion. All excerpts are presented exactly as found in the original documents with only minor punctuation or reference points added, and then so in brackets [ ], to aid in readability. Parenthesis, ( ), and underlines, (__) are maintained if they were used in the original document. Any misspellings, odd capitalizations, abbreviations of words, or terms which have since lost their meaning or have been deemed inappropriate by current cultural standards, have been recorded here as they appeared in the originals. Punctuation, proper grammar, and political correctness were often in short supply on the frontier.

It is my purpose in writing this book to provide the reader with a glimpse into the reality of another time that was in some ways slow and simple, yet in so many other ways was severely treacherous and unforgiving. The pages that follow will spotlight the qualities of people — bravery, cowardice, heroism, philosophy, and even humor — through the telling of their stories. These are not meant to be definitive biographies. They focus on periods of these people's lives that proved to be intriguing, insightful, and often heroic. Even a few animals played a part in the history of the frontier and their tales will be told as well.

Heroic people do extraordinary things everyday. Through modern technologies we see and hear about them as we scroll through our daily news feeds. That is a perk of our twenty-first century world. But time shouldn't erase good deeds no matter how long ago they may have been done; and intrigue can grip a reader centuries after the fact. Therefore it is my hope through this book to resurrect just a few of the profound people and the curious turns their lives took while they lived in and around the Northwest Territory of the United States of America. ♦

THE AUTHOR

ACKNOWLEDGEMENTS.

Writing a book is not a one-man endeavor. Left exclusively to one's own thinking in an enterprise such as this can lead to a less-than-desired outcome. Perspective is essential. I often found myself so deep in the details of a story, that I lost sight of the big picture. That is why I welcomed another pair of eyes to repeatedly review my progress. It's a wise practice for any author. I have several people to thank for the use of their eyes; as well as their knowledge, insights, and encouragement.

Of course I thank God, Jesus Christ, who I truly believe steered my thoughts and research in the directions He wanted this book to go. Only the reader can judge if I made proper use of the talents He has allotted me.

The scrutiny which most profoundly influenced this work and gave it its proper tone and direction came from my ever-encouraging wife, Debra. If not for her keen sense of style and her own knowledge of history I would not have been able to complete this project in a professional manner.

Several other family members and friends provided valuable insights as well. Topping the list is my daughter and son-in-law, Sara and Doug Wegrzyn; and my son and daughter-in-law, Matthew and Sadie Kuron. Their willingness to give me honest opinions along the way have made this a better read for everyone.

I've had a lifelong bond with the family of my true friend and fellow author, John Curtin, who has always been supportive of my efforts. Because of John, brother Bill Curtin, late mother June Curtin, and relative Joyce Tuckerman Zeigler; the story of Ezra Brown was able to be told within these pages. They are all descendents of the intrepid Ezra.

Judith Justus, historian extraordinaire, author, and mentor, kept me on my writing toes with constant votes of confidence. Friend, Roger Throckmorton, known to the Shawnee as *Plain Talker*, has provided invaluable insights into the Native American culture with refreshing frankness and humor.

An extra special note of thanks goes out to two brothers, Bob Hamlin and Vance Hamlin, who have become like family to me. These men have performed extensive, lifelong, genealogical research into the heritage of the Hamlin family and as a result the story of their ancestor Isaac Hamblin is featured in this book for the public at large to appreciate as much as I do.

In 1990, with her husband James, Pat Appold saved the grandest hotel in Toledo, Ohio, circa 1859, from demolition. Known as The Oliver House then and now, it was built by William Oliver. Because of her love of history and willingness to share her insights and resources, Pat allowed me to add some extra splashes of color to the canvas depicting William Oliver's life.

Further understanding of life in early America has come to me through the innumerable conversations I've had over the years with fellow history enthusiasts. For this book, special thanks go out to Julia Wiley, current president of the Fallen Timbers Battlefield Preservation Commission; Xavier Allen, the Regimental Drum Major of the Essex and Kent Scottish Regiment of Canada; Rusty Cottrel, renowned historical interpreter; Michael Zeiler and Bill Kramer, authors and expert eclipse chasers; Randall Gittinger of Melmore, Ohio, and Tonia Hoffert, Director of the Seneca County Museum.

The anonymous staff of several institutions have provided advice and documentation that is critical to this book. These include: The Toledo/Lucas County Public Library, The University of Toledo Carlson Library, The Bowling Green State University Jerome Library, The Kentucky Historical Society, The Filson Historical Society, The Library of Congress, The Ohio Historical Society, The Cincinnati Museum Center, The Rutherford B. Hayes Presidential Center Library, The William L. Clements Library at the University of Michigan, The Wright State University Dunbar Library, The Chatham/Kent Museum, The OhioLink Digital

Library, and the Internet as a whole for the substantial travel time and expense it spared me. An extra "thank you" goes to the numerous historical sites, societies, organizations, and libraries across the Midwest who have invited me to speak on various history topics over the past several years. These opportunities have incentivized me to continue writing.

Finally, I want to posthumously thank the people written about in the pages ahead. If they, or their close friends and family, had not left a record of their thoughts and activities we would have a much dimmer view of what life was like in the old Northwest Territory. ♦

SKETCHES
OF
INTRIGUING PEOPLE.

INTRODUCTION.

Since the early thirteenth century agreements, charters, accords, and most often treaties, have been negotiated at one particular site — Paris, France. Diplomats the world over, for no less than eight hundred years, have repeatedly favored gathering in this city of love to discuss viable solutions to various conflicts. In fact, more than sixty documents bear the title, "Treaty of Paris," differentiated by the year they were signed and the details they contain. Several were agreed to during the turbulent 1700s when settlement expanded across the North American continent. One was penned on September 3, 1783, and gave birth to a new nation.

The Treaty of Paris of that year officially removed the colonies in North America from the control of England's king and declared them to be independent states, united as a new republic.

Boundaries were established for these United States. The Atlantic Ocean defined the eastern end. The Mississippi River marked the western edge. The south shores of the Great Lakes provided the northern border and Spain's Florida territory stopped the new country's stretch southward. It wouldn't be until the Louisiana Purchase of 1803 that the lands beyond the Mississippi River would become the West that we know today. At the birth of this country in 1783 the region just over the Appalachian Mountains and up to the Mississippi River was the West, and it had been beckoning settlement for a long time.

How was it that this massive amount of land was still essentially a wilderness in 1783? Why hadn't the colonies spilled over the Appalachian Mountains by this time? Why hadn't the French, Spanish, or Dutch trading posts ever blossomed into bustling communities like the original colonial villages had done along the coast?

There were several reasons for this phenomenon, and a brief step back in time will reveal them.

We all know that Europeans from several countries began arriving in North America as explorers and settlers as long as a millennium ago. From Leif Erikson of Iceland in the year 999, to Christopher Columbus of Spain in the late 1400s, to Sir Walter Raleigh from England in the late 1500s, the voyagers came and the numbers of their expeditions accelerated.

Sailing vessels from across the world anchored at points all along the Atlantic coast. From those shores the adventure seekers moved inland. The Spanish entered through the southern regions. The Dutch navigated their way into what is now the New York State area. The French descended from Canada and eventually progressed to the middle of the continent via the Mississippi River. And the English nestled along the rivers of the current Chesapeake Bay, eventually spreading north, south and west toward the Appalachians.

Explore they all did, but it wasn't until 1565 that the Spanish established what would become the very first lasting settlement within the boundaries of the future United States of America. They named it San Augustin in honor of the saint on whose feast day they had spotted the land. Spanish interests remained primarily in the southeast and southwest regions of the continent, except for a brief possession of the trading post at St. Louis throughout the American Revolution and a few years beyond.

Dutch colonization in North America was quite limited in comparison to the others. Their settlements were predominantly in what would become New Jersey and eastern New York. Perhaps the most famous of their holdings was an island they had purchased from the Lenni Lenape Indians known as Mannahatta — the land of many hills. Today it's the land of many people, the most populated city in the United States. This and other possessions were held by the Dutch for several decades through the 1600s. However, their ownership of New Netherland transferred to the British in 1664 as a result of several Anglo-Dutch wars.

The broad middle swatch of the continent was known as New France for quite some time. The French had plunged into the heart of North

INTRODUCTION

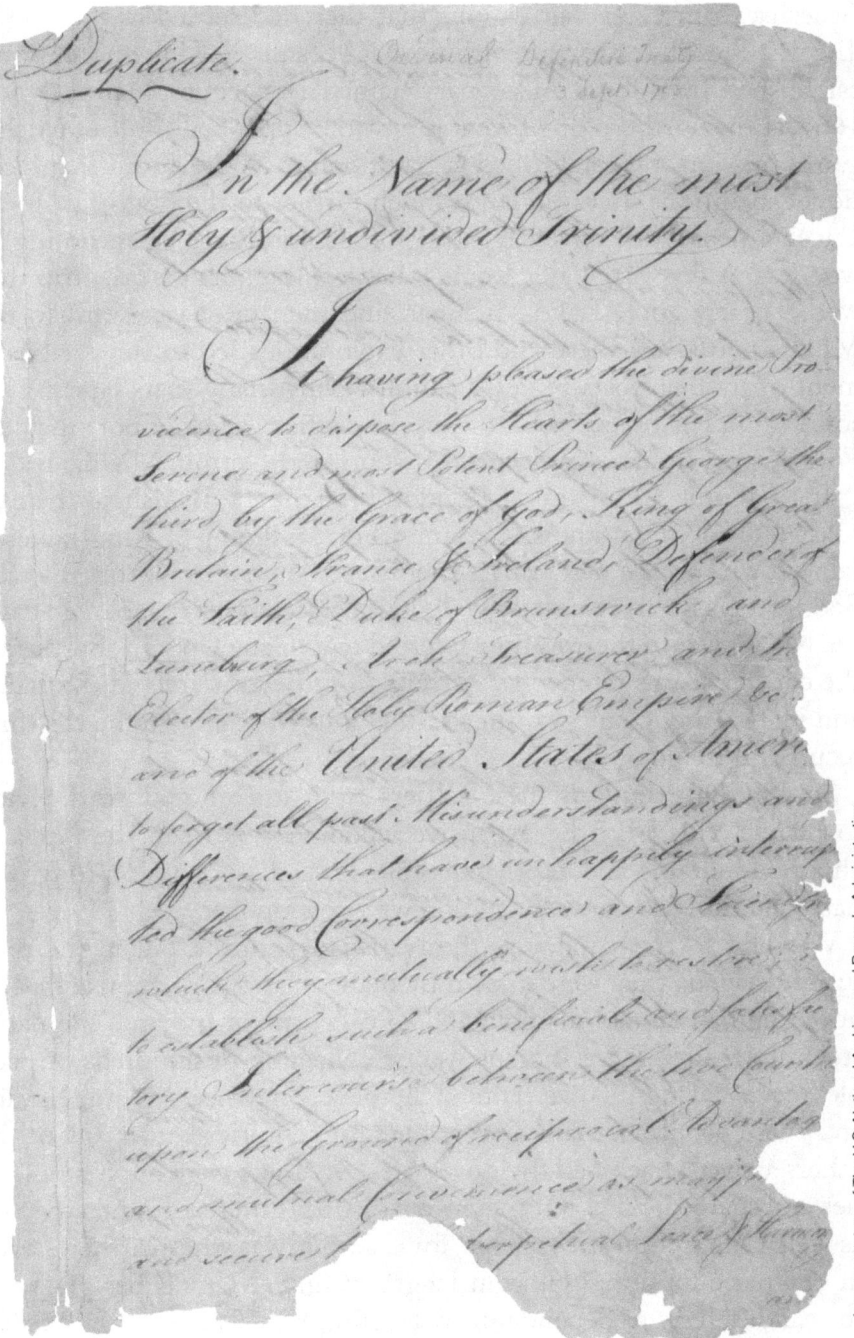

The first page of the Treaty of Paris signed on September 3, 1783.

America from Canadian regions that they had settled in the 1600s. The first French settlement within what became the United States was established by a Jesuit missionary named Fr. Jacques Marquette. In 1668, at the northern tip of what is now the upper peninsula of Michigan, a mission was established at Sault Sainte Marie. From that location, expeditions surveyed lands much further to the South. In 1669, Cavelier de LaSalle travelled through the Ohio River Valley noting its wonders. A few years later Louis Joliet left the mission on a trip that would nearly circle Lake Michigan and then head westward to the Mississippi River. These and other explorations led to the establishment of trading posts in key locations. Only many years later would some of these sites evolve into American cities. A few of note include: Fort Wayne, Indiana, St. Louis, Missouri, and Detroit, Michigan.

The Virginia Company of London brought the British to the east coast in 1607. First known as James Fort in honor of King James I, Jamestown was the first lasting English settlement in North America. Soon, others fleeing England's religious persecution disembarked from the Mayflower in the area now referred to as Cape Cod. In short order the continent was flooded by citizens from Britain, Ireland, Scotland, and many other countries. They settled into what grew to be the thirteen British colonies.

So why didn't any of these settlers from foreign countries decide to plant a village in the expansive wilderness between the Appalachian Mountains and the Mississippi River before 1783? Maybe it had something to do with a nation we've overlooked.

We refer to them today as the Native Americans, but in the centuries previous they were known by many names. Columbus first believed he had landed in India and so called them Indians. The name stuck. In reality, these Indians were a collection of hundreds of peoples; each having its own name: Cherokee, Shawnee, Miami, Navajo, etc. These peoples, or tribes, were here for centuries before any of the others arrived. Each had their own lifestyle. There were many similarities and shared beliefs, but there were distinct differences and attitudes as well. One significant variable, for example, was whether they stayed in one place for any significant length of time. Many tribes preferred to wander, heavily dependent on hunting and fishing; only putting down roots for the short term in any one location. Others did settle into communities for the long term where their farming was extensive enough to supplement hunting efforts.

Relationships invariably developed between these Indian tribes and the newly arrived European peoples. Interactions were mixed. Some Native Americans welcomed the newcomers, others were wary. Likewise, many of the European settlers genuinely sought friendship, but others rushed to judgement, unable to shake an attitude of disdain.

Breakthroughs in these interactions came through the trading process. Many tribes quickly discovered that the goods these white men had to offer could make their lives more comfortable. The white men found the business very lucrative. And so, the trading posts themselves acted as an active conduit, not only for the exchange of goods, but of ideas between the two cultures. In this way many lasting friendships were forged. Potentially volatile, polarizing perspectives could often be diffused through discussions. But each person was an individual – for every relationship that came to a peaceful coexistence, another failed because no effort was made to change their prejudices.

All this being said, the tone of individual relationships between the two cultures played little part in the big picture. On the broad political stage the European countries who were colonizing North America repeatedly ignored the input of the Native Americans. In fact, as white men fought each other upon Indian lands, over the rights to own those Indian lands, the treaties to end such battles over the Indian lands never included an Indian's opinion. Can you not envision the average Indian incredulously throwing up his hands and shaking his head upon hearing the ludicrous news that some foreign country thinks they now owned their land?

That being the case, on paper at least, the mid-section of the continent remained primarily in dispute between the large and powerful countries of France and England. The metaphorical "elephant in the land," the Indian, was generally used only as a pawn in their games of war with each other.

Through the 1600s and the first half of the 1700s several conflicts and short-lived wars did occur. The more recognized ones were known as King William's War, Queen Anne's War, and King George's War. These lesser clashes proved to be stepping stones to the more intense French and Indian War of 1754. Through that war of nine years, the

Map showing the British colonies and the line drawn across the Appalachian Mountains establishing the Indian Territory in the West per King George III's Proclamation of 1763.

British would fight the French with whom many Indian tribes had allied themselves. Finally, a Treaty of Paris was signed in 1763 ending the conflict. It announced that, as victors, the British would be awarded all lands east of the Mississippi River. New France was no more. This was a huge expansion of British holdings, and a devastating blow to France. Though several tribes fought right alongside the French for all those years, no Indian had a say in the negotiations and terms of the treaty.

With this victory, adventurous British colonists expected to now make the precarious trip over the Appalachians in order to start a new life. But within a few months, that notion was squashed by the King of England. He would, by a royal decree, block colonials from settling in the newly won lands.

Why? The British had overlooked, or at least underestimated, the factor the Indians played in this land. These Native Americans had been allies to the French for quite some time, in some cases for over a century. Ties between these two peoples ran deep in their daily lives. In fact, over the years many intermarriages had taken place. Trade between these tribes and the French was as natural as a sunrise. And now the British suddenly owned the land? The French were going away? You can imagine how quickly the frustration and anger against the British rose in the hearts of the Indians.

Almost immediately after the implementation of the Treaty of Paris on February 10, 1763, these disgruntled Native Americans took matters into their own hands. Chief Pontiac of the Ottawa, in an alliance with many tribes in the Ohio Valley, strategized a war plan to take the vital British forts of Detroit, Pitt, and others. Their efforts ultimately proved unsuccessful, but they certainly opened the eyes of King George III. The British lost many men in the conflicts and became keenly aware of the Indians' ability to unite against them. The king had to do something to tamp down the tensions. On October 7, 1763, just shy of eight months after the treaty took effect, he issued his major proclamation. Its purpose was multi-facetted.

This Royal Proclamation of 1763 drew an imaginary line across the central peaks of the Appalachians over the entire length of the colonies. It separated the colonists from the wilderness in the West which the king now designated as the Indian Reserve.

One purpose of this action was to appease the Indians. With colonists now forbidden to cross the mountains, the Indians had the land to themselves. In the king's eyes the West was land held by the Crown, but allotted to the Indians. It's interesting to note that in this document the king addressed the Indians in terms that implied that they too were his subjects, deserving of his protection.

Another reason for this ruling was to contain the colonists. This was an essential maneuver. It was already becoming increasingly difficult to govern the growing colonies. The populations were swelling and becoming unruly. King George III felt that if these colonists were to spread west, he would never be able to reign them in. They had to be restricted within a manageable region.

Land grants awarded to British military personnel for their service in the previous wars were rescinded. Colonists who had been eyeing the land with the lust of a speculator were held in check. As you might imagine, no one was happy.

The reality was that this proclamation deterred many of the colonists, but not all. The British had no way to enforce their own rules on the frontier. The most hardy and adventurous colonial souls went west anyway. It certainly was not a flood of would-be settlers, just a handful, because no one could secure legal title to the land. In other words, they could go, declare ownership of whatever parcels they wanted, but they were actually just squatters.

In hindsight, this proclamation of King George III could be considered the flash in the pan of that, "Shot heard 'round the world,'" a dozen years later. England was flexing its muscles and ramping up its imperial power play over the colonists. Resentment and anger continued to fester up and down the Atlantic coast.

The settlers who did cross the mountains often put down roots south of the Ohio River in what would grow to be Kentucky. This created a major problem since the Native Americans were promised this wouldn't happen. In an effort to dissuade further encroachment the Indians attacked many of the settlers. Tensions rose. Now both the Indians and the colonists were quite unhappy with the king of England.

After five years of turmoil on the frontier, the Crown tried to quell the fighting by signing yet another agreement. This time it was with the Iroquois confederation of tribes. Known as the Treaty of Fort Stanwix, it opened the land south of the Ohio River to settlement by the colonists. But there was a major glitch in this treaty.

The Iroquois nation lived in the colony of New York, not in the Ohio Valley. Their authority to sign away this land was not recognized by the tribes who actually lived in the area. That would be the Shawnee, Seneca-Cayuga, and Delaware who refused to acknowledge this treaty. These tribes didn't claim to own the land, but it was the land they lived and hunted upon. They were adamant that neither the Iroquois, nor any other tribe, had any right to sell it. The Treaty of Fort Stanwix only had validity in the eyes of the British and their colonists. And so, the confrontations continued between the frontiersmen and the Indians of the region.

In spite of the continued potential of Indian attacks, this treaty encouraged the colonists who were inclined to settle, to do so only below the Ohio River. They started spilling over the mountains in greater and greater numbers; and it was not an easy feat to get through the Appalachians. The pivotal passageway for Virginians was through a natural break in the mountain range known as the Cumberland Gap. Northern colonists navigated the Hudson and Mohawk rivers toward the Great Lakes before following river systems into the Ohio Valley. Pennsylvania colonists likewise followed various river routes as well as British military roads that had been blazed during their wars with the French. No matter how they came, they indeed were beginning to settle, legally, in what was formerly part of the Indian Reserve.

Finally we arrive at 1783. At this point in time, as citizens of the United States, people were totally free to explore, lay claim, and settle the lands over the mountains at their own risk; all the lands. This included those north of the Ohio River as well as those already becoming populated to the south of it. The northern lands were considered Indian territory and so anyone choosing to settle there took on significantly more risk than those who chose the already dangerous grounds south of the river.

In the Kentucky region, forts and trading posts multiplied. More and more cabins dotted the landscape. These scattered homeowners freely opened their doors to new travelers who were making their way to lay claim to their own plot of land further west. Their dwellings acted as stations of rest and recuperation as the would-be settlers moved along. Besides, there was some safety to be had in a structure with more hands available to stave off a possible Indian attack.

It's significant to note that the British continued to hold posts in the Indian wilderness to the North. This was not sanctioned by the Treaty of Paris that had just ended the war, but the new United States didn't have the capacity, nor really the stomach, to confront this infraction so soon after the revolution. These posts were big business for the British to carry on trading with the Indians.

What needs to be understood through this transitional time is that from the moment of its conception the United States government was broke. They had to find ways to raise money, and fast. Spain, France, and the Netherlands had funded much of the Revolution and it was pay back time. To generate income, the new government went to extreme measures. They stopped credit to farmers. Taxes were raised. Debtors, many who were the very men who put their lives on the line for this new freedom, were now losing it as they were locked away in prisons. By the country's tender age of four in 1787, rebellions against the fledgling government's heavy-handed practices were becoming all too frequent.

To acquire wealth the government had to come up with a new plan. The Ohio Valley was gorgeous and fertile on both sides. To the South, the hills and valleys of what would become Kentucky were teeming with wildlife and rich soil. It was the first area to be populated due to the progression of treaties which opened it to settlement. But, likewise, the country above the Ohio presented a spectacular landscape of lush vegetation fed by an extensive network of rivers. It is this area, lying north and west of the Ohio River, that would later become the states of Ohio, Michigan, Indiana, Illinois, Wisconsin, and Minnesota.

To generate an income stream, in 1787 the government declared that the area above the Ohio River and below the Great Lakes, lying between the Mississippi River and the Appalachians, was no longer to be considered a simple wilderness, nor just Indian lands; rather it was now a territory of the United States — the Northwest Territory.

The Northwest Ordinance declaring this fact brought more than a name change. It established the framework for these lands to eventually become states; and more importantly gave the federal government control over the sale of this prime real estate. In due time, with the signing of treaty after treaty with various Indian tribes, lands were officially sold to the United States in exchange for goods, money, and peace. Surveys were made, tracts delineated, and ultimately income was flowing into the government's coffers from the sale of former Indian acreage to adventurous Americans. This legislation officially put the population and financial expansion of the United States on the fast track.

Settlement in the Northwest Territory accelerated almost logarithmically. The forts, or stations as they were called, grew into villages, villages into small towns, and small towns eventually into cities. But the transition was by no means easy. The Native Americans still resided in this territory. Many tribes disavowed the treaties that other tribes had agreed to. Resentment over being excluded from the negotiations that ended the Revolution still burned in the Indians' hearts. They found themselves yet again, at least on paper, under the control of another country. This time it was the United States. They hadn't agreed to this, and most were determined not to accept it.

And so it happened that within a vast wilderness, the original inhabitants had to deal with a change of the status quo. The Americans were coming into their lands and staking claims to it parcel by parcel. And settling here was no small feat of bravery for those Americans who had to risk the anger of the Indians, the attack of wild animals, and numerous deprivations for the freedom of beginning a new life. Conflict became the norm but it would propel many individuals to new heights of bravery and accomplishment. ♦

ANECDOTE.

An Irish gentleman, deranged in his mind made two attempts one morning to drown himself; but as he was an expert swimmer, in spite of his wish to die he could not help emerging from the water, therefore making to the land he tucked himself up in his garters on a neighboring tree. Soon after a party of his friends came hotfoot after him and seeing him dangling in the air whilst an Irish cow-keeper was whistling on a stile [step] very near, perfectly unconcerned —, "why you thief (said one of them to the fellow,) [how] could you be after standing here whistling, and see the Jontleman tuck himself up, without offering to cut him down? — "Arrah," pon my conscience (says paddy) I was not so impartinent; for as I saw the Jontleman come out of the river as wet as a drowned rat, devil burn me but I thought he had only hung himself up to dry."

In the Centinel of the North-Western Territory, August 1, 1795[1]

I.
AN AMERICAN IN CANADA.

Only after long, fierce labor pains did the United States of America come into the world. Over more than seven years of gestation, a total of nearly 80,000 people lost their lives in the conflict. The form of freedom that was born, however; became a benchmark of world history.

This new country was the first to espouse liberty for all through a representative government from individual states. This was unique. No nation before it had ever borne quite the same characteristics. Its spirit was contagious and admirable. It was proud and confident of a long and healthy life ahead; but it was also immature. It had to act as its own parent, setting up rules for itself, only to rewrite them as it learned from experience. Like any child, it floundered for several years before it could stand on its own two feet. None-the-less, it was a good kid.

The stumbles occurred almost immediately as the colonies transformed into states. This metamorphosis was downright awkward. Sure the war was over, but confusion and new conflicts replaced the outright killing that the rebels and loyalists had been engaging in.

The peace treaty negotiations dragged on for over two years once the decisive battle at Yorktown had initiated them in 1781. As the new American government began to establish itself, those former colonists who had until now steadfastly supported Britain had to make a very tough decision. Most owned property. Should they maintain their allegiance to the king of England and as a result give up their claim to the land they had lived on for years? Or, should they keep their holdings by becoming citizens of this new country? What were their neighbors, friends and relatives doing? Just as would happen during the Civil War in the years to come, the Revolution had turned relationships upside down. Family members agonized over parting ways with their kin. This was a life-changing event with very emotional and tangible implications.

When the count was tallied, a small number of the British residents signed on to the ideals of the new republic and applied for U.S. citizenship. Most, however, packed up their belongings and sailed back to England to start over. But, there was a third group of several thousands, labeled as Loyalists, who moved north to the British Province of Canada. The majority of this latter group went to sites in Quebec which was just north and northwest of Maine and Vermont. Others went to Upper Canada, now the province of Ontario, and settled the lands lining the Thames River which flowed somewhat parallel to the north shores of Lake Erie.

Looking at a map, one might wonder why land situated at the bottom of this huge country was known as Upper Canada and not the more logical Lower Canada? It's because this moniker is determined by the flow of the St. Lawrence River which originates at Lake Ontario in the southern lands of Canada, and happens to flow north and eastward to the Atlantic. Hence, the upper, albeit southern, end of the St. Lawrence River defined this region as "Upper" Canada.

For the new Americans, the transition to autonomy was no less confusing. The peaceful, romantic scene of a white picket fence surrounding a quaint home with a hot apple pie cooling on a windowsill was hardly the reality of 1783. That came a bit later. The fledgling state and federal governments had a lot of kinks to work out. Not all of their policies were having a positive effect on the citizens.

The external conflict with the British may have ended, but new battles were erupting internally. Some disputes were simple individual incidents that could be easily settled either by a meeting of the minds or a session in a local court. Others, however, were of a more serious nature and broader in scope. When new laws became much more than a nuisance, and in fact life-threatening, it did more than raise the hair on the backs of citizens' necks. Folks took to arms en masse to express their discontent with the government policies.

One of the earliest of these types of rebellions was an insurrection led by Daniel Shays, a former captain in the Continental Army. Shays'

Rebellion, as it became known, saw the farmers of Massachusetts rail against their state government officials who were putting a financial squeeze on them.

The root of the problem stemmed from a national economy that was horrific throughout the war years and still hadn't recovered as of 1786. After the Revolution, many people had purchased lands to farm in the western areas of their states. But just a few years in, they were finding it impossible to make their mortgage payments. That was exacerbated by the imposition of new taxes, the very thing over which they rebelled against Britain. In fact, the taxes were demanded in full, lump sum payments. As a result, the already struggling farmers were being foreclosed on and many thrown into debtor's prisons. Ironically, most of these people were the very men who had won the country's freedom as soldiers in the Continental Army. Special consideration for their service, however, was not to be found. They felt betrayed.

The pressure to generate revenue originated with the foreign parties who had financially underwritten the Revolution. France, Holland, and Spain had not only been key moral supporters, but also investors in the new United States. Now that the fighting was over they wanted, and needed, a return on their investment. Each of the new states was required to pay back its fair share of this wartime debt. Nationally, our foreign credit was still on shaky ground. The Massachusetts business community felt particularly strong about keeping their credit in good standing, and so they lobbied the state to raise taxes to cover their debt. Thus the demand for money snaked its way down to the lowly farmers.

By 1786 the situation became so dire for citizens living in western Massachusetts that people like Daniel Shays surfaced and gained a large following. At first the angry farmers simply held town meetings and lodged formal complaints, but that proved useless. So, they began gathering together at courthouses and interrupted proceedings that involved foreclosures on farmers. When these tactics still proved to be ineffectual, citizens took things to the next level. Under Shays' lead, prisons were stormed and debtors were freed. Bullets flew when they even tried to steal arms from a government stockpile, only to be met by state militia. Skirmishes like these were luckily short-lived, occurring only over the winter months of 1786-87, but they led to several significant and long-lasting changes in government policies. Not the least of these adjustments was the writing of the our existing Constitution in place of the original and comparatively loose Articles of Confederation.

One of the prominent figures in Shays' Rebellion was a man named Perez Hamlin. It was Hamlin who on February 27, 1787, led a force of approximately a hundred men through the streets of Stockbridge, Massachusetts; rampaging through the homes of prominent citizens who were government supporters. Taking many of these residents as prisoners, Hamlin moved on a few miles to the town of Great Barrington where he helped debtors who were imprisoned to escape. On his way back to New York, Hamlin and his men were attacked by a nearly equal force of militia. The battle resulted in several deaths, including that of Perez who was fatally wounded and died in prison a short time later. Though many of the captured rebels were scheduled to be hanged, the arguments of George Washington and others toward leniency, spared all but two from the gallows.

In 1773, some fourteen years before Perez's uprising occurred, another Hamlin was born in nearby Connecticut. The son of Elisha and Rachel Hamlin, Isaac grew to maturity in the town of Brookfield. His home was only sixty miles from Stockbridge, Massachusetts, where Perez had created a name for himself. In fact, having the same surname, in the same region of the country as such a noted rebel was a double-edged sword. It may have given Isaac instant popularity with the outlying farmers of the region who thought he was somehow related to Perez; but it likewise may have put a bulls-eye on his back for law enforcement.

Isaac spelled his name Hamblin with a "b" in the middle. Records show his father spelled it both with and without the "b". Perez never used the "b" at all. There is some speculation that Isaac may have always used the "b" to purposefully disassociate himself from Perez, even though there is likely to be no biological connection between them. The spelling issue, if there was purpose behind it, was at best superficial because in the eighteenth century there were only few occasions requiring anyone to write their names anyway. Many people were illiterate and spellings were often conjectured by the one hurriedly writing it down on a roster or such. It was the spoken word that mattered, and in Isaac's case, the verbalization of the name was identical whether spelled Hamlin or Hamblin. It is pure speculation therefore whether Isaac's spelling preference of his surname had anything to do with Perez, but it is interesting to make note of it considering Isaac's next move.

That was a literal move. Sometime during the 1790s Isaac found a new home in Canada. It may seem odd to many that just a few years after the country's independence had been won, anyone would move out of it and resettle in the British possession of Canada. Isaac's own grand-uncle, James Bradshaw, had moved there; but then again he was a Loyalist who served the Crown as a Captain in the British military. His service like many others' secured him a gift of property in Upper Canada. However, Isaac was American. Was his action unique?

It's lesser known and widely forgotten, but many Americans besides Isaac, while retaining their United States citizenship, moved to Canada in the early days of our country. Even fewer realize that they did so at the explicit invitation of the Lieutenant Governor of Upper Canada, Sir John Graves Simcoe.

In 1792, this Canadian leader made a proclamation which would award lots of two hundred acres to any American who wanted to settle upon it so long as their intentions were to, "Cultivate and improve the same." Further it stated that the only cost was to, "Promise and declare that I will maintain and defend to the utmost of my Power the Authority of the King in His Parliament as the Supreme Legislature of this Province." [1] This allegiance was generally taken lightly by the Americans as they were not anticipating another conflict between the two countries so soon after the Revolution. Free land was worth a half-hearted pledge that they believed would probably never be put to the test.

Lieutenant Governor Simcoe was deeply committed to the established rule of the British Empire and its expansion in Canada. He additionally had a romantic vision of Upper Canada blossoming into the ideal British colony even though reality was working against him. There were several factors at work stifling his dream. The economy in England was not flourishing at this time, so the notion that any of the

Portrait of John Graves Simcoe by George Theodore Berthon. Simcoe served as Lieutenant Governor of Upper Canada from 1791-1796.

common people living there would relocate to Canada was just a wishful thought. In the least a financial enticement would be needed for each family considering it, but that was never offered. Further, many were not adventurous enough to take on the challenge of settling into what they knew would be a very rugged lifestyle. Most were simply content to stay in their homeland. Besides, some government heads in England had cast aspersions against such a move as they saw future conflicts on the horizon for which they needed their population of young men readily at hand.

It was evident to Simcoe that most of the Americans were industrious self-starters who were already experienced in turning a piece of wilderness into productive farmland. He sought to take advantage of this. His vision saw communities expanding, surplus goods being produced, and trade developing. He expected Upper Canada to become a superior and lucrative colony of the Crown in no time. Besides, he reasoned, speculators from the United States were already buying up Canadian land with no intention of settling upon it, only to re-sell it at a profit sometime down the road. Simcoe merely accelerated the inevitable growth.

Further evidence of the size of the migrations to Canada and its potential political causes is found in a news report in the *Salem Impartial Register* in 1800.

> Again, as to the emigration to Canada, we noticed the fact more than 8 months ago, that a vast number of families had been enticed out of the counties of Bucks, Berks, and Northampton, to go into Canada.
>
> In the first week of June last, above sixty wagons, carrying the families and furniture of emigrants from those counties, passed thro' the Genessee country on their route to Niagara. Indeed so numerous have been the passengers of this description, that the people in that country complain their roads being cut up by the number of them passing that way and through the wilderness.
>
> These are serious facts — and they exhibit a very remarkable contrast between the policy of our sinking administration and that of the English colony of Canada. They hold out immense offers to emigrants. We hold out terrors and discouragements. ²

The population of Upper Canada in 1790 was a mere 20,000 Loyalists and Indians. Over the next twenty years, thanks to Simcoe's plan, it swelled to nearly 100,000, and the vast majority were Americans. Whether it was the heavy handed fiscal policies of the fledgling American government, the high cost of U.S. farmland, or an escape from potential harassment because of his last name, Isaac Hamblin was among those Americans who took Governor Simcoe up on his offer.

Though he was living in Canada, Isaac Hamblin was a devoted American. It was in his blood. His father Elisha served three terms with the Connecticut State troops between 1776 and 1779, honorably discharged after each stint. His uncles also served; as well as his grandfather, William, Jr., who enlisted in response to the triggering battle of Lexington Green in Massachusetts. But Isaac's family was one of the many which was conflicted by a division of loyalties. While his father's side served in the Continental Army, uncles on his mother's side supported the king.

In the late 1790s Isaac settled along the Thames River, just east of the present-day city of Chatham, Ontario. Reports say that he brought his wife and family with him, but it is unclear whether the family included children or other relatives such as his parents, siblings, or others. He was a hard worker as evidenced by the large farm and orchard he had established over the next twenty years. He was known to have had a fine team of horses and an impressive wagon which were considered prized and necessary possessions at that time. Historic accounts imply that Isaac's prosperity lasted until the fall of 1813. It was then that the war declared in June of the previous year would drift right into Isaac's backyard — and not metaphorically. When it did, Isaac's response to it would prove epic.

As June unfolded into July of 1812, General Hull marched his United States troops around the northwest corner of Lake Erie and into Canada on a mission to capture Fort Malden, a British stronghold situated at the mouth of the Detroit River in the British shipbuilding town of Amherstburg. As he entered Upper Canada, Hull issued a proclamation to the Canadians and Americans living in the vicinity. It succinctly explained that those who were loyal to the American effort, or those who looked forward to the true freedom which the Americans had recently won, need do nothing but carry on as usual.

> The army under my Command has invaded your Country and the standard of the United States waves on the territory of Canada. To the peaceful, unoffending inhabitant, it brings neither danger nor difficulty. I come to find enemies not to make them, I come to protect you not to injure you.

Hull further explained:

> In the name of my Country and by the authority of my Government I promise protection to your persons, property, and rights. Remain at your homes, pursue your peaceful and customary avocations. Raise not your hands against your brethren, many of your fathers fought for the freedom and independence we now enjoy. Being children therefore of the same family with us, and heirs to the same heritage, the arrival of an army of friends must be hailed by you with a cordial welcome. You will be emancipated from tyranny and oppression and restored to the dignified status of freemen... If contrary to your own interest and the

just expectation of my country, you should take part in the approaching contest, you will be considered and treated as enemies, and the horrors, and calamities of war will stalk before you. [3]

Thus, the efforts of Hull met no opposition from the wary residents of Upper Canada. Instead resistance manifested itself in Hull's own mind in the form of fear. After a few brief skirmishes against the 300 men of Fort Malden, who were under the command of the British Colonel, Henry Proctor, Hull ordered his 2,500 men to retreat. Yes, retreat back to Fort Detroit having achieved nothing.

In his defense, Hull's supply lines had been cut, and his written campaign plans were literally stolen by the British when they were discovered on an American vessel that they had captured earlier. Rumors of an Indian force on their way from the Lake Huron area clinched his decision to get out of there. However, while at the walls of the enemy fortress he had an eight-to-one advantage of men and was likely only hours away from taking possession. Misguided evaluations of his mens' and his own capabilities combined with his hyper fear of the Indians had created a doomsday scenario in his mind. And so, Hull fled Fort Malden. Upon his arrival at Fort Detroit, it only took a matter of days before he was intimidated to surrender it as well. The most important U.S. post in the region was handed over to the legendary figure of Major General Isaac Brock of England. Citizens of the United States living in the region, including Isaac Hamblin, must have been incredulous at this news and left fearing what would happen next.

After Hull had shamed himself and jeopardized his country in this manner he faced a court martial. He was found guilty and a death sentence was pronounced for his treason, cowardice, and neglect of duty. It was only his long friendship with then President Madison that spared his life. Ironically, British General Henry Proctor, whom Hull had run away from at Fort Malden, had a similarly questionable military history. As we will see, he likewise faced a court martial from his government for cowardice at the Battle of the Thames just over a year later.

As Hull returned home in disgrace, Proctor took command of the Canadian and British forces in Upper Canada. Meanwhile, Major-General William Henry Harrison, as commander of the U.S. military in the Northwest Territory, took on the mission to regain Fort

Detroit. The Americans and Canadians living in the area stretching from Detroit to the east end of Lake Erie became very apprehensive about their future. Hull's proclamation which promised no problems to anyone who minded their own business, now seemed meaningless. Everyone knew, including Isaac Hamblin, that Harrison would soon be on his way to Detroit. Even though his home was a hundred miles from that potential conflict, Isaac feared things could get very messy in his own neighborhood, and he was right. But before Harrison arrived, Proctor took the offensive and crossed the Detroit River to attack U.S. forces in the Michigan territory.

What became known as the Raisin River massacre took place in today's city of Monroe, Michigan. In January 1813, Major-General Henry Proctor led British and Indian forces from Fort Malden against an American encampment situated along the Raisin River. Victory went to the British. Over 300 Americans were killed. The ones who survived and who were able to make the fifty-mile trek back to Fort Malden, which was still in British hands because of Hull's previous cowardice, did so as prisoners of war.

Those Americans who were so seriously wounded that they could not walk were left behind. Proctor promised he would send sleds back the next day to transport these men. He also promised to leave British guards to defend them against any anxious Indians remaining in the area. Captain William Elliot, a major player in the British war effort, did linger behind with a few interpreters. But in the morning, the good captain and the others were no where to be found. Unprotected and unable to defend themselves, the desperate, disabled American men were easy prey for anyone intending to do harm. And as they say, the rest is history; disturbing history.

Most of the wounded were incapable of even getting out of their beds or off the floor that they had been laid upon. Trouble began midmorning as several of the homes that these men were being kept in were ransacked and set ablaze by the Indians. Some men burned to death. Others were dragged out and tortured. Months later many of their bones would be found strewn across the area. The few survivors were force-marched by the Indians to Malden. If their ability to walk

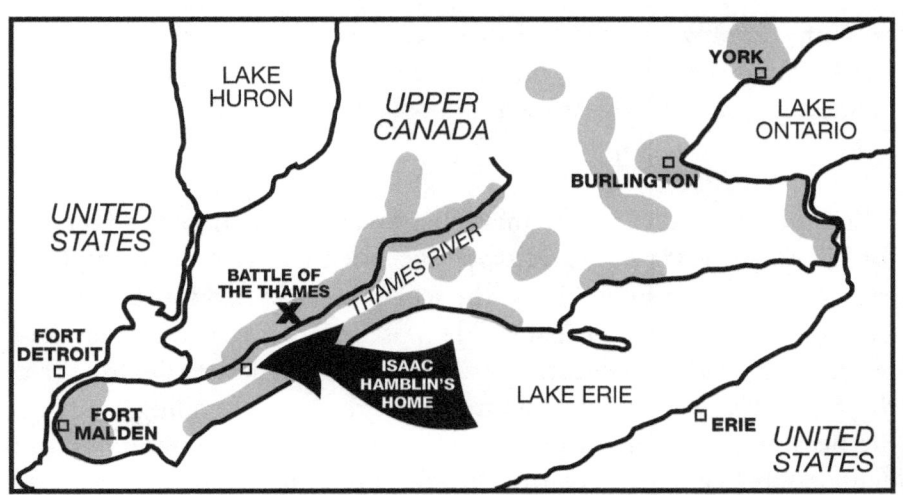

Map showing where Isaac Hamblin is believed to have lived near current-day Chatham, Ontario. Gray areas are regions of Upper Canada populated by both Loyalists and Americans through 1825. (Based on map by John Bartholomew & Son, Ltd./ The Edinburgh Geographical Institute, in An Historical Atlas of Canada, 1927.)

failed, they were dispatched along the trail.

One has to wonder why these Indians were so bloodthirsty that they would attack defenseless, wounded men. There could be little pride in such an act. Some history stories report that they were crazed by alcohol. Possible, but unprovable. Some say it was simply the heat of battle. Maybe; many of their own had been killed in the previous day's encounter and revenge is understandable. Others say it was their strong, persistent resentment toward any American, especially those from Kentucky, whom they perceived had been stealing their land over the previous decades. Likely. These particular POWs were indeed Kentuckians, and young ones at that, most mere teenaged boys.

It was in Kentucky that most of the recent years' conflicts between settlers and Indians had occurred. Kentucky was the prime hunting ground for Indians of numerous tribes for as long as anyone living could remember. Although there were occasional conflicts about hunting rights between the tribes themselves, the Kentucky lands were generally considered open to all tribes. It was the American frontiersmen, who suddenly appeared and decided to set up permanent residences on this land that had created a problem. The situation that had presented itself along the Raisin River that cold January morning of 1813 offered these Indians the chance to take vengeance out of God's hands and put it into their own.

Proctor returned to the Thames River region as a Brigadier General for his Raisin River effort. His presence seemed more imposing than ever to Isaac and his neighbors. The scorn this man had for the Americans in residence was palpable. He was keenly aware that they had never renounced their citizenship and so he could never fully trust that they would at least remain neutral through any impending conflicts. He became determined to hold the advantage in the situation and so deliberately began intimidating Isaac's community.

It began with restrictions on the Americans' movements. Until now, they had been able to travel back to the United States at will. No longer. Proctor eliminated their right to leave. Americans were constrained to their Canadian properties and everyday movements were carefully monitored. Further, Proctor, "with some Canadians on the Upper Thames, commenced plotting the destruction of all the defenseless Americans in that region."[4]

What? Yes, a plot was devised by Proctor to murder the Americans in Upper Canada. The plan was well-developed. It was to unfold with the help of two groups: Indians and certain Canadian residents. While the unknowing Americans went about their daily business, albeit troubled that war may be coming their way soon, Proctor was deviously planning their mass execution.

First he contacted, or better stated contracted, the Indian nations living east of Lake Huron in the northern regions of Canada. Several tribes may have been involved but most likely it was the Ojibwe and/or Ottawa tribes who lived in that region. Proctor instructed them

> to come down on the Thames on a certain day, to a place designated, where the inhabitants (who) adhered to the English [the Canadians] should have a good feast of roast beef prepared for them, and plenty of whiskey to prepare them for the work of death.[5]

The other party to Proctor's impending crime was the band of Canadian collaborators in the area. Proctor met with these neighbors, who had been friends with the Americans, soon after he took command of the region. They were likely not to act directly against the Americans, but instead they were to be involved with the preparation of the feast promised to the Indians. Regardless of the exact part these Canadian accomplices were to play, after their talks with Proctor they, "were to return home and wait for the mail from Detroit, which would bring them news and letters, giving them all needful information for the completion of the dreadful plot."[6]

This evil scheme was a well-kept secret from Isaac and his American neighbors living along the Thames. That was until a particularly close friend of Isaac's came to visit him. A Canadian friend.

Isaac and this man had associated for years. Both were deeply devoted to their Saviour, Jesus Christ. Many a day they spent discussing spiritual and practical issues closest to their hearts. At this time, however, Isaac's friend began coming around much more frequently. With each visit he tried to persuade Isaac, "To take his friends and move away to the States."[7] Isaac had to be puzzled by his friend's repeated suggestion. Of course everyone was anticipating some sort of military action, but it was still speculation. Besides, even if Isaac was convinced that fleeing the area was the best action to take, it would be nearly impossible with Proctor's restrictive orders in place. Isaac stayed put while his friend knew that the clock was ticking. Finally, the Canadian decided to clearly lay out to Isaac as much as he knew of Proctor's evil plan.

Shocked by the disclosure, Isaac's first response was a solemn promise to his friend that he would never divulge to anyone his identity. And he never did. As a result, to this day we do not know the name of this life-saving Canadian.

Immediate action was required by Isaac Hamblin and he did not hesitate. That night he discreetly made visits to several of his American neighbors' homes. The discussions were strained but deliberate. All were determined to develop a plan of action before sunrise. There was no ignoring the direness of their situation. Without permits to leave, an attempt to escape to the States was suicide. It was a small miracle that Isaac was even able to visit his neighbors without drawing undo attention from British soldiers about the area.

In spite of their understandable panic and fear, the neighbors came to an agreement on a plan that night. The most strategic move they had

Portrait of Isaac Hamblin
believed to have been done between 1852 and 1859.

any chance of successfully making was to stop those letters of instructions from reaching their Canadian destinations. In Upper Canada, it is believed that the mail service had become a military operation at this point in time due to the war. The postman who was expected periodically from Detroit was likely to have been a member of the British forces. Deliveries were more sporadic due to unforeseen complications of the war, but a postman was known to be due, and soon. Isaac and his friends had to make sure this fellow did not complete his rounds. But how? As a man of deep faith, Isaac trusted God to provide the means, and He did.

A coincidence, or in Isaac's view an act of Divine Providence, had occurred a few days earlier. It was this: amongst the neighbors, three of their cows had run off. This was quite an unusual thing to happen, but it would prove fortuitous. Isaac and a couple others were able to use their search for the lost cows as a pretense to leave their homes.

This provided the means of executing their own plot to intercept the in-coming mail — the mail that could lead to their destruction.

And so they went out in search of their stray cows. These common farmers took to the Detroit Road which ran all along the Thames River from its origin at the fortress of the same name. This was the usual path of mail delivery in Upper Canada.

Several days would pass, each spent a short way off the road in quiet anticipation. Lying in tall grass or tucked behind trees, night and day the farmers advanced and waited for the rider. Finally, the night came when they discerned the glow of a fire in the distance. The farmers cautiously moved closer. Soon the silhouette of a single male figure presented itself to them against the dancing flames. His small movements led them to presume that he was preparing his dinner over the fire. Nearby was a horse saddled on either side with bulging bags. Then it happened. "The sound of one solitary rifle broke the awful stillness of the night, but soon its sounds died away, and all was still again as death; the little fire, too, mysteriously went out." [8]

The ball that took the life of this lone man, spared the life of hundreds, maybe thousands of others. The owner of the gun from which the fatal shot was fired is unknown. However, as Isaac and his friends opened the post bags and read the letters, "they found, as had been told them, the agreement of their massacre, the time, the place, the names of those who were to be their murderers." [9]

As it happened…

> In a few days the Indians came on, according to the contract, but there was no dinner and no whiskey, and they cursed the whites as lying dogs, and could hardly be restrained from falling on the Canadians. They obtained a little whiskey, got drunk, and killed a few of their own number and then decamped. [10]

Proctor had known Isaac Hamblin and always suspected that he was somehow involved in the demise of that postman, and by extension the ruin of his murderous plot. Though we don't have details beyond those given here, one has to wonder if those cows were ever found and driven home by Isaac and his friends? And further, did anyone take note of whether they were or were not? Perhaps the answer to these questions triggered Proctor's suspicions.

Isaac's Canadian residence was well-maintained and apparently functioning profitably. He worked acres of farmland, owned some cattle, and had grown an extensive fruit orchard. And like anyone, he had horses, farm equipment, and at least one exceptionally American-built wagon. The fact that records make note of something as ordinary as a wagon makes one assume that it was a great source of pride for Isaac and was far better than anything his neighbors may have owned. Perhaps it was akin to someone in today's culture having a Ferrari or other highly prized vehicle sitting in their driveway.

Unfortunately for Isaac, however; after the murderous plot was foiled a suspicious eye was cast toward him. Proctor, who needed additional means of transportation viewed Isaac's possessions as his own. Soon the General would confiscate whatever he desired. Ironically, General Harrison, as well, would eventually make use of Isaac's things as the war crept up the Thames River.

As 1813 unfolded, William Henry Harrison was in full command of the Northwest Army. Taking Detroit back from the British was a key part of his agenda, but he wanted even more. He was determined to alleviate the entire threat to America by annihilating the alliance of Indian warriors led by the famous Shawnee leader, Tecumseh, and the British troops who were commanded by Proctor.

Along the banks of the Maumee River in northwest Ohio, the enemy attacked the Americans at Fort Meigs. Unsuccessful assaults were made in May and again in July 1813. Frustrated by their failure, Tecumseh and Proctor led their forces forty miles further into Ohio to attack a much smaller garrison known as Fort Stephenson in today's city of Fremont. Again, the Americans held their own and the enemy could do nothing more than retreat to Fort Malden.

A few weeks later, on September 10, Oliver Perry attacked the British fleet on Lake Erie. At Fort Malden, Tecumseh and Proctor could hear the cannon blasts as the battle transpired. When word came that Perry had won the day, they were mortified. In practical terms this meant that the supply lines of the British were now in jeopardy. Goods, ammunition, and reinforcements weren't going to arrive any time soon in Upper Canada. The inhabitants of Fort Detroit and its surroundings fled as they knew American troops under Harrison were on their way to re-occupy the garrison and more.

Portrait of Henry Proctor by J.C.H. Forster.

Sometime after Proctor had returned from his misadventures in the Ohio country, he had gotten to work preparing for the anticipated fight. The American naval victory was simply the final indicator that it was on its way. He apparently needed every bit of equipment he could find including what was owned by Isaac Hamblin and his neighbors.

Already bitter and distrusting of Isaac, Proctor had no qualms about taking his things without asking. He demanded the use of Isaac's horses and his grand wagon. In fact, he forced Isaac to haul for him. But that didn't last long. Soon, Isaac was able to stop working for Proctor because he was officially made a prisoner of the General. It was mid-September when he was bound within the walls of Fort Malden. The reason for this move is unknown, though it wouldn't be a stretch to suppose that evidence of Isaac's encounter with the postman may have surfaced. Or perhaps Proctor didn't want the man he suspected of that treachery to be moving freely about with Harrison only days or weeks away.

Isaac's stint as a prisoner was not pleasant.

They wound him up in a large rope, like scythe blades are usually wound up, commencing at his feet, and passing the rope round his body, arms, and legs, up to his neck. In this condition he lay seventeen days and nights...[11]

In case you can't picture this scene, research the 1960s cartoon series of Dudley Do-Right. In that show was a character known as Snidely Whiplash who frequently would tie up a damsel by the name of Nell in much the same distressing manner.

Besides the physical torture of being bound in rope for such an extended period of time, Isaac had to endure a bit of emotional abuse as well. "While thus tied, he said Proctor and Tecumseh came to him every day to kick, cuff, and curse him."[12] Because of Tecumseh's extensively documented history of not torturing those who were defenseless, it might be safe to assume that most of this taunting was Proctor's doing.

Over the final days of September, the American forces made their way to Upper Canada. They came from the south shores of Lake Erie's Sandusky Bay. Some would ride around the lake and cross the Detroit River toward their objective. Others would board boats and cross first to the islands of the lake and then beyond. On October 1 they arrived. To their surprise, the enemy was no where to be found and what had been Fort Malden now lay in ashes.

In the interim, Isaac had been moved to one of the dozen or so British supply vessels that ran upriver alongside the troops as they made their retreat. Yes, Proctor's forces, and reluctantly Tecumseh's, were in full flight along the Thames River. Proctor hoped to reach Burlington, on the western edge of Lake Ontario, where he expected reinforcements. Tecumseh, who had wanted to do battle at Fort Malden, grew angrier with Proctor as each day had passed without them turning to engage their pursuers.

Harrison and his troops closed the gap more each day. By October 4 they drew very near to the enemy; so close that they knew a battle might begin that night. They made camp across private properties near present-day Chatham, Ontario. Two thousand or more men take up a significant amount of space. And as it happened, one end of their expansive camp was on Isaac's land.

The soldiers had to create a hedge of protection in case of an overnight attack. They grabbed whatever they could find to make an abatis that would encircle the entire camp. And so, while Isaac lay tied up in a British flat boat on the night of October 4, his fellow Americans were cutting down his orchard. In fact, they destroyed much of his property; pulling wood from his home, barn, and fences to fortify their position. After losing his horses, wagons, and dignity to Proctor; ironically he now lost his life's work to the very men there to protect him.

The British had set fire to a few of their own flat boats to prevent their excess supplies and ammunition from getting into the Americans' hands. Other vessels were grounded by the shallow waters of the Thames in this area. One of them held Isaac and other American prisoners.

> The prison boat, however, could not run; consequently, it was soon hailed by the advance guard of the American army, and ordered to shore. Brother Hamblin had prevailed with the [British] soldiers to put shirts over their regimentals to prevent the [American] guard from firing at them, which was the means of saving their lives. [13]

In this way, Isaac spared the lives of his captors as well as his own. He never fully recovered from the ordeal. In fact it took a few hours for him to stand and walk properly once he was untied. Yet, that very day, he would bear arms in the fight that ever since has been known as the Battle of the Thames.

Some sort of communication transpired between Isaac and Harrison after being released early that morning, because as a civilian he would not otherwise have been allowed into the battle. Harrison had to have been impressed with this farmer's stamina and patriotism. So much so that he placed Isaac in the front lines of the fight. Few of the Americans present had ever seen Tecumseh. Perhaps Harrison requested Isaac to take a more precarious post because he was familiar with the Shawnee leader and could monitor his movements. Whatever the reason, Isaac indeed fought amongst the men in the forefront of the battle. As a result, he provided history with an account of Tecumseh's death that has been used by historians ever since to make a solid case for Richard M. Johnson having taken out this fiercest of warriors. His narrative reads that he

> was standing but a few feet from Colonel Johnson when he fell, and in full view and saw the whole of that part of the battle. He was well acquainted with Tecumseh having seen him before the war, and having

Though the name is in dispute, (supposed to be the captured American *Erie*, *Miamis*, or *General Myers*), this vessel was torched by the British on October 4, 1813 to avoid its arms and ordinances from being captured by the Americans. In 1901, the remains (pictured) were raised and found to still have a considerable number of cannon balls and shells onboard (a few of which have been preserved in the Chatham-Kent Museum in Chatham, Ontario). On a similar British-held vessel, Isaac Hamblin had been bound and held captive for over two weeks until General Harrison rescued him on the morning of the Battle of the Thames.

been a prisoner seventeen days, and receiving many a cursing from him. He thinks Tecumseh thought Johnson was Harrison, as he often heard the chief swear that he would have Harrison's scalp, and seemed to have a special hatred toward him. Johnson's horse fell under him; he himself being also deeply wounded; in the fall he lost his sword, his large pistols were empty, and he was entangled with his horse on the ground. Tecumseh had fired his rifle at him, and when he saw him fall, he threw down his gun, and bounded forward like a tiger sure of his prey. Johnson had only a side pistol ready for use; he aimed at the chief over the head of his horse, and shot him near the center of his forehead. When the ball struck, it seemed to him that the Indian jumped with his head a full fifteen feet into the air; as soon as he struck the ground, a little Frenchman ran his bayonet into him, and pinned him fast to the ground.[14]

There are plenty of accounts of Tecumseh's death at this battle, but Isaac's was one of the few by an eye-witness and not by speculation or here-say.

Something equally as intriguing about this historic battle was the behavior of General Proctor. As the opening shots were fired, Proctor deserted his men. Yes, the head of the British forces went AWOL. Maybe he knew how exhausted his men were at this point. He certainly knew they were outnumbered. For some reason, he had no faith in a victory and so he speedily road off to an eventual court martial.

After the battle,

> Hamblin, by permission from Harrison, made a search for his team; the wagon was found, but so completely riddled with balls that it was unfit for further use; his horse he never found, and was told by one British prisoner that Proctor had ran away with one of them.[15]

Proctor had not fled alone. Members of his personal staff accompanied him. One of them may have been riding one of Isaac's fine steeds. A band of Kentucky militiamen pursued them for six or seven miles, but never caught up. Along the way, however, they discovered Proctor's abandoned carriage and many of his personal items strewn along the road in his haste to escape. A few miles further the Kentuckians came upon wagons carrying women and children who were kept away from the battlefield for their safety. The wagons were likely the ones taken by Proctor from the Americans living along the Thames.

When the battle ended it is believed Isaac came back to the U.S. in the company of Harrison and the troops. He had lost everything.

> General Harrison gave him one hundred dollars, and that was all he saved out of a good living of at least three thousand dollars. In that fearful strife and race for his life he seemed to have lost all relish for worldly gains, only so far as the pressing wants of his family were concerned.[16]

Isaac settled in Franklin County, today the heart of Columbus, Ohio, where Harrison had a military base. The wife he had moved to Canada with some twenty years earlier was not with him. Her fate is not known. In 1815, just two years after leaving Canada, Isaac, Jr. was born. Isaac and his new bride, Hannah, would go on to have nine children.

The Hamblins moved many times over the years; throughout Ohio, Wisconsin, Iowa, and finally Indiana. It is believed that Isaac put his mason skills to use in the building of Kenyon College of Ohio in the 1830s. Otherwise, he farmed the lands he lived on.

Always a devout Christian, Isaac's faith deepened with age and spread through his descendents. Isaac, Jr. became a minister and started the Sylvania church near Bloomington, Indiana. It is there that Isaac Hamblin was buried after passing on to his creator's care in 1859. He was eighty-six years of age.

According to his minister, Rev. Abraham Wright, Isaac would often be found

> like Jacob of old, leaning on his staff, worshipping God. Several times during my stay in the Bloomfield charge he walked to the (church) meeting, when it took him at least half the day to go and come, though it was only a mile. Often he would say he was just waiting the Master's will, and when he talked of going, his eyes would sparkle with delight. [17] ♦

ANECDOTE.

> Dr. Clarke was preaching to a large congregation, and after dwelling in glowing terms on the freeness of the Gospel, and telling them that the water of life could be had "without money and without price," at the conclusion of the sermon, a person announced that a collection would be made to support the Gospel in foreign parts. This announcement disconcerted the worthy doctor, who afterward related the circumstance to the lady of the house where he was staying. "True, doctor," replied the hostess, "the water of life is free, 'without money and without price, 'but they must pay for the pitchers to carry it in."
>
> *In Harper Magazine's Book: American Wit and Humor, 1859* [18]

II.
THE MELMORE MAN.

The clouds of war loomed over all the American settlements in Upper Canada as the year of 1812 unfolded. At the opposite end of the province from Isaac Hamblin's farm was another American family nervously wondering what might happen next in the course of the war. Ezra Brown had been living just west of the St. Lawrence River for over a decade. In 1800, with his wife Elizabeth, he had left Chatham, New York. The couple had followed in the footsteps of his parents and his siblings who were lured earlier to Canada by the offer of free land.

They all had a stable, peaceful existence in a town named Athens. Their already large family was, as they say, fruitful and multiplying. Elizabeth alone eventually bore Ezra nine children. But as 1812 unfolded, the rumor of war became a fact and it rocked the Brown's stable world.

The middle child of seven brothers, Ezra, as all able-bodied Americans of military age living in Upper Canada, would have his patriotism put to an extreme test. British recruiters were now drafting these American residents into the defense of the Crown. Imagine the seriousness and consternation that this situation afforded. Here were Americans who had been enjoying, developing, and growing their families and farms for years; never anticipating another conflict with Britain so soon after the Revolution had ended. Yet now war was indeed threatening to wipe out their way of life. And, to complicate matters even further, they had to choose sides in the conflict when the unpredictability of war itself pointed to the futility of such a decision. For no matter the victor, all may be lost. Even further, each choice had serious immediate consequences. If they remained loyal to America, they were likely to be imprisoned or worse. If they fought for the British, they could find themselves aiming at the children of the very men who gave them the freedom they now knew.

As events transpired, and battles occurred on Canadian soil near the St. Lawrence River, some American residents were shocked to see their fellow countrymen plundering and even burning their American neighbor's properties in the heat of battle. Such actions embittered a few, and turned some to take the British side. The Brown brothers, however, made a quick decision. They would leave their possessions and property and return to their homeland in the United States. Betraying their country of origin was something they just could not abide.

On the surface, it might have seemed to be a simple venture. Afterall, they were merely ten miles from the St. Lawrence River which marked the divide of the two countries. But British soldiers were on high alert regarding the Americans. The tension in the air was easy to discern and the authorities were not going to tolerate any overt defections. None-the-less escapes were attempted.

Ezra, his friend Richard Jaqua, and eight others, probably many of his brothers, celebrated New Year's Eve of 1812 by crossing the St. Lawrence to their freedom under the cover of darkness. What a grand way to bring in the new year. According to an 1880 historian named William Lang:

> Jaqua carried a small feather-bed and bed-clothes, and Brown carried the clothing for both. When the party arrived on American soil, they traveled on foot through the snow, and reached an American picket-fort late in the night. The next morning the whole party of run-aways were sent, under guard, to Ogdensburgh [a fortress along the St. Lawrence just a few miles north of where they crossed], in the state of New York, where Major Forsythe was in command. The Major examined each man separately, and being fully satisfied of the truth of their statements, gave each man a pass. [1]

Ezra's younger brother, Daniel, was not quite so fortunate. He was captured by the British and put on trial for treason. Luckily, he was acquitted and eventually found his way back to the States. Elizabeth and the children remained in Canada with Ezra's parents until the conflict ended.

Portrait of Ezra Brown.

Ezra parted ways with his friend Richard for a short time, but in April they met up in Morristown on the shores opposite their former Canadian homes. From this location they decided to team up and help their fellow countryman escape across the treacherous river. They acquired a punt-boat, a flat bottomed and squared end canoe of sorts that is especially designed for shallow waters as were common in this area of the St. Lawrence River. The boat was maneuvered with a long pole that was pushed off the river bottom rather than by oars or sails.

It was risky business, but they were quite successful; so much so that by late summer British authorities decided enough was enough. A small contingent of soldiers were sent to the riverfront to end the transports by abducting these men. What the British party did not expect to meet up with was Ezra's cunning.

One night, Jaqua, Brown, Patterson, and five others crossed over to Gibway Point and secreted themselves until morning. Patterson walked along the beach to attract the attention of the [British] guard. Immediately, three men were seen putting out from the island in a punt-boat, and landing on Gibway Point, pulled their boat on shore, and then made for Patterson. These men and Patterson, getting into sharp conversation, Patterson receded from the British and the shore, and when they were far enough away to be considered safe, Jaqua, Brown, and the other men who were secreted with them, jumped up, and with cocked guns and the help of Patterson, took the men prisoners and handed them over to a militia captain at Rawsee. This captain detailed a guard, consisting of Sergeant Whipple, Jaqua, Brown, and several others, to take the prisoners to Sackett's Harbor, which they did. [2]

And so, after escorting their captives some forty miles to Sackett's Harbor, the men returned to their business of shuttling American escapees across the river. This continued into the autumn months until one day when two messengers from an American post further north had arrived. One of the two surprise visitors was quite ill and needed immediate medical care. The other explained their mission. American General Wilkinson and his reinforcements were at this time based further upriver and required help navigating the waters of this region, known as the Thousand Isles. Because these waters were so shallow with an extraordinary number of rocks deceptively hidden just below the surface, it was a very treacherous stretch for the inexperienced boatmen. To this end, Ezra and Richard stepped up yet again. Having lived in the area much of their lives, they were expert at maneuvering vessels through this watery gauntlet.

For weeks the two friends led teams of U.S. soldiers through miles of dangerous river water to their destination. This was a much speedier and preferred route for the soldiers, rather than making a trek on foot through the wilderness of upper New York State.

Ezra continued serving his country throughout the war years. His grand-daughter, Laura Everett, explains how his spunk nearly cost him his life on more than one occasion.

He acted as a spy and assisted in transferring supplies and men across the St. Lawrence River. He came near to losing his life when he swam the St. Lawrence on a barn door, and another time he was taken prisoner. As the enemy was taking him over to Canada, he managed to upset the boat and swim to the American shores.

At another time, Ezra was taken prisoner by British soldiers and was taken on board a British ship; and was guarded by two soldiers. He told them if he could get into the water, they could shoot at him as much as they chose. He dared them to do this, but they did not accept the proposal. Later, he jumped overboard as they were approaching shore and swam underwater until he reached the shore in safety. [3]

When the war ended, Elizabeth and the children came back to the United States and they all settled for a few years in the Genessee County area of New York (between today's cities of Buffalo and Rochester). But Ezra and his brother Case had their eye on land in the heart of the Ohio country. Case went first and settled, well, squatted, on land along Honey Creek; so named because the color of its water resembled the nectar when it was high.

In 1820 a land act was passed which ended the practice of using credit to buy public lands. This meant no more mortgages. All sales had to be made with payment in full. Though this seemed harsh, there was a trade off. The usual price per acre was cut almost in half and the minimum size of lots was indeed cut in half. All these moves triggered a much needed cash flow for the government while making Ohio land more affordable for the would-be settler. Ezra took advantage of the policy changes. In 1821, he was moving onto land next to his brother Case, and within the year they built a gristmill. It was this kind of entrepreneurial thinking that served Ezra well throughout his days, as the mill spared the swelling number of residents a treacherous trip of ten to twenty miles through the wilderness to the next nearest town where they could have their grains ground.

Just three years later the brothers would become part of the team of surveyors to officially lay out the new town of Melmore. Colonel James Kilbourn, former 1812 officer and founder of Worthington, Ohio, led the effort. Situated just five miles southeast of today's Tiffin, Ohio, the name Melmore was created by the colonel who united the Latin word "mel" for the English "honey" with the English word "more." Thus the town name of "more honey" became an expansion on the

The Masonic Meeting House built by Ezra Brown in 1824 is still standing as seen in this photo taken by the author in 2020. It has been renovated over the past 200 years and is now a private residence.

Honey Creek name already given to the waterway running through the village. The town grew from a dozen or so squatters before 1820 to nearly 1,500 by 1840. As of 2019, it's a cozy community of 150. A poem written by Colonel Kilbourn lives on as a testament to the spirit of the people who grew the town of Melmore.

> MELMORE
>
> Where honey-dews from the mild Heaven,
> Distil on the foliage below —
> Where Honey creek's waters are given,
> T'enrich the sweet bosom of flowers —
> There Melmore is seen, on a hill,
> With fragrance and health in her bowers.
>
> This country and village to prove,
> Of pleasure and health the abode,
> Kind Nature has formed in her, love,
> And on her good children bestowed.

> The fees to her agenda are small.
> For titles in form which they give;
> Then come, men of enterprise — all,
> Accept, and in happiness live.
>
> Merchants and laborers come,
> A fortune is offered you near;
> Here make it your permanent home,
> The country will cherish you here.
> Come, taste the Melmorean springs,
> Possess the Melmorean lands,
> Wealth, honor, and pleasure they'll bring,
> To strengthen your hearts and your hands.
>
> So healthy the country is, round,
> That doctors have little to do;
> So moral the people are found,
> They live without ministers, too;
> So honest our neighbors we call,
> So peaceful and happy at home,
> They've need of no lawyers at all,
> And none are desired to come. [4]

By 1824, Ezra was in building mode again, this time constructing a beautiful brick structure of two stories to serve as a Masonic Hall. Nearly 200 years later it still stands. Elizabeth, Ezra's wife, most likely never saw the construction of this structure as she is known to have passed away shortly after their settling in the area. The town cemetery was on a portion of Ezra's property and his beloved bride was only the second person to be laid there. In 1829, Ezra took a second wife, Sabrina (Ransom) Parks, herself a widow of several years with five children. The couple would have three more children between them, making Ezra the proud father of twelve.

Ezra fancied himself a good judge of the value of land for farming. He travelled throughout the Northwest Territory evaluating prospective new lands to invest in or move to. After a trip to Chicago, he is famously quoted as saying that he, "wouldn't accept land there as a gift," for it was nothing but a "muddy hole." [5]

A testament to Ezra's character and brush with death are related by his daughter Elizabeth "Betsy" (Brown) Tuckerman.

While living in Ohio in the early 1830s, Ezra had travelled to Michigan on foot. On his way to Detroit, he followed the Raisin River and stopped at a Trading Post, an Indian came in and wanted some food and something to drink.

At this time, the Michigan region was still heavily populated by the Native Americans. In fact as the state of Ohio continued to be settled by white men, the Michigan territory was one of the last areas where they still had a strong presence before the Andrew Jackson's Indian Removal Act was fully implemented.

The man in charge would not serve the Indian as he did not have any money. Ezra paid for the food and drink and left. On Ezra's way back to Ohio, he lost his way and he knew that if he could find the river he could find his way home. He came upon a group of Indians and they captured him. The reason that he felt he was not harmed was, that the Indian he had befriended in the Trading Post was with this group of Indians. This Indian recognized him, and after some discussion, this Indian took Ezra to the river, where he got his bearings and was able to find his way home. [6]

Ezra was a restless soul. It is inferred in records that he may have moved his family around a bit after settling in Melmore, but the only change that is certain came twenty years after marrying Sabrina. In 1849 they relocated just a few miles north to Republic, Ohio. In that same year, at the age of sixty-seven, the ever-spry Ezra joined his step-son, William Henry Parks, on a trip to California.

It was the famous "Gold Rush" that Ezra partook in as he traveled in a one hundred man, oxen-driven excursion that took five months to complete after they had gotten to St. Louis. It's unclear whether he came by any of the fortune that others had found in "them there mountains," but he certainly approved of the land and its prospects. Eighteen months later he was back in Ohio. But not before stopping in Iowa to spend the winter with one of his sons. He was known to spend many a day running barefoot in the snow around the house in order to toughen his feet. Why? Because he was going back to California the next year, on foot. Yes, in 1852, at seventy years of age he walked from Ohio to California. He spent several years there until he went back one more time to collect his family and escort them to the town of Marysville in 1861. Ezra managed to locate his

The western mining town of North San Juan, Nevada County, California, circa 1858, where Ezra Brown spent his final years and continued working as a miner into his 90s.

family in the shadow of the gold-filled hills; a stone's throw from that mystical, far-away place that no one else ever seems to get to: Timbuctoo. Really. Just a few miles east of Marysville was a mining town that Ezra probably worked in and it was named after the original Timbuctu in Mali, Africa. Today it's a ghost-town.

Census records show that Ezra continued moving several more times while living in California, but always within the mining regions and always with fellow family members. One record listed Ezra's occupation as a "miner," and lists a Chinese person acting as their cook living with them. This leads to the speculation that he had found some success in the gold business. He spent his last days in North San Juan, California a certified mining town that was booming during the years he lived there.

It's easy to see that Ezra was one of the most robust specimens of the era and continued to exhibit unusual stamina until shortly before his passing at the age of ninety-four. His obituary attests to this fact.

> He was of very vigorous constitution, defying hardships and exposure. Enthusiastic... but for a few years the infirmities of age and disease and

lack of hearing bore heavily on him. He was trying to live a Christian life, and longed to depart to that "better land." During months of acute suffering, he was tenderly cared for by two daughters. He passed away quietly as a babe to sleep, and as he lay in the casket looked scarcely 70 years old.[7] ♦

ANECDOTE.

Origin of the Name Yankee. — Anbury, an author who did not respect the Americans, any more than many others who have been led captive by them, has the following paragraph upon this word — "The lower class of these *Yankees* — apropos, it is derived from a Cherokee word, *eankke,* which signifies coward and slave. This epithet of yankee was bestowed upon the inhabitants of N. England by the Virginians, for not assisting them in a war with the Cherokees, and they have always been held in derision by it. But the name has been more prevalent since (1775) the commencement of hostilities; the soldiery at Boston used it as a term of reproach; but after the affair at Bunker's Hill, the Americans gloried in it. *Yankee-doodle* is now their poean, a favorite of favorites, played in their army, esteemed as warlike as the grenadier's march — it is the lover's spell, the nurse's lullaby. After our rapid successes, we held the yankees in great contempt; but it was not a little mortifying to hear them play this tune, when their army marched down to our surrender."

But Mr. Heckewelder [Missionary to the Delaware] thinks that the Indians, in endeavoring to pronounce the name *English,* could get that sound no nearer than these letters give it, *yengees.* This was perhaps the true origin of *Yankee.*

In Samuel G. Drake's, Biography and History of the Indians of North America, 1848[8]

III.
AND THIS LITTLE PIGGY WENT TO WAR.

In the course of the War of 1812 the men of Kentucky: farmers, merchants, even preachers, were called upon to yet again grab their guns, saddle their horses, and travel north. Their charge was to defend their families from the British and Indian alliance now at war with the United States. These were not trained soldiers, but they were certainly skilled with weapons. And their bravery was off the charts. They were the offspring of the men who ventured over the Appalachians to settle in this unsettling land in the first place. They became the Kentucky militia.

General William H. Harrison, in August of 1813, told Kentucky Governor Isaac Shelby that he needed his men who had already served so heroically in the past to return for another term. In fact, Harrison needed more men than ever alongside the army of the Northwest Territory. Shelby responded by having Colonel Richard M. Johnson, who would command the mounted regiment, solicit his Kentucky brothers once again. The request read in part:

Great Crossings, Aug. 15th, 1813 --

> The Mounted Regiment is again under marching orders, the deepest regret is felt that the occasion ever existed for the Regiment to leave the North Western Army. I have received the order of General Harrison to join the N.W. Army without the delay of a moment. The vital interest of the country demands dispatch. Already distinguished for its promptitude, the regiment will imitate its former example…
>
> As it is probable that arms may be scarce the companies will begin at Newport to arm themselves and procure such accommodations as they may need. The officers and men of the mounted Regiment will accept

my sincere thanks for their exemplary good conduct. The spirit of subordination which they have manifested, the spirit of enterprise which they have displayed — the firmness with which they have encountered difficulties and dangers, and the patience and fortitude with which they meet with losses. I have reason to congratulate myself in the selection and command of such a corps and from the experience of the officers I make great calculation of aid and support.

The mounted Regiment has aided the protection of a vast and extensive frontier altho they have never avoided danger, the Regiment was never permitted to meet a foe in the field — that opportunity will no doubt be afforded in the splendid campaign now opening against the enemy about Malden and Detroit, the campaign will be interesting — the mounted Regiment will have its part to act — what ever it may be let every movement be distinguished for its merit, and in case of an engagement let us unanimously resolve to finish the work assigned us.

(Signed) RH. M. JOHNSON, Col. R. M. V. [1]

They arrived from all over Kentucky at specified meeting places. In total the recruitment effort brought in more than 2,000 men who would eventually travel well over 1,500 miles before their commitment would end some three months later. They didn't know their fate, but as it played out they were the ones who would be responsible for a momentous turning point in the history of the United States. They would successfully defeat the forces of the British and Indians along the Thames River in Upper Canada; extinguishing any further organized Indian resistance to Americans' settlement.

One of the gathering points of the volunteers was Harrodsburg, Kentucky. From there, they were to march toward Newport, a small town on the southern shores of the Ohio River opposite Cincinnati. At the beginning of their trek, only a couple miles out of Harrodsburg, they had to make an unplanned stop due to a battle that was in progress just ahead of them. This was not anticipated. With amazement and incredulity they watched as two wild pigs engaged each other in a grueling fight.

When the contest ended, the loser ran off while the men applauded the winner. With the distraction over they reformed their lines. Soon after resuming their march to Newport they were surprised again, this time by the sight of the winning hog picking up their rear in full stride. After a significant march of probably twenty miles the men camped for the night, and so did the pig. The men were intrigued at the stamina the pig had shown. Now, rather than running off to find familiar grounds, she nestled nearby into a bed of her own making.

As dawn broke, orders echoed through the woods for the men to form up. As if she felt the command was for her as well, the pig took her place with the men and again followed along. Another night and day would pass and the pig behaved as before. The men grew quite fond of this tough gal who continued on with them for the full 120 miles to Newport.

After gaining fresh supplies and a brief rest the men prepared to make multiple ferry crossings over the Ohio River. They expected that this was where they would part ways with the pig. However, she approached the riverbank and assessed the situation, quickly deciding that the ferry was not for her. Diving into the current the pig made a determined swim to the other side. There she shook off the water and patiently waited until all the Kentuckians made their safe crossings without so much as getting their feet wet.

At this point the men considered this wild creature more than a curiosity, she was a Kentuckian. Even Governor Isaac Shelby himself took a keen interest.

All the way up to the south shores of Lake Erie, the full length of the state, the pig marched along day after day. Sometimes she couldn't quite keep up, but would always eventually waddle into camp to the cheers of her fellows. Often she danced before the men, running in circles, squealing and almost prancing with pride for having made it through another tedious hike.

Though their rations were meager at times, the men agreed that she should get a full share of her own in order to keep up her strength. Even when hunger pangs struck, "no one thought of putting the knife to the throat of their fellow soldier". [2]

When the Kentucky militia reached Lake Erie, they settled into a large base camp with federal troops who were arriving from other locations. Some militia would march around the lake, but these Kentuckians would board flatboats to the islands before sailing on to Fort Malden. Their horses were corralled on a large grassland at the Sandusky Bay so they could feed while the men were gone.

The pig didn't seem to care much for the idea of grazing with the horses, and after surveying the vastness of the lake she dismissed the idea of a very long swim as well. She boarded a vessel with the men who landed on Bass Island. But this wasn't the final destination of the troops. In a few days the men cast off from the island for the Canadian shoreline. This time the pig refused to board. "Some of the men attributed her conduct to constitutional scruples, and observed that she knew it was contrary to the constitution to force a militia pig over the line." [3] At this time, militias were a local defense mechanism, sometimes a state one. The president had no federal authority to make them serve outside of their home regions, but they could do so voluntarily. These Kentuckians were a volunteer regiment crossing into Ohio and then internationally into Canada by their own choosing. This pig was not going to become Canadian bacon.

The battle along the Thames River proved victorious for the American militiamen. About ten days after they had left Sandusky Bay, they had returned. Now preparations were made for the long trek back home. Supplies were gathered and horses were mounted. "As soon as the line was formed, to the great surprise of many, and inspiring a deep interest in all, there was the pig on the right of the line, ready to resume her march with the rest." [4]

It was now mid-October and winter was moving in fast. Snows and cold made travel difficult and took a serious toll on all, including the pig. After many days of marching under such harsh conditions the Kentuckians reached Maysville on the south side of the Ohio River.

They were still a hundred miles from home near Harrodsburg. The pig was in the care of Governor Isaac Shelby himself at this point. He determined that his friend could go no further and so arranged for her to recuperate with a responsible party. Once she was nursed back to her full strength, she was taken to the Governor's home where she lived on for quite some time as his special pet.

This story was originally noted in 1816 by Robert McAfee, a participant in the campaign to the Thames River, in his *History of the Late War in Western Country*. It is picked up again in 1847 by the historian Lewis Collins in his *Historical Sketches of Kentucky*. Collins further notes that the tale could be verified by many sources who had witnessed it and were still alive at the time his history was published. ♦

ANECDOTE.

Two Englishmen were disputing about the moon, one insisting it was an inhabited element, the other contending with him, a Yankee standing by attended to their discourse, replies with confidence, it is not: one of the gentlemen being a little displeased with his interferrence with a look of disdain, says how do I know sir? (replied the Yankee) because if it had been, the British would have had the folly and persumption to have laid siege to it long before this time.

In the Centinel of the North-Western Territory, January 9, 1796 [5]

IV.
THE JERSEY BOYS.

———— ✦ ————

Perhaps the most recognized New Jerseyans of our day are the ones that came together in the 1960s as the acclaimed musical group the *Four Seasons*. But, there were a few other boys from New Jersey who deserve notoriety of their own. The guys I'm referring to predate the singing quartet by more than 200 years. They weren't famous for their melodic tones, but rather for the courageous service they gave to their country and the heroic personal survival skills they demonstrated many times over as they settled into the Ohio Valley. Their names were Benjamin Stites, Ephraim Kibbey, and Robert Benham. No creative writer could get away with offering up some of these Jersey boys' adventures as believable, yet they are as true as blue.

You'll soon learn that these men had much in common. Perhaps on the deepest level the most significant bond they had was the fraternal one shared through freemasonry. In 1791, a petition was made to the Grand Lodge of New Jersey to form a second masonic lodge in the Ohio Valley, where all three of them were living at that time. They were amongst the founding fathers of several new villages in an area that would soon be known as Cincinnati. Just months earlier the first lodge was sanctioned in the newly settled town of Marietta some 200 miles upriver from their site. It took a few years, but in 1795 the Nova Caesarea Harmony Lodge No. 2 was in operation. The name cleverly revealed its roots, as the Latin "Nova" translates to "New," and "Caesarea" to "Jersey." Once all the officers were properly installed, Ephraim Kibbey became its first brother. Ben Stites and Robert Benham would soon follow suit.

Stites was the oldest of the three, born in 1746. Benham was four years younger, and Kibbey ten years his junior. They all participated in the American Revolution and the Indian engagements on the frontier. It's not certain whether they knew each other during their childhood days in New Jersey; but by the mid-1780s they would all be found along the Monongahela River in far western Pennsylvania. Several small settlements were popping up very close to each other in this region; Tenmile and Redstone were two of them. Eventually a gentleman named Thomas Brown and his brother Basil would purchase land nearby and establish a town bearing their name, Brownsville. Here the three Jersey boys certainly must have become acquainted with each other because in a short time they would all be found together aboard flatboats heading down the Ohio River to start a new life. They were just three among the many other New Jerseyans who took on the adventure of settling the Ohio Valley, but they made a special impression on their fellows.

As one can already see, the stories of these men overlap because of their common home state, the associations they joined, where they lived as young adults, and their decision to move into the Indian country of the Northwest Territory. But they have intriguing individual stories that deserve to be told. So, let's begin with the one who initiated the idea of settling lands on the northern banks of the Ohio River, Benjamin Stites.

Ben descended from a stout line of Englishmen who were blessed with genes of longevity. This can be attested to by his great, great grandfather, John Stites, who it is said lived for 122 years. But genes don't protect you from bullets. Ben was living in a rough, dangerous world that he refused to run from. In fact he aggressively defended the peace. When he reached his mid-twenties he was found living near Redstone and there was serving as a Captain of the First Battalion of the Pennsylvania Militia. Stites would spend the Revolutionary War years protecting the settlers of that region, including his first wife and their four children, from the assaults being made by the Indians. He was stationed at a garrison known as Jackson's Fort in present-day Waynesburg, Pennsylvania. It was a small structure as forts go, but provided a refuge for the residents to run to in the event of an Indian attack. It served its purpose far too often.

When the war had officially ended Stites would settle back into his home in Redstone and for a short time would work as a tax collector, before becoming a merchant. However, his old job of Indian fighting would never cease. Some of his encounters reveal both his character and his good fortune. As told by his daughters Phoebe Miranda and Rachel Kibbey, one incident nearly cost the young Stites his life.

> In the summer of 1778, of a Sunday, three men went out of Jackson's fort to a mill on the opposite side of the Creek (Hathaway's mill) and one of them, Caleb Rinehart, was killed, the bullet striking a sapling, glanced and struck him on the side of the head. Rinehart fell, only stunned, and before he could recover, the Indians ran up and tomahawked him (and very likely, as Mrs. Kibby says, shook the scalp defyingly) and ran off. The other two whites escaped.
>
> Capt. Stites and several of the men in the fort ran out with their guns, and while crossing the causeway over a low wet spot between the fort and creek, when the Indians shot from over the creek, and a ball passed between Stites' powder-horn and shot-pouch and cut both, but without injury to Capt. Stites. His party returned the fire, and the Indians decamped. Some seven or eight of them were in view, their whole number not known. A few days after, a dead Indian was found in a hollow log near to where he had evidently crawled and died of his wounds, which was through the body. [1]

Sometime later another Indian raid was made in the Redstone area. The frightened settlers again sought protection within the walls of Jackson's fort. Major Stites and his men took up their arms and rode away from the safety of the fort to hunt down the attackers. The Indians were successfully run off, but when the militia returned Stites discovered that he had cheated death once again for his shirt and hat were riddled with holes made by Indian balls that had barely missed their mark.

By 1785, Ben was found selling his wares in Washington, Kentucky (also known as Limestone and later Maysville) on the banks of the Ohio River. As happened far too often, one day a band of Indians suddenly appeared racing through the town. This time they hadn't harmed any of the residents, but were getting off with several of their horses. Stites and others immediately mounted up and rode in pursuit. The chase went on much longer than they had anticipated, a couple days in fact. After some eighty miles they had to give up. Their horses were exhausted and the stolen horses were nowhere to be found. They had ridden as far north as what is now Xenia, Ohio, near the source of the Little Miami River. Disappointed, they turned back toward Washington, ambling along more leisurely to give their horses a rest from their hard runs.

The ride home proved inspirational and life-changing for Stites. This was country he hadn't seen before. The slow pace gave him time to look about and study it. He became enamored with the land; maybe obsessed would be more to the point.

Like a case of love at first sight, the enchanted Stites decided this was it. This was going to be his new home. He was determined to establish a settlement on the land between the two Miami Rivers which wove their way through the territory's wilderness before emptying into the mighty Ohio River. Almost immediately after his return to Washington he headed off to New York where the Continental Congress was in session.

Along with four other associates, presumably potential fellow investors, Benjamin Stites made this formal request to Congress on December 27, 1785. It's titled a "memorial" which is a term that was used more frequently during the 18th and 19th centuries than today to label a communication between lesser bodies and the houses of Congress. That included ordinary citizens like Stites.

> To the Honourable
> The United States in Congress assembled.
>
> The memorials of Henry Delay of Harrison County, State of Virginia, John Holes of Essex County, State of New Jersey, Cornelius Ludlow of Morris County, State of New Jersey, Benjamin Stites and Henry Enochs both of the County of Washington and State of Pennsylvania.
>
> Humbly Sheweth,
>
> That whereas from various informations received of the proceedings of the Indians in the Western territory of the United States it is greatly to be feared that danger will arise to the said States unless suitable measures are speedily adopted for counteracting the apparent design of our Enemies and it is supposed that a settlement established by Congress on said frontiers will effectually secure to the United States equal part of that extensive territory is therefore proposed.
>
> That a tract of Country beginning at the grant given the inhabitants

of Post Vincent [Vincennes] from thence running up both sides of the Wabash River extending to the grant given to the Indians so as to include one hundred miles breadth. That the tract of Country where described be given to the settlers as an encouragement to settle in said Country on as reasonable terms as Congress may prescribe.

And as the situation of the first adventurers will be an exposed one that they should be entitled to _____ Acres of land as reward for settling said Country. And for the better enabling the first adventurers to guard and defend themselves and their Country from the Enemy and to assist its population it is therefore petitioned that no person be allowed the privilege of purchasing any of said Country for the space of five years but those who became settlers on the land.

That all such as are willing to become immediate settlers in that Country shall meet together next spring at any place that Congress may appoint as a place of rendezvous and those to come under military direction and march into the Country in a body.

That Congress appoint a certain Gentleman whom they shall think proper as Commander in Chief of the company of said adventurers; also appoint such other officers under him as they shall judge expedient to conduct a plan of that importance.

That the first adventurers be governed by military law until such an establishment is made upon the land as will admit of a change after which the inhabitants shall be governed by the civil law which is more friendly to freedom and compatible with republican principles.

Whereas, one main object of the proposed settlement is to form a barrier against encroachments of the Enemy and to secure to the United States the land comprehended within those limits we therefore humbly request that Congress provide the first adventurers with one years provision, ammunition and artillery justable for that purpose; all other necessary articles to be furnished by the first adventurers at their own expense. That no person be admitted to settle in said Country who cannot give satisfactory testimonials of his attachment to the American cause during the late struggle for Independence.

Should it be thought wise and necessary to form a settlement on the foregoing plan may it please Congress to publish it in the papers that each State may have an equal opportunity of settling.

Your memorialists apprehend that their request being granted will greatly promote the public good and answer the end proposed.

Your memorialists therefore as in duty bound, shall ever pray. [2]

It was 1785 and two land ordinances had just recently been passed by the Continental Congress which laid the groundwork for the government to begin surveying and parcelling out acreage north of the Ohio River. That made Stites's timing absolutely perfect. John Symmes of New Jersey, serving his last term as a representative to the Continental Congress listened to Stites's ideas and heard opportunity knocking. So impressed was Symmes, that he made a trip down the Ohio to personally check out the lands. Soon he was moving into the Ohio Valley as a judge for the newly declared Northwest Territory. By forming the "East Jersey Company," Judge Symmes purchased over 300,000 acres, 10,000 of which, situated near the mouth of the Little Miami River, were sold to Stites.

The land became known as the "Symmes Purchase" or the "Miami Purchase." However, the Kentuckians had a far more sinister name for it due to the decades of deadly encounters they had there with the Indians. They called it the "Miami Slaughter House."

The daring pioneers who chose to settle this new territory came into Maysville, Kentucky through the summer of 1788. Many were from New Jersey and New York where Symmes, Stites and other investors had stirred interest in the new lands. There they waited for the seasons to change before attempting to make the seventy mile cruise to the site. The delay was strategic as they knew that the Indians typically headed to their northern villages for the winter. Even through autumn it would still be too dangerous to travel the Ohio River with Indians potentially hidden along its banks. But waiting posed another dilemma, a frozen river. This November was cold and much of the river froze early. When it began breaking up, three flatboats took their chances voyaging downstream.

Stites captained one of the vessels, dodging icy buildups much of the way. Ice flows during thaws can be very treacherous as anyone living near a river in northern states will attest to; but for these adventurous souls the risk of being hit by a floating rock of ice had understandably more appeal than being hit by an Indian's bullet.

An account by a descendant of one of the men on Stites's boat, a Mr. Ferris, relates some precaution that had to be taken as they arrived at their new home.

Previous to their leaving Maysville, a report had been in circulation

Portrait of John Cleves Symmes as it appears in the book: *Centennial History of Cincinnati and Representative Citizens*, 1904.

that some hunters had returned from the woods who had seen five hundred Indians at the mouth of the Little Miami, and that the Indians had heard the white people were coming there to settle, and intended to kill them all as soon as they should arrive. On its being announced at break of day that they were near the mouth of the Miami, some of the females were very much alarmed on account of the report alluded to. To allay their fears, five men volunteered their services to go forward in a canoe, and examine. If there were no Indians they were to wave their handkerchiefs, and the boats, which were kept close to the Kentucky shore, were to be crossed over and landed. If there were, the men were to pass by and join the boats below. The token of "no Indians" was given, and the boats were crossed over and landed at the first high banks (about three-fourths of a mile) below the mouth of the Little Miami, a little after sunrise on the morning of the 18th of November, 1788. [3]

Ben Stites and Ephraim Kibbey were in this brave group of five. Once the rest of the people came ashore, a few of them, including

Stites, thanked God for their safety.

> After making fast, they ascended the steep bank and cleared away the underbrush in the midst of a pawpaw thicket, where the women and children sat down. They next, as though to fulfil the commands of the Saviour [to] "watch and pray," placed sentinels at a small distance from the thicket, and, having first united in a song of praise to Almighty God, to whose providence they ascribed their success... upon their bended knees they offered thanks for the past and prayer for future protection; and in this manner dedicated themselves (and probably their thicket) to God, as solemnly and acceptably as ever a stately temple, with all the pomp and splendor attending it, was dedicated. [4]

Because they felt that they had discovered a new world of sorts, the people chose to name their new settlement Columbia, in honor of Christopher Columbus. It was the first of three nearly adjacent settlements to grow at this time along the riverfront. Today the Cincinnati Municipal Airport covers most of the original site, and a neighborhood still known as Columbia-Tusculum keeps the name alive.

A month after Stites's group landed, another settlement was being erected just a few miles further down river on land owned by Matthias Denman. An associate of Denman's company, the scholarly John Filson, named their town Losantville, a name created as a play on words from four different languages. The town was located directly across from the mouth of the Licking River, so the English "L" began the name. The Latin "os" for "mouth" was next. The Greek word "anti" translates to "opposite" and the French "ville" means "town." Put it all together and you get the "town opposite the Licking River."

A little footnote to this part of the story explains how this name quickly vanished:

> Shortly after its occupation, by General Harmar, who built therein Fort Washington, the little town of Losantville was chosen by Governor St. Clair to be the seat of government for the Northwest Territory. But, so the record runs, the Governor in his trip of inspection down the river [1790], arrived near the incipient village: standing on the roof of his flat-boat and looking at the collection on shore of two small hewed log houses and several cabins, he asked, "What in Hell is the name of this town anyhow?" On being given the linguistic potpourri he threw up his hands in astonishment and at once rechristened the place "Cincinnati,"

in honor of the society of that name which had just been formed by the ex-officers of the Revolutionary Army.⁵

Soon, both Columbia and Losantville would be absorbed into the expanding metropolis of Cincinnati.

A few months after these two towns were established, and about fifteen miles further down river, North Bend was settled by Judge Symmes himself, who also had previous experience as a surveyor. His town has retained its original name to this day.

Though Stites apparently had a deep faith, some moral issues in his family life would plague him. His first wife, Rachel, did not make the move to Columbia. She remained at Redstone and on paper remained married to him for ten years. In Ben's case, distance didn't make the heart grow fonder, as he would illicitly marry two more women in that period and father six additional children.

As unusual as his marriage life played out, there is little else to question in Stites's character. All his life he would put himself between others and any type of danger. He demonstrated this yet again a few years after Columbia was established.

While on a trip to Cincinnati with a friend named Reeder, a band of six Indians sprang from the woods along their path and commenced shooting at them. Stites, nearly fifty years old, was still dextrous enough to launch himself out of his saddle. In stunt man fashion he continued his ride while holding and hiding himself along the side of his horse. Luckily he and his horse dodged the Indians' shots. Reeder was less fortunate. He was hit in both his leg and arm. Stites raised himself back into his saddle and road to his friend's aid, ducking the flying balls along the way. He kicked Reeder's standing horse to spur him on and then road as a human shield between his friend and the attackers. As Divine Providence or luck would have it, the Indians' ammunition ran out. All they could do was give chase on foot with tomahawks raised high; but soon they saw the two men shrink into the distance.

Though Stiles continued to perform heroically in his later years, he would do so only in the due course of handling the business affairs of his town. No longer did he serve in a military capacity, though the Indian Wars continued on a much broader scale all around him through the early 1790s. After the signing of the Greenville Treaty in 1795, Ben would move about thirty miles up the Little Miami River and help survey the town of Deerfield, now South Lebanon. Finally he returned to Columbia where he spent his final days until 1804.

From a note in a small manuscript book on the Stites family, "... the major died a violent death in the aforesaid year [1804] when returning to his home from Fort Washington."[6]

It seems no one knew how to spell his name. In the history books and genealogical documents it is recorded as Kibbe, Kibby, Kibbey and even a few other variations. We'll refer to our second Jersey boy as Ephraim Kibbey, the most often found variation. I would submit that a Kibbey by any other spelling is still an intrepid man of character.

Mr. Kibbey was as skilled and noble as any of the frontiersmen who settled in the Ohio Valley and certainly one of the most driven. He is worth knowing about, and posthumously appreciated.

Born in 1756, Kibbey must have sensed the tensions growing between the colonists and the British soldiers as he was growing up in New Jersey. When things came to a head after his twenty-first birthday, he chose to enlist in the Continental Army. Within just a few months he would become hardened into manhood; for after the British had captured Philadelphia in July of 1777 Ephraim's regiment was stationed just a few miles northwest of that city, at Valley Forge. He endured the historic suffering from disease, malnutrition, and severe weather conditions for six months and yet continued on active duty for more than three years. He was discharged in 1781 having attained both the rank of Sergeant and the resolve to tackle any new challenges that might come his way.

As a civilian once again, Kibbey returned to New Jersey where his wife, Phebe, bore them three children through the middle 1780s. Many of his neighbors had already headed west and with the end of the war the Kibbey family decided to do so as well. They ended up in the same region Benjamin Stites had chosen, the Redstone and Tenmile area of Pennsylvania. This region was on the edge of the Indian Territory. It was seen as a strategic point from which Easterners coming through the mountains would begin their excursions into the wilderness via the Monongahela and Ohio Rivers. It was here also that Kibbey would begin to learn the ways of the Indians who were not especially fond

Pioneers' Flatboat – A wood engraving by Alfred R. Waud. Published in *The Century Magazine*, 1916.

of the settlers moving onto their lands. Unfortunately, his lessons were often learned through conflict.

Just a few years after settling along the Monongahela, Kibbey was found heading down the Ohio River on the flat boat captained by Benjamin Stites. Their destination was the mouth of the Little Miami River where he would immediately begin surveying the new town of Columbia; dividing it into lots that would soon be sold to one settler after another. Perhaps as a metaphor for his strength and individuality, Kibbey constructed his house of stone rather than wood which was the norm for the others. In time he would be a key surveyor of several regions in the Symmes Purchase. Besides laying out Columbia, it is certain he marked off properties in Losantville and Ben Stites's second settlement of Deerfield.

As the Americans plunged deeper into the Ohio Valley the trouble they had experienced with the Indians near Tenmile would seem petty. As noted earlier, there was a large contingent of Indians watching as they landed at what would become Columbia, but fewer than the

Fort Washington circa 1790. Drawn by Captain Jon. Heart.
As seen in: *Sketches and Statistics of Cincinnati* by Charles Cist.

five hundred that were rumored to be about the area. However, their numbers would increase to thousands very soon. The rise of villages along the north shores of the Ohio River did nothing but provoke the Indians to act defensively. Their land was being settled by the white men. This wasn't a transient thing. It was permanent and in their eyes meant still more of their hunting grounds were being usurped.

By the late 1780s tensions were at a fever pitch. Rather than the random horse raids and individual attacks that had been going on for years, both the Americans and Indians were now preparing for organized warfare. The so-called Indian wars of the frontier would take many lives over the next five years until the signing of the Greenville Treaty of 1795 finally brought it to a temporary halt. Ephraim Kibbey would proudly be a part of it all, and survive.

In the summer of 1789 construction of Fort Washington began in the heart of Cincinnati, (Losantville). It was designed to be a depot for the supplies that would be needed by the American forces being formed under Josiah Harmar, as well as protection for the three new villages along the riverfront. Eventually Ephraim would participate in both General Harmar's and then St. Clair's efforts against the Indian coalition, but in what capacity it is uncertain. Only in 1794, do we know any details of his service under General Anthony Wayne.

As Fort Washington was completed and its population of troops growing, food was needed on a larger scale than the Army was providing. Along with other hunters in the settlements, Kibbey was hired to provide meat to these men. But the search for wild game was often deadlier for the hunter than the hunted. On one occasion a group of six men were chasing their prey in the woods north of the fort when they were suddenly ambushed by a band of Indians. All of them were slain except one, Kibbey, who managed to escape and eventually make his way back to his home. On another occasion, Kibbey had gone out alone on a hunt when he was again discovered by Indians. Because he understood his enemy's tracking methods, he was able to out maneuver them. In this way, and following his own instincts, he managed to weave his way through the forest for over twenty-four hours. Finally his pursuers gave up the chase.

This account from the *Centinel of the North-Western Territory*, the first newspaper published in the region, highlights one of the many such escapades and their frequency. This one occurring just weeks before Kibbey would begin his march north under General Wayne:

CINCINNATI, April 26 (1794)
On Tuesday last the Indians stole out of the stables of the inhabitants of Columbia, four horses; early the next morning, Capt. Kibbey set out with ten men in pursuit of them; from the characters of the party we flatter ourselves we shall be able to give a good account of them in our next.

Last week some boats belonging to the Contractors, on their passage down the river, a few miles above Limestone (Maysville) were fired upon by the Indians and one man killed. [7]

Although the next issue of the newspaper did not make note of the stolen horses incident, the skills of Kibbey in dealing with the Indians was evident in this excerpt. After serving with the first two military campaigns, his knowledge and reputation had swelled. Kibbey felt that his expertise could serve Wayne's new effort as well.

The force at Fort Washington had been training for some time and were already at a significant strength of 2,000 regulars and Kentucky militia. But Kibbey wanted in; and he knew his fellow Columbians were like-minded. He solicited the General to consider taking advantage of their experience and let them serve as a squad of rangers running miles ahead and alongside the main body of troops. The high words of praise and endorsements from several men whom Wayne held in high regard, persuaded him to employ Kibbey and his frontier militia. Over seventy men signed on under Kibbey's command; most of them from Columbia. They were men with whom he had hunted both wild game and Indians in years previous.

In a history written by Henry Howe in the late 1800s it is noted:

> General Wayne, having a bold, vigilant and dexterous enemy to contend with, found it indispensably necessary to use the utmost caution in his movements to guard against surprise. To secure his army against the possibility of being ambuscaded, he employed a number of the best woodsman the frontier afforded to act as spies. Capt. Ephraim Kibby, one of the first settlers at Columbia, who had distinguished himself as a bold and intrepid soldier, commanded the principal part of this corps. [8]

More praise for Kibbey and an explanation of the corps duties comes from one of the volunteers, John McDonald:

> In April 1794, my brother Thomas and myself joined Gen'l Wayne's army as spies or rather as rangers. The command of the rangers, seventy-two in number, was entrusted to Captain Ephraim Kibby, a true Jersey blue, a man who was fully addequit to the performance of the responsible, important, and dangerous duty assigned him. It was the duty of rangers or spies as they were commonly called to traverse the Indian country in every direction in advance of the army in which an enemy could approach. This was a dangerous and fatiguing business. The spies were constantly on the look out. They were divided into small squads, and were kept, constantly on the alert. Some were sent east, others sent north, and others west of the main army to discover if any body of the enemy were collecting to meet our army. The spies often traversing the country in every direction would return to the army like bees to their hives to make their reports. That they performed their various and complicated duties with ability and intrepidity is proven by the fact that every ambuscade attempted by the enemy was discovered and frustrated. [9]

Kibbey's band proved to be a rugged, reliable bunch; garnering not one but two nicknames among the troops. Some called them the "forty famous scouts." That was the number directly under Kibbey's command after others were sent off in smaller spy units. Other troops referred to them as the "Columbian Scouters" for obvious reasons. No matter their name, their espionage and surveillance of the land ahead and around the troops was key to the campaign's success. Per Wayne's orders, numerous Indians that they had discovered in their searches were not to be shot, but instead brought back to camp for interrogation. Key intelligence was gained by this practice, repeatedly giving Wayne the advantage.

William Clark, soon to make his own mark on history, kept a journal along the way of the campaign. This note makes clear that Kibbey's work did not end with the battle on August 20.

> 12th September 94. A preparitory order for the move of the army, the Q. Masters with the Pioneers, under the cover of Capt. Kilby's [Kibbey's] Spies ordered to proceed in our front & cleare the Road up the Miami [River][10]

Kibbey thus guarded the troops who were cutting a road westward to the Miamis towns where the Miami (Maumee), St. Joseph, and St. Mary's Rivers meet. When the troops arrived they began construction of a new fortress, named in honor of their general. Fort Wayne would be completed on October 20, 1794. Clark's journal entry certifies that Kibbey was still on scouting detail just days before the fort was completed.

> 14th Oct. 94. The Voluntiers set out at about 8 o'clock after bureing 2 men that Died the last night, a faire day, worm. I should have mentioned that Capt. Kilbey [Kibbey] with some spies went in serch of some Camp thirty miles distance on Wabash. [11]

Late that November, Ephraim was finally back home in Columbia. There was a general sense in the region that the victory at the fallen timbers site was decisive enough to put an end to further Indian confrontations, at least for a while. Assuming this would be the case, Kibbey returned to civilian life. He was well-known and well-liked throughout the area, and his recent heroics simply added to his gritty reputation. As the story goes, upon his release from military duties, he soon sought a bit of well-deserved relaxation at a Cincinnati tavern. As he approached the doors to the establishment the raucous laughter and its volume brought a smile to his face and clued him that the guests inside had not just recently arrived. Then he…

....heard the boastful proclamation, "I am the best man in Ohio!" Before anyone inside could take issue with the speaker, if indeed any were so inclined, the door whipped open and the newcomer in ringing tones demanded to know what was said and who said it. "Captain Kibbey!" went up a shout in recognition, then silence.

From among the mixed crowd representative of a border town that filled the place, there stepped forth a tall English officer, evidently a stranger in the vicinity, who proceeded to a cool inspection of him who dared challenge his claim to the aforesaid title. He faced a man of forty, inch for inch his equal in height, dressed in picturesque fringed deerskin, splendidly proportioned, keen-eyed, with features bronzed to the color of an Indian from a life in the wilderness, an ideal type of the American frontiersman, Captain Ephraim Kibbey, leader of Wayne's scouts in the campaign against the savages then recently closed.

"I say I am the best man in Ohio," repeated the Englishman, undaunted by his survey. "If you had said you were as good a man as there is in Ohio, there would be no room for dispute, but as it is, I dispute it," was the response of the American.

"Captain Kibbey, step into the room," suggested the other, and opened a door which led into the long room of the tavern. This the captain was prompt to do, being followed inside by his opponent and all the onlookers, intent on seeing the "fun."

The Britisher, undoubtedly a man of experience and reputation in duelling, had things all prepared, for on the table lay two long flintlock pistols, primed and ready for use. Pointing, he ordered, "Captain Kibbey, take one of them." At the latter's ready compliance he picked up the other with the words, "Name your time and distance." Removing the handkerchief from his neck, the American held to one corner with his left hand and cocking the weapon in his right, reached the other end for the Englishman to take and likewise prepare, at the same moment exclaiming, "Here is the distance and now is the time!" Completely taken aback at such unusual, if not positively unheard of, conditions, his rival wilted, whereupon Kibbey reversed his pistol and with the butt knocked him to the floor, while the house rang with shouts of "Hurrah for Captain Kibbey!"

Little, perhaps, when making his challenging boast did the Britisher figure on the possibility of catching a Tartar [an ill-tempered person], even in a rough frontier town as Cincinnati then was, where, as in all places of such character, trouble could be had for less than the asking. However, that he backed down before his American antagonist need

The Centinel of the Northwest Territory. The earliest newspaper of the Northwest Territory whose motto reads: "Open to all parties – but influenced by none." First published in Cincinnati on November 9, 1793, "by W. Maxwell, at the corner of Front and Sycamore Streets, where Subscriptions, Essays, Advertisements, etc. are than[k]fully received – and Printing in general performed, with accuracy and dispatch."

not necessarily stamp him as being deficient in courage. Rather it would prove an unacquaintance with the ways of the West, where the favorite method of settling disputes and questions of supremacy was to engage at close quarters. Some of the more fierce among the backwoodsmen are said to have even gone to the extreme of tying their left hands together and fighting it out to the death with knives. [12]

Almost a full year after the successful campaign at the area of the fallen timbers, a major treaty was signed at Fort Greenville with the warring Indians. Much of what would become the state of Ohio was relinquished to the Americans. Kibbey's Indian fighting days were behind him, but not his indomitable spirit to challenge himself.

For a few years during and after the military actions against the Indians he was the appointed clerk of the newly named Columbia Township. His taste for politics must have been wetted as he would be elected in 1803 to the new legislature of the state of Ohio. Ephraim would be elected twice to this body as a representative of Hamilton County.

Before settling into the Ohio realm of politics, however, Kibbey just couldn't seem to sit still. For two years, 1799-1800, he led a team of men who blazed a road from his home in Cincinnati to the burgeoning city of Vincennes in the Indiana Territory. His endurance was tested yet again as this report in the *Western Spy*, another of Cincinnati's earliest newspapers, attests to:

> Captain E. Kibbey, who some time since undertook to cut a road from Vincennes to this place, returned on Monday, reduced to a perfect skeleton. He had cut the road 70 miles, when, by some means, he was separated from his men. After hunting them some days without success, he steered his course this way. He had undergone great hardships and was obliged to subsist upon roots, etc., which he picked up in the woods. [13]

Beaten but not destroyed, Kibbey recuperated, went back to his team, and finished another eighty-five miles of road to Vincennes. Almost immediately it would become the main thoroughfare for travel between the two cities. Just months after completion, William Henry Harrison, the newly elected Governor of the Indiana Territory, would use it to transport his children and wife Anna Symmes, daughter of Judge Symmes, to the city where he would build a mansion famously known as Grouseland that is still standing today. There is little direct evidence of this road remaining today except for segments that historians tentatively believe traverse parts of Scott, Martin, Dearborn, and Ripley counties in Indiana.

Ephraim Kibbey certainly had a life of accomplishment and was never known to back down from a challenge of any sort. After successfully completing what would become known for some time as Kibbey's Road he moved his family to Deerfield, the town a little north of Cincinnati which he and Ben Stites had plotted. There he would spend his last days in political circles until he passed away, probably from exhaustion, in 1809 at the young age of fifty-three.

Jacob Burnet, an early Ohio Supreme Court judge and U.S. Senator described him as, "Possessed of great activity, muscular strength, and enterprise: had a sound, discriminating judgment, and great firmness of character."[14] He was speaking of Robert Benham, the third Jersey boy.

Born in Monmouth County, Benham remained a New Jerseyan only until his early twenties. As we've seen, people were starting to move westward just before the Revolution began, and Robert was one of those who felt that call. By 1772 he married and settled, like his two other Jersey friends, in the Tenmile/Redstone area on the Monongahela River. Soon he would entice other relatives and friends from New Jersey to join him.

Benham was no loyalist to England. He enlisted to fight against them during the Revolution. Attaining the rank of Captain, his battles were mostly against the British-supported Indians on the frontier. Few details are known about the Indian encounters he may have had except for one, but it stands as sufficient proof of Benham's character and virility.

So incredible is his story that it has been retold many times through history. Theodore Roosevelt detailed it in his *Winning of the West* account of early westward expansion. Noted historian Henry Howe records it in his expansive *Historical Collections of Ohio*. Though the story needs no embellishment, it was somewhat fictionalized and published with a bent toward the adventure-seeking appetite of young boys growing up in the early decades of the 1900s by both the Boy Scouts of America and the creators of *The Exploits of Daniel Boone* comic book series.

The story being referred to here is actually the end scene of an even bigger adventure that holds just as much intrigue throughout its telling as its more famous conclusion provides. In its entirety, this tale reveals the inherent dangers of travel, the difficulties of communicating, and the subversive dealings between countries during the American Revolution.

The scene begins as Patrick Henry, then governor of Virginia, makes a deal with the Spanish for material aid that his troops require in their fight against the British. A plan is devised to send a small contingent of men, under the command of Colonel David Rogers, down to New Orleans to obtain Spanish material goods and ammunition. From the Redstone area, some fifty miles up the Monongehala River from Pittsburgh, the men were to travel to Fort Pitt. From there the volunteers would board two keel boats and make the trip along the river system, first down the Ohio and then the length of the Mississippi River to New Orleans.

Cincinnati circa 1800.
Lithograph by Strobridge Litho. Co., Cincinnati, based on painting by A.J. Swing.

Though there were many heroes on this mission, Robert Benham and his friend Basil Brown would become the most celebrated personalities. Years later, Brown told his story directly to historian Lyman Draper and here's his account of how it all began.

In the year 1778, the government of the state of Virginia ordered Col. David Rogers with about fifty men, with two large keel boats to decline the [Ohio] river to New Orleans for the purpose of obtaining clothing and ammunition for the troops of the Virginia line. The boats were procured at Pittsburgh; one of them was brought up to Brownsville, then called RedStone Fort, to receive the baggage and provision for the voyage. The detachment left the fort in the month of June, 1778. [15]

The excursion wasn't exclusive to obtaining the Spanish goods, though that was its main objective. It was also a floating communication system between American military strategists in the colonies and those on the frontier, like George Rogers Clark. In fact, as they were sailing on the 4th of July, Clark had won the strategic post of Kaskaskia. This fortress, located just above St. Louis on the Mississippi, was held by the British for years. International correspondence was also being carried on with important officials like Bernardo de Galvez, the Spanish Governor of Louisiana. Based on letters of Patrick Henry and other Virginia manuscripts in Lyman Draper's collection:

In addition to conveying dispatches to Governor Galvez, he [Colonel Rogers] was to act in the capacity of private ambassador in behalf of Virginia, consulting with the Governor as to the most suitable point on the Mississippi for establishment of an American garrison; making to him a full representation of the resources, strength, and condition of Virginia, the progress of the war, together with any additional information he might desire. Colonel Rogers was, on his return, to take into his care such supplies as Governor Galvez, or Mr. Pollock, the American commercial agent, might have to transmit for the use of the State. He was furthermore, to be the bearer of despatches to Colonel G. R. Clark, connected with his expedition against the Illinois country; who, when [Colonel] Rogers should ascend the Ohio, was directed to furnish him a proper escort for the safety of his vessels and cargo. [16]

Colonel Rogers had raised the company of men for this journey from the residents of his home settlement at RedStone. Brown and Benham were two of those who volunteered. Benham was appointed to be the Commissary; a deputy of sorts to the captain and charged with coordinating acquisition and distribution of food and other supplies.

With a plentiful stock of flour, the commissary [Benham] had to rely for wild meat upon the success of squads of hunters, who took their turns, in following along the margin of the streams, while the boats were being carried down by the current, aided by oarsmen of the party.

Arriving, at length, at the Arkansas Post, fifty miles up the Arkansas River, where a Spanish garrison was established, Rogers and his party were kindly received by the commandant, and informed that the goods he sought had been sent up to St. Louis; but that it would be necessary for him to go to New Orleans to get the proper order for them. Selecting half a dozen of his men, among whom were Robert Benham and Basil Brown, Colonel Rogers descended the Arkansas and Mississippi in a canoe, and narrowly escaped capture in passing the British post of Manchac [Natchez] in the night. [17]

After leaving the Ohio, the sail down the Mississippi River began with ease. Approximately halfway to their destination they came to the Arkansas, then known as the Ozark, River where they turned off and headed upriver to a Spanish post. There Colonel Rogers left the two large keel boats and most of his men to wait for his return from New Orleans. With only a handful of men, Rogers took a large pirogue, a canoe-type vessel common in New Orleans, back down the Arkansas and onto the Mississippi. Over this leg of the journey they had to pass a British fortress known as Natchez (Manchac). Presumably, Rogers had hoped this smaller boat would not draw undo attention as it sailed past. The maneuver worked.

As they approached New Orleans, the Americans were surprised to find a British war sloop in the Spanish port. The British, likewise, became wary of a boat full of Americans, albeit a small one, who dared to move downriver into this deep south locale. Suspicions of both parties were piqued.

At this point in time, though tensions were rising between the two countries, Spain was not yet officially at war with England, and they didn't want this secret transfer of goods to trigger a change of that status. In fact, this sale of ammunition to the Americans was a violation of international law. Therefore their planned assistance to the Americans needed to be handled with great discretion. This would explain their sending most of the goods up to St. Louis with the transfer coordinated by an independent broker, the Mr. Pollock mentioned earlier. However, it is believed that the timing of the actual transfer of powder and other goods coincidentally occurred just after the official declaration of war was made by Spain in May of 1779.

The unexpected British presence at New Orleans also called for a change of protocol between the Americans and the Spanish. Rogers felt so strongly that Virginia officials and others needed to be alerted to the situation that he sent a messenger, in stealth fashion through the woodlands, all the way back to the St. Louis area on foot. Robert Benham was that courier.

> The situation of Major [Colonel] Rogers was truly critical and perplexing; under these circumstances, he found it necessary to send Captain Benham through the appalling extent of Indian country, on the west side of the Mississippi, with despatches (it is conjectured) for the government of Virginia. Benham, with the hardihood characteristic of the times, subsisting principally on Indian corn boiled in lye, to save it from the weavil, passed through the Indian wilderness, reached Kaskaskia, then under the American arms; proceeded to the falls of Ohio [Louisville], in the spring of 1779. Soon after his arrival at this place, owing to some unexplained success, Colonel Rogers, with two keel boats, ascended to the same place, on his return to Pittsburgh, and most joyfully took Captain Benham on

board. The latter gentleman was then placed in command of one of the boats, and the little American squadron, the second escort of military supplies procured by our coutrymen from New Orleans, moved on its destination up the Ohio. [18]

In his deposition, Basil Brown explains how he, with Colonel Rogers and the other men, made their way back sometime after Benham had snuck away.

Having arrived at the place of their destination [New Orleans] and procured the necessary order to the proper officer or authorities for said stores, munitions of war, etc., Colonel Rogers & his party, owing to the danger of navigating the Mississippi in consequence of the British post at Natchez, were compelled to return to the Post on [the] Ozark [Arkansas River] by an inland trip, which was accomplished with great hazard & fatigue, the entire country being a wilderness, & the journey several hundred miles in length. Having reached Ozark they re-entered their boats & ascended the Mississippi & procured said stores, etc. Col. Rogers & his party returned to the mouth of the Ohio & ascended that river a considerable distance above the Falls where Louisville now stands, nearly to the mouth of the Licking river... [19]

Though Brown states that the men went by land back to their base on the Arkansas River, they apparently travelled in their pirogue at the beginning of the return. Letters written by Colonel Rogers to Governor Henry and others give further details to this part of the journey and the lengths they had to go to avoid British suspicion.

It was near the close of the year before Colonel Rogers took his departure from New Orleans, going about ninety miles by water, to the point where Plaquemine village is now situated, a little distance below Manchac and Natchez, where all passing boats were rigidly overhauled; and the bare suspicion that any party was friendly to the American cause, was very certain to subject them to seizure and imprisonment, with confiscation of all their property. After leaving the river, their course lead them about sixty miles to Opelousas, and thence about one hundred and twenty miles to Natchitoches on Red River, where (they) arrived on the first of February, 1779. Their journey had been much impeded by almost continual rain, and consequent high waters, which compelled them to tarry a couple of weeks at Natchitoches. Resuming their toilsome travels they passed through the wilderness — partly by canoe, and partly by land — in a north-eastern direction, over two hundred miles, and, at length, after great hazard and fatigue reached their point of destination. Over this route some goods were conveyed, which seem to have been brought from New Orleans. [20]

Having finally reached the Spanish post on the Arkansas, Rogers's full crew, except Benham, set sail in the two keel boats down river to the Mississippi where they turned upriver for St. Louis. Upon their arrival, they had little trouble making the appropriate contacts to acquire the goods they were promised. Some time after August 5, 1779, well over a year into their adventure, the boats made off for the Ohio and then on to Louisville where they would take on a number of new passengers.

Benham was found at the Falls [Louisville], and there rejoined the expedition. Colonel [George Rogers] Clark, then making his head-quarters at that place, assigned Lieutenant Abraham Chapline, and some twenty-three men of the Illinois regiment, together with an additional boat, to escort Colonel Rogers, with his two boats laden with supplies, to Pittsburgh. Colonel John Campbell, of Yohogania County, Virginia, and perhaps others, there took passage with Rogers, as affording a supposed safe opportunity of returning to the Pittsburgh country. There were also half a dozen British prisoners, who had, in some way, come into Clark's possession, and were now ordered up the river, where they could be used in effecting exchanges. A negro woman, and two negro boys, probably employed as cooks, were attached to the expedition. Thus, including all classes, Rogers' party must have numbered about sixty-five persons. [21]

At this point Brown begins the most incredible part of the story:

On the 4th of Oct., 1779, the boat reached the mouth of the Licking [River], opposite the site of Cincinnati. A little before the landing of the boats, some Indians were discovered crossing the river from the Indian [Ohio] to the Kentucky shore. As soon as the boats were landed, about forty men ascended the bank, and went up the bottom to try to kill them. The Indian canoe, the only one seen by our men, contained only seven Indians; and as soon as they landed on the beach of the river, they were fired on, but at too great a distance for doing much execution. The party (of whites) was instantly attacked by about one hundred and seventy Indians, who in less than two minutes almost surrounded them; only thirteen escaped, two of whom were left wounded in the woods. Those who escaped unhurt made the best of their way to the settlements in Kentucky. One of the boats was taken by the Indians. The other having

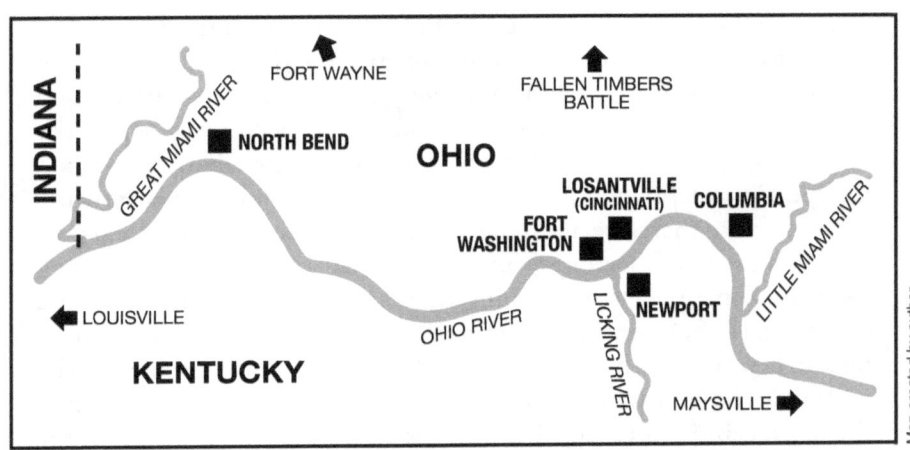

three or four men on board was rowed off during the battle. Two men were killed in the captured boat in attempting to push her off.

Thus ended the project for supplying the Virginia troops with clothing and ammunition. The greater number of the men were killed by a rash exposure to ambuscade — a trick of war which the Indians often executed with great skill and adroitness. The captured boat furnished a rich booty to the half-naked Indian conquerors. The other boat returned to Louisville, and furnished a seasonable supply of clothing and amunition to the destitute troops of Gen'l Clark. [22]

Simon Girty, the notorious turncoat, was leading this Indian contingent band which killed Colonel Rogers and most of his men. He is said to have recognized Colonel John Campbell and so escorted him as a prisoner to Detroit. But unknown to anyone, even each other for some time, were two disabled men hiding under the cover of the forested land. These were two very strong-willed men — Basil Brown and Robert Benham; the heroes of this story.

According to historian John McClung, who provides one of the earliest records of this event:

> Among the wounded was Captain Robert Benham. Shortly after breaking through the enemy's line, he was shot through both hips, and the bones being shattered, he instantly fell to the ground. Fortunately a large tree had fallen near the spot where he lay, and with great pain, he dragged himself into the top, and lay concealed among the branches. The Indians, eager in pursuit of the others, passed him without notice,

and by midnight all was quiet. On the following day, the Indians returned to the battle ground, in order to strip the dead and take care of the boats. Benham, although in danger of famishing, permitted them to pass without making known his condition, very correctly supposing that his crippled legs would only induce them to tomahawk him upon the spot, in order to avoid the trouble of carrying him to their town.

He lay close therefore, until the evening of the second day, when perceiving a racoon descending from a tree, near him, he shot it, hoping to devise some means of reaching it, when he could kindle a fire and make a meal. Scarcely had his gun cracked, however, when he heard a human cry, apparently not more than fifty yards off. Supposing it to be an Indian, he hastily reloaded his gun, and remained silent, expecting the approach of an enemy. Presently, the same voice was heard again, but much nearer. Still Benham made no reply, but cocked his gun and sat ready to fire as soon as an object appeared. A third haloo was quickly heard, followed by an exclamation of impatience and distress, which convinced Benham that the unknown must be a Kentuckian. As soon, therefore, as he heard the expression "whoever you are, for God's sake answer me!" he replied with readiness, and the parties were soon together.

Benham ... was shot through both legs! The man who now appeared, had escaped from the same battle, with both arms broken! [23]

The man who emerged was Basil Brown. He had been shot through his left shoulder and his right arm. He told Draper that he

was wounded on his retreat. He had followed a buffalo path some distance, and had descended a steep bank of a little branch, and had thought himself pretty well out of danger, when two Indians at the distance of about thirty yards, sprang up and shot at him nearly at the same time. He attempted to return the fire, but both his arms refused to obey the command of his will. The Indians instead of rushing up and dispatching him with their tomahawks as he expected, both ran off. After running some distance, he fell and fainted from the loss of blood. After he came to himself, he heard the report of a gun on the opposite side of the Licking River. He hallooed and after some time was answered by Benham, but before he could reach his companion in misfortune he had to travel three miles up the Licking before he could cross it. [24]

Can you imagine the mix of emotions as the two of them met? First each gained relief that they were not alone. Then they discovered the ironic nature of their injuries. They may have had a momentary chuckle of incredulity through the pain. The reality was that

> each was enabled to supply what the other wanted. Benham having perfect use of his arms, could load his gun and kill game, with great readiness, while his friend, having the use of his legs, could kick the game to the spot where Benham sat, who was thus enabled to cook it. When wood was near them, his companion would rake up brush with his feet, and gradually roll it within reach of Benham's hands, who constantly fed his companion, and dressed his wounds as well as his own — tearing up both of their shirts for that purpose. They found some difficulty in procuring water at first; but Benham at length took his own hat, and placing the rim between the teeth of his companion, directed him to wade into the Licking, up to his neck, and dip the hat into the water, by sinking his own head. The man who could walk [Brown]. was thus enabled to bring water, by means of his teeth, which Benham could afterwards dispose of as was necessary. [25]

Luckily the river bottom was full of small game. Wild turkeys were herded by Brown toward Benham who never failed a successful shot. Squirrels and birds also provided sustenance.

The accounts of their rescue scene after weeks in the woods vary slightly. One highlights Benham's part in persuading a passing boat to pick them up while Brown explains his own part in seeking help. Most likely they both made the efforts attributed to them over the course of the time it took for the rescue to unfold. McClung explains:

> On the 27th of November, they observed a flat boat moving leisurely down the river. Benham instantly hoisted his hat upon a stick and halooed loudly for help. The crew, however, supposing them to be Indians; at least suspecting them of an intention to decoy them to ashore, paid no attention to their signals of distress, but instantly put over to the opposite side of the river, and manning every oar, endeavored to pass them as rapidly as possible. Benham beheld them pass him with a sensation bordering on despair, for the place was much frequented by Indians, and the approach of winter threatened them with destruction, unless speedily relieved. At length, after the boat had passed him nearly a half mile, he saw a canoe put off from its stern, and cautiously approach the Kentucky shore, evidently reconnoitering them with great suspicion.
>
> He called loudly upon them for assistance, mentioned his name and made known his condition. After a long parley, and many evidences

Exploits of Daniel Boone Comic Book No. 3, March 1955.
This issue includes a story titled, "Strange Ordeal" which relates the adventure of Robert Benham and Basil Brown in a youth-oriented writing style that remains true to the facts.

of reluctance on the part of the crew, the canoe at length touched the shore, and Benham and his friend were taken on board. [26]

Brown's testimony is a bit different.

On the nineteenth day after the battle, they heard the whooping cough of some persons in a family boat. Brown went to the shores, hailed the boats, and was answered; but the people in the boat, afraid of an ambuscade by the Indians, declined coming ashore.

A project was hit upon for the safety of both parties. Some distance below them a [sand]bar put out a long distance into the river. The river then being quite low, it was proposed to Brown that he should go to the point of the bar, and if they found things as he represented, they would take him in; but if they discovered any sign of a decoy, they would shoot him, and make their escape. After they had taken Brown into the boat, it was with considerable hesitation they sent out two men to bring in his companion, Benham. [27]

The bottom line is that they were both indeed rescued and taken down river to Louisville. There they received medical treatment for their injuries and in a few weeks had recuperated enough to travel.

Basil Brown was only about sixteen years old at the time of this adventure; but it seems that although he had a long life, he never fully recovered from the experience. In his later years, James Bowman, a native of Brownsville and acquaintance of Basil, told Lyman Draper a version of this tale as he remembered it, albeit decades after the fact. He apologized to Draper for not interviewing Basil directly at that time by noting that Basil was

> an eccentric old bachelor of a morose disposition, [and] it was seldom he could be found in a proper state of mind, disposed to relate such events. [28]

Thomas Brown, Basil's brother, seems to get most of the attention in the historical records as the founding father of the town of Brownsville, though Basil had to have been invested in its origin as well. One historian explains how Michael Cresap, a famed frontiersman, had

> retained the title to this land for years, and at last disposed of it to Thomas and Basil Brown, two brothers from Maryland, from whom the present town of Brownsville takes its name. [29]

Thomas's gravestone reads "Here lies the body of Thomas Brown, who once was owner of this town." In contrast, James Bowman notes that:

> [Basil] Brown rec'd a small pension from the state of Virginia until the time of his death in 1835. There is no tombstone from which to ascertain his age. I suppose however about 75 years. [30]

In fact Basil Brown did receive a pension, and near the end of his life in a deposition he gave to strengthen his case for it, he stated the fact that he

> was himself severely wounded in the right arm and the left shoulder in said engagement, by means whereof he has always been disabled, and from the nature of his wounds must continue through life. [31]

Having fully recovered from his wounds, Robert Benham succeeded in having a much more active and full life than Basil Brown was capable of. Just a year later, in 1790, Robert's brother moved his family to the new town of Losantville, and Robert was right behind him with his wife and kids. The brothers must have made several trips prior to this permanent move, perhaps on the boats of Stites and Kibbey. The Benham brothers names are on deeds dated 1789-90. One source states that Robert built the first log cabin in Losantville, which would certainly place him in the company of Stites' original flotilla. His properties were in the heart of today's downtown Cincinnati, in fact some were practically next to Fort Washington which was built in the summer of 1789 just as Losantville was being settled. Today the home of baseball's Cincinnati Reds marks this area.

Another interesting fact is that:

> Old deeds in the County Court House at Alexandria, Ky., show that his [Benham's] property partially consisted of "certain lots in the said town of Newport, aforesaid and county of Campbell situate[d] at the conflux of the Ohio and Licking Rivers." His son, Joseph S. Benham, was born while the family was living in this area, and it was also to Robert's home here that his brother, Peter, brought his family when they came from Washington Co., Pa. [32]

What this brings to light is that Benham ended up buying and living on land in the very woods where he almost perished just a couple years previous. With properties on both sides of the river it is no wonder that he soon established a ferry service over the Ohio connecting Cincinnati to Newport, Kentucky.

All this settling in and creating of businesses was occurring as tensions with the area's Indian forces were rising. A series of Indian battles were about to take place. General Harmar would launch the first campaign from Fort Washington in 1790. Benham was a part of the effort, but it is not clear in what capacity.

The next year he would serve under General St. Clair in the second and most disastrous confrontation for the Americans. He was appointed to be Commissary General of the Army. One of his many duties was to purchase horses for the artillery and several brigades of pack horses. He was coordinating such purchases and the movement of supplies from Fort Washington to the many posts being built north toward the Indian villages. But he also stepped-up as a soldier. At the battle's most dire point, as the remaining American troops were surrounded by the Indians, St. Clair requested Benham, who was already in the thick of the fight, to help him charge through the enemy's lines and lead the remnant of the troops in an escape. Robert rode hard directly at the enemy, breaking through the line ahead of many men who would live to see another day. He was again wounded in the effort, but again recovered.

Upon his return home in 1792, he began his ferry business, but again was called on by the government to serve in the same capacity of Commissary for General Anthony Wayne's campaign in 1793 and 1794. After the success of this effort, Benham retired from military/merchant service. He became one of the original justices of Campbell County, Kentucky where he was living in 1794. He moved back to Cincinnati in 1798 and was elected as a representative of Hamilton County to the first Northwest Territory legislature. Finally in 1802 he bought land in Warren County, Kibbey's neighborhood, and there spent his last days until he passed away in the same year as Kibbey, 1809.◆

ANECDOTE.

A Dutchman and his wife were travelling; they sat down by the road, exceedingly fatigued. The wife sighed: I wish I was in Heaven — The husband replied: I wish I was at the tavern — Oh, you old rogue, says she, you always want to get the best place.

In the Centinel of the North-Western Territory, April 9, 1796 [33]

V.
JANE THE PIOUS.

"Her Christian life was a reality."[1] Does that line cause you to pause? No matter whom it is said about, it implies that the opposite could be true; the Christian life of some could be "unreal." Some professed Christians may secretly admit that their spiritual life is more hope than true belief; more about the after-life than the present life. Such was not the case for the woman referred to in this quote. She was a Christian who applied her rock-solid faith to every minute of her earthly life, as well as her eternal one. Her name was Jane Allen Trimble, a frontiers woman living in the Northwest Territory.

It was the Reverend D. W. Clark who made the above observation of Jane's life as part of his introduction to a book of her memoirs. He would go on to explain:

> Mrs. Jane Trimble was one of God's noble women. She stands preeminent as a pioneer woman both in the State and in the Church. Of good descent, favored with an education, and an early training and experience peculiarly adapted to the times in which she lived, she added to these a keen and quick perception, a vigorous reason and sound judgement, an endurance that never tired, and a courage that never quailed. When we add to these an unbending sense of justice, and the whole overspread with the sunshine of a loving heart and a living faith, we may well inquire what element essential in a truly-heroic character was wanting to her? This character did not flash out merely on some heroic occasion, but was sustained to the close of a long and nobly-conducted life. [2]

The sorrow incurred by the death of family members was felt early in Jane's life. Two of her uncles were killed in battles of the American Revolution. Her father's distress over the loss of his two brothers was obvious to young Jane, and so she attempted to console him by reciting verses from the Bible. A prolific reader with a great memory, she was said to have committed the four gospels to memory when yet a mere teenager. So unquenchable was her thirst for knowledge that she would set a book upon a frame in close proximity so that she could read while using her hands to knit. She was Presbyterian for many years, but later became Methodist due to the conversion and teachings of her husband's half-brother, Colonel James Moffitt.

An amusing episode in her young adult life points to her sense of fairness and patriotism, not to mention her ability to act. It seems that during the Revolution there was in her neighborhood one family who was not so neighborly. While all able-bodied men in the area had volunteered to serve on the side of the Americans, the sons of this particular German family remained at home. Further, though the household was relatively successful in their farming business, they never offered any help to the needy families of the town; many of whom had boys who were killed or wounded in the war. The townspeople would never openly espouse it, but most believed them to be Tories; loyal to the British cause.

One evening, while a soldier from the old neighborhood was home on a visit to his parents, a friendly gathering took place with Jane and many other women in attendance. The standoffish neighbor became a heated topic of conversation. Many thought that this was the night to run them off! But Jane felt otherwise. She explained that should they be forced out of the town they might join a larger community of Tories in the region, adding to their numbers and giving the Americans a few more enemies to worry about. Another young women agreed with her. The crowd retorted that if the girls felt so about it, they should come up with a better idea. They did.

Their plan was to dress in full military garb and approach the family as recruiters. They would first demand the immediate enlistment of their boys; which they suspected would be balked at vociferously. When that occurred, they would then offer an alternative means for the family to do their part in the war effort. They would be told that instead of losing their sons, they could give a regular donation of money or goods in support of the poor in the county. The plan was agreed to and the girls were soon disguised as soldiers

and mounting their chargers, dashed off at a gallop to the house of the

Portrait of Jane Allen Trimble as it appears in the book:
Memoir of Mrs. Jane Trimble, written by her son Joseph M. Trimble, 1861.

German, two miles distant. The dogs announced their approach. It was late in the evening, and the family were all at home. The old lady, who was the master-spirit of the establishment, stood at the door in perfect astonishment at the sight of two officers in regimentals and armed to the teeth, approaching the house at a rapid pace. The old man and boys took to the loft, the grown daughters stood behind their mother, and the smaller children ran under the beds with palpitating hearts.

The officers rode to the door and inquired for the men. No answer — an occasional bow-wow from the dogs. "Well, madam, we must inform you that Gen. Washington's requisition for men is not filled. He wants, and must have, more soldiers. Yes, he must have them. You have at this house four capable of bearing arms — you can spare two. We would prefer that they volunteer, but if not, you may select those you choose to send to the army."

The old woman seemed paralyzed. "Madam," continued the officer, "your family has been saved from the tomahawk and scalping-knife of the savages by your worthy neighbors, many of whom have been slain in battle, leaving widows and orphans dependent upon the charities of others for the supply of their wants. Your family has refused, as we are informed, to contribute a penny to relieve the sufferers. You have been left to cultivate your lands, raise full crops, and sell to your neighbors at high prices, and then refused to aid the needy, whose protectors have fallen in saving you. This conduct can no longer be tolerated. You must either furnish men for the army or supplies for the neighborhood, and your decision must be made at once."

Having uttered this command in a stern tone, the pseudo officers drew their swords as if to enforce it. This gave the old lady power of articulation, and, clasping her hands, she cried: "Mine Fader, mine Fader, vot vill we do?" A voice from the loft cried out: "O, give de money or provision, and let the men be at home to raise more." "Come down," said one of the officers, "and ratify the contract." This was done in short order. It was agreed that, thereafter, this family give their full quota, according to their means, for the supply of all cases of suffering requiring help, in that neighborhood, during the war.

The officers returned and made their report, which was heard with acclamation, and yet much astonishment. Profound secrecy was enjoined and preserved as to the persons engaged in the enterprise. The evening's entertainment was closed by singing a hymn of praise to God, then all joined the good man of the house in fervent prayer, imploring the Divine blessing upon Washington and his brave soldiers, and humbly entreating the Most High to give to the colonies the blessings of civil and religious liberty.

It is said that the German family kept the pledge so bravely forced upon them.[3]

By the end of the war in 1783, Jane had married Captain James Trimble; a long-term officer and resident of her neighborhood. Payment for Captain Trimble's military service came in form of a government land grant in Kentucky. It wasn't long after James' return home that he led his family and a company of about ten other families from their Augusta County, Virginia neighborhood into the expanses of the "West."

All rode upon horses, and upon others were placed the farming and cooking utensils, beds and bedding, wearing apparel, and provisions, and last, but not least, the libraries, containing two Bibles, half a dozen testaments, the Catechism, the Confession of Faith of the Presbyterian Church, and the Psalms of David. Each man and boy carried his rifle and ammunition, and each woman her pistol, for their long journey was mostly through a wilderness, and that infested by savages. [4]

While many of us might be hard-pressed to remember the message our minister delivered as recent as a week previous, it's interesting to note that in Jane's memoirs, written decades after the fact, she recalled the topic of the sermon given by their pastor before they left for Kentucky. Appropriately, it was on the effects of separation from loved ones. The spiritual send-off signaled the beginning of an adventure that would mark Mrs. Trimble as a bold and courageous soul.

They left from Staunton, Virginia in the autumn of 1784. By the time they travelled two hundred miles to Abingdon, Virginia their numbers had increased by three hundred. After another hundred miles, another two hundred would-be pioneers joined the caravan. The majority were women and children. Now at Bean's Station, in today's state of Tennessee, General Knox took charge of the group; the same general who would have the famous army camp and gold depository named after him years later. He was a renowned Revolutionary War hero momentarily between jobs; having left the post of senior officer in the Continental Army and anticipating becoming the national Secretary of War. The company was fortunate to have him as their leader. He knew there would likely be trouble with Indians from this point forward, for they were entering their lands. The dozen or so men whose horses were not burdened with additional bundles of supplies, were divided into two groups; one to lead the front of the line and the other to guard the back. They would alternate these positions daily. Captain Trimble was assigned to a special advance guard to reconnoiter the path ahead, and so was separated from Jane and his children.

The Trimble family

> consisted of a wife (Jane) and three children, and four colored servants. The eldest child was a daughter by a former marriage. The other two were sons, the older one three years old, the other eleven months. These the mother carried, one on her lap and the other behind her. [5]

Generally, the women and children were positioned first in line behind the front guards, then followed the pack-horses, and finally the rear guard. The path was very narrow permitting the horses to move only in a single file that stretched nearly a mile in length. The stronger horses, and riders with more endurance, tended to move faster and eventually spread out from the rest. Jane soon found herself at the head of the line astride her fine Narragansett Pacer; a treasured breed of horse known for its surefootedness, easy gait, and stamina.

When they arrived at Clinch Mountain, about fifteen miles out of Bean's Station, the column began its ascent. It was a treacherous climb and many horses lost their footing or gave out completely. The narrowness of the course caused bottlenecks and confusion as the front of the line continued in motion. At the same time, General Knox, in the rear, feared they were being followed by Indians who might soon attack. The spread of the line left all quite vulnerable. He sent a messenger forward with orders for the front to stop once they made it over the mountain and arrived at its western base. They hoped to find suitable grazing land for the horses. The messenger, however, could only get so far; blocked by fallen animals and a narrow, restricted path. At some point the runner decided that the order had to be sent ahead orally, person to person, in the hope it would soon reach its intended recipient.

> Unfortunately, Mrs. T. and a few others were so far in advance as not to hear the order, and gained the foot of the mountain sometime before the main body. When Mrs. T. came to the brink of the river Clinch, which was near the mountain, she halted. The river was swollen by the continued rains, and dashing over and against rocks, some of which projected above the rapid waves of a stream three hundred yards wide. The front guard [with Mr. Captain Trimble] had entered the river at this point, but finding it past fording, they had gone up the margin [of the river] and crossed at what was called the Horse-shoe Ford. They supposed that General Knox, who was well acquainted with the river and its fordings, would be with the advance, and did not think it necessary to leave a guide [for the upcoming company of women and children]. But the General had been detained by difficulties that occurred in the rear, and he did not reach the front in time to guide it to the safest ford.[6]

The men in this advance group were in new territory that few but the General had ever traversed before. They were uncertain about the best place to ford the river, especially because it was running so high. Once they had crossed it at a shallower spot, they spread out to survey the area ahead for any further impediments or signs of Indians. This area is believed to be somewhere in the vicinity of Raven Hill, Tennessee today. Captain Trimble was part of this company, and once satisfied he crossed back over the river at the Horse-shoe ford and began riding back through the underbrush to where he expected Jane and his family to be approaching the river. Unfortunately, Mrs. Trimble arrived at the river before her husband had returned and she made an assumption, and you know what they say about that.

She seeing some of the guard on the opposite bank, and noticing the place at which they had entered the river, supposed that the ford was in the direct line across. Her horse, also, espying animals that he seemed to recognize, was anxious to encounter the turbid stream. She indulged him and ventured in.

Her husband, some hundred yards above, saw her enter the river, and hallooed at the top of his voice, but it was drowned by the roaring of the water against the rocks, and she heard him not. Mrs. Erwin, wife of William Erwin, of Woodford, Ky., then followed Mrs. T. They were soon in swimming water. Mrs. E.'s animal was washed by the strong current against a ledge of rocks, and he wheeled round with his head to the shore he had left, which he gained with great difficulty. Mrs. E. carried two little negro children in a wallet [saddlebags] thrown across the horse. These the waves took from her. Mrs. T. saw the peril in which her friend Mrs. E. was, and the loss of the children, and she called to those on shore to save them. Fortunately, Captain T. at that moment arrived, and succeeded in saving the little negroes.

But his wife was fully into the current of the deep and dashing stream, with two children, the one infant in her arms, (Allen,) the other four years old, riding behind her. How terrific a sight! Mrs. T., with that decision and firmness which characterized her through life, when she found her horse was in swimming water, determined not to check or attempt to turn him, but to give him the rein, hoping he would make the opposite shore. Then, grasping firmly the bridle and mane of the horse with her right hand, and her infant with her left arm, and calling to her little son behind to take a firm and sure hold of her clothes, and committing herself and children to Him who rules the winds and the waves, she maintained her position and self-possession until her noble Narraganset struck the opposite shore. When the multitude, who had witnessed this thrilling scene, saw Mrs. T. and her children safely landed, they could not restrain their feelings. Some wept, others shouted for joy. The balance of the day was occupied by the rest of the party in crossing the river. Mrs. T. always spoke of her preservation in this instance as a very signal display of the goodness of God, and his power to save in any emergency.[7]

Portrait of Allen Trimble, the Eighth and Tenth Governor of the State of Ohio, by Freeman Thorpe, as it appears in the book: *History of Ohio - The Rise and Progress of an American State*, 1912.

The perils, however, continued throughout the journey.

Shortly after the crossing, a band of twenty men on horseback passed the caravan rather than join it. In a few days, on land approaching the Cumberland Gap, their dead and mutilated bodies were discovered by the pioneers strewn across their camp. It was the work of Indians. General Knox had these men buried and then prepared the camp against the attack he anticipated to come on them that night. All the travelers were determined to hold their own against any enemy. Even some of the women took up guard duty through the night. Mrs. Trimble was one of them. This evening, under more serious circumstances than just rousing a neighbor to behave ethically, she once again gave the illusion of being a man. After placing her children in the care of an elderly lady in the camp, she donned her husband's great-coat and loaded her pistol. Parading slowly in front of the fires in camp, she formed an intimidating silhouette figure of a man to any Indian who might be peering in from the woods. Fortunately, no attack came that evening, but in the morning's light a disturbing number of moccasin prints were found encircling the camp.

Fears of attacks continued through the journey, but none of significance occurred. On November 1, 1784, one month to the day from their departure, the entourage reached the Crab Orchard village in the lands of Kentucky. Here they would begin to go their separate ways. Their leader, General Knox, gave a touching farewell before going on to other affairs. He praised the men for their bravery and

> he said the women were especially entitled to high praise for the fortitude and daring displayed on every trying occasion. They were equal, he said, to the Spartan mothers and their daughters; and one of them, alluding to Mrs. Trimble, for horsemanship, courage, and firmness of purpose, was equal to any heroine of ancient or modern times. It was a subject of remark, that Mrs. T. was the only person who had not been dismounted by accident or fear during the journey. She, with her two children, stuck to her trusty horse over every step of the difficult and rugged passes they had to encounter. [8]

And so, the new pioneer families eventually ventured away from Crab Orchard singly or in groups to stake claims to land on which they would create a new life. Captain Trimble's land grant was in the northwestern region of Kentucky where the population of Americans was very sparse and the Indian presence was quite dense. Therefore, he opted to purchase additional land owned by relatives of Jane's family which was located just west of Lexington, Here, where more people had settled before them, the strength of their numbers provided a sense of safety and camaraderie.

The rugged life they had chosen, and the ever-present danger of Indian attacks, kept the thought of death at the top of everyone's mind, and unfortunately Jane would soon see her share of it. But faith defined Jane. She constantly longed for a deeper understanding and relationship with God's spirit, and wanted to make certain all her friends and family were saved. Over the twenty years she spent in Kentucky, she would continue to bear children, seven more, bringing the family total to ten overall — three girls, (one from James' previous marriage) and seven boys. All would be reared diligently in their mother's spiritual beliefs.

> ... in no place did she seek, with more anxiety, to minister religious

instruction than at her own fireside. So frequent were her efforts made at this point, that she was often subjected to the reply from some of her family, "Mother, you talk to us too much about religion." No mother was ever more solicitous for the spiritual welfare of her children, or took more pains to cultivate their hearts and minds for happiness in the present life, and a state of free pardon for happiness in "the life that is to come." She cared for their bodies, their reputation, their usefulness in society; but her all-absorbing interest was their conversion to God. [9]

Ministers of the Methodist, Baptist, and Presbyterian persuasion were traveling the wilderness at this time. Many came to her area of Kentucky and it is little surprise to know that Jane sought them out when they arrived. She seemed to have never gotten her fill of spiritual encouragement. But likewise, just as she reached out to the preachers, she acted as one herself within her circle of friends and neighbors. Always, she was seeking to comfort those in any type of distress and always she was eager to share the word of God with anyone who would listen. In early 1801, word swept through the Kentucky settlements that a number of ministers of all denominations would be gathering in the fall to preach at a place only forty miles northeast of them. It was known as Cane Ridge. Jane and her family would be in attendance that August. Such camp meetings, as they were called, had been growing in popularity over the previous couple years, but this one would garner the largest crowd yet, nearly 20,000.

> A large majority of them were hauled there in wagons, bringing with them food and fixtures for their own accommodation by day and night… The multitudes used their wagons for sleeping apartments. The religious services commenced by the delivery of a sermon from a stand in the center of the encampment. It was soon seen that but comparatively a small number of the vast crowd could hear the speaker. [Therefore] Several stands were erected and occupied by different ministers at the same hour. [10]

It was on the second day of this revival that participants witnessed some very odd occurrences. They were called manifestations of the spirit and had been heard about by some because they had happened at previous meetings. This day they had occurred at Cane Ridge. For some, these "manifestations" were extremely beneficial and life-altering, for others they were simply disturbing, still others found them to be nothing more than outrageous antics.

Some fell like dead men, and remained for hours apparently lifeless. Others would stagger, and if not caught would fall, and rise, struggle and scream, as if in the greatest agony. Some would jerk till they were quite exhausted, and sink into a state of unconsciousness. Some of these thus variously exercised, would rise as from a trance and cry for mercy; others awakened, shouting the praises of their Redeemer, while a few manifested no concern whatever, and after lying helpless for hours would rise, and walk off as though nothing had occurred. [11]

One report states that a skeptical young man, though the son of a clergyman, called it all nervous excitement. That was until while he was watching others in the throes of it, he himself was struck down, face to the floor. Jane's son, Allen, happened to be near this fellow and turned him over. He appeared dead. The man's father who was nearby came and prayed over him for two hours. To the preacher's chagrin, when his son woke up he was merely perplexed, but otherwise unchanged in his lack of faith.

However, there were plenty of others who underwent stark conversions. It was this dichotomy of experiences that to this day baffles people's understanding of what really happened. One example that Jane noted in her memoirs is when she encountered a friend who was quite disturbed by what was happening.

She took his arm and asked him to accompany her to a tent she had just left. He consented, and they entered the tent where lay a lovely girl of his acquaintance, pale as death. A few female friends were about her singing, with sweet and subdued voices, "Jesus, my all, to heaven has gone." The prostrate girl opened her eyes, clapped her hands, and shouted a few times, "Glory! Glory! Glory!" She sprang to her feet, and in a moment clasped the Presbyterian gentleman in her arms, and besought him, in the most eloquent strains, to lay aside his prejudices and his formality, and seek the salvation of God. She assured him that her prejudices were once as strong as his, but now they were all gone. The Lord had converted her soul and filled her with his love. His heart was touched, melted into tenderness. Mrs. Trimble, observing his tears, called on him to join them in prayer. They kneeled down, and his heart was so drawn out in prayer that he ceased not to call upon God, till the light beamed into his soul and he felt the renewing power of God's Spirit. Then was he willing to join with others in pointing sinners to Christ. [12]

Mrs. Trimble would participate in a few smaller camp meetings held in the region after her Cane Ridge experience and she would always be found guiding whomever she could in the ways of the Lord. She noted that similar unexplainable events occurred at these gatherings as well, but with each successive meeting they were less and less until they ceased.

In 1802, the Trimbles came to a new realization. Their faith would not allow the status quo in a key area of their life. They were convicted, "That slavery was not right, that it must be a moral and political evil. After carefully examining the subject they determined to free their slaves."[13] They submitted paperwork to emancipate their slaves but the courts refused it. They appealed a second time and were again rebuffed. However, this time the officials referred the matter to a young lawyer who was just beginning to gain a reputation on the frontier. And so it happened that Henry Clay, with no hesitation, advised:

> Grant his wishes; he is right. I know him; he is a good and true man. The time will soon come when such acts will be looked upon not as freaks of a bewildered man, but as the promptings of the better feelings of our moral natures. Grant his request, or you disgrace yourselves.[14]

Through the difficult process of trying to free their slaves, the idea of removing to the Northwest Territory where slavery was illegal, came up. Neither of the Trimbles really wanted to uproot themselves at this point in their lives. Both were in their mid-forties, and eight of their children were still in their formative years, ranging in age from one to eighteen. Their Kentucky home was in the midst of a developing society, complete with its perks of social interaction and schooling. A move meant connections to friends and relatives would be severed.

> Yet slavery was not compatible with their views of the law of love, the law of God, and they thought it better to make sacrifices to please God, rather than enjoy all their advantages and offend against his Divine Majesty. The purpose was soon formed to seek a new home.[15]

The site selected by James Trimble was north of what became downtown Hillsboro, Ohio. While Jane took care of the family in Kentucky, her husband cleared ten acres of his Ohio land, built an extra-large cabin, and planted crops in preparation for the move-in. However, Jane would never share the new home with James. He passed away shortly before the trip was scheduled to take them to the Northwest Territory.

Cane Ridge camp meeting illustration by H. Bridport circa 1829. In August of 1801, upwards of 20,000 people from across the Northwest Territory and beyond assembled for six to seven days to hear Baptist, Methodist, and Presbyterian ministers preach during what became known as the Second Great Awakening.

Grief-stricken as would be expected, Jane leaned on her faith, as she always had, to get through. Over James' coffin at the gravesite she was heard to say, "Peace to thy slumbers, my husband, I shall see thee in the morning; for the morn of immortality shall dawn on the night of thy grave, and thou shalt awake in the likeness of thy Saviour." [16]

Suddenly finding yourself a widow with eight minor children would be a daunting situation for anyone, but Jane worked through it. Stepping up to handle the settling of James' estate, which involved business dealings unfamiliar to her, was her son, Allen. Yes, this was the baby she desperately clutched to her bosom as she trusted her horse to carry them across the raging Clinch River twenty years earlier. The other boy, John, who had clung to his mother's clothing in that adventure had been accidentally killed later in his childhood.

With all the transfers of real estate and goods settled, and all eight children in tow, in October of 1805 Jane made the journey to the home her husband had prepared for her. It was truly a brand new start, but she bore it all bravely. Soon her new neighbors introduced themselves and made her feel welcome. One day she learned of a traveling preacher coming to the area. She made a lengthy trip to hear him preach and invited him to come to her home to preach to her children and friends. He did so and in the process convicted her daughter Margaret to recommit her life to her Saviour. As a result, her son Joseph, Jane's grandson, was so influenced by the lifelong examples of his mother and grandmother that he became a preacher himself, a renowned one.

Jane never ceased educating herself in the word of God and in-turn would share it with everyone she met. Sometimes she came off as overbearing in her concerns for the salvation of friends and family, but eventually would almost always win them over and leave a mark upon their hearts for Christ.

In the year following the move to Ohio, Allen, the oldest of the siblings, married his sweetheart from Kentucky and both of them moved back into his mother's home to help her raise the children and handle other affairs. Allen's wife, Margaret, was adored by Jane, appreciated for her gentle and pleasing spirit and practical help. But as wonderful as the family unit had become, another tragedy loomed over it. In 1809, just three years into her marriage to Allen, Margaret became gravely ill and died. On her deathbed, Jane promised her daughter-in-law to raise her and Allen's two children to live for the Lord, and she made every effort in that purpose.

Besides the many daily challenges of raising so many children, Jane became heavily involved in the Methodist community of her area. She somehow always made herself available to teach or help someone in need. She started a Sunday school in which she instructed her children, and the children of the town, in the ways of the Lord. Over her lifetime, she would make several trips back to her original home of Augusta County, Virginia, where her primary purpose was to make sure her sisters and old friends truly knew the power of God in their lives. Her testimonies and sermons while there, resulted in the local congregations blossoming in both numbers and in their faith.

When the War of 1812 broke out, as only a mother can, she feared and prayed for the safety of three sons who enlisted. All survived their terms of service, though one, William, suffered an injury that would plague him throughout his life.

The years passed and Jane had finally reared all her remaining children to adulthood. With their coming of age and her responsibilities lessened toward them, she sought to broaden her horizons of influence on behalf of the Lord. She approached her son, Allen, seeking his approval of her desire to join a missionary team that was reaching out to the Wyandot Indians in what is now Upper Sandusky, Ohio. It was being led by Methodist ministers Rev. John Stewart and Rev. James Finley. Jane

> felt that she could aid them in their work of enlightening and Christianizing the red men of the forest. Her son replied, "Mother, you are too old — over sixty years of age; you have feeble health even with the comforts of a home; how could you endure the exposure and fatigue of such a situation? No, mother, there are fields of usefulness white to harvest nearer home, where you may profitably spend your time and strength." [17]

She conceded to his insight and continued tending to the needs of those in her community.

It's historically interesting to note that the mission that Jane wanted to teach at had been deeded to the United Methodist Church by the Wyandottes in 1843 when, like other tribes, they were forced to move west by the government. The three acres of land had a mission building and small graveyard of Wyandotte people which the Church had maintained as a historic site. But in September of 2019, this land in the middle of a larger Upper Sandusky cemetery was deeded back to the Wyandot nation. As a result of this rare move, the tribe once again owns land east of the Mississippi – their ancestral land.

In 1820, on her return journey from one of her visits to Virginia, a wave of bad news would begin to lash at Jane's soul. Suddenly her son Cary had taken ill and died.

> A loss so unexpected, and an uncertainty whether his soul was prepared for the great change, proved an almost unbearable burden for her poor heart; but the remembrance of God's promise to the widow — the afflicted widow — and of the counsel she had given others, restored her faith, and with loyal trust she said, "The Lord gave, and the Lord hath taken away; blessed be the name of the Lord." [18]

The pain she bore over Cary was barely fading when more distressing news arrived. It was shortly after she had arrived back home when

Portrait of Eliza Jane Trimble "Mother" Thompson, grand-daughter of Jane Allen Trimble, a leader of the Temperance movement circa 1900.

she learned that another son, William, a sitting Senator in Congress, passed away in Washington City from complications of that wound he had suffered during the late war. This blow hit her hard, but she took some comfort in knowing that through years of her efforts, she had finally witnessed his acceptance of Jesus as his Saviour.

Then:

> Just as the sunlight came back to her spirit a messenger brought tidings that her fifth son, Doctor Cyrus Trimble, living in Chillicothe, was very ill. This was in August, 1822. With a mother's affection she hastened to his sick-room, where she found him in a most critical condition. His physicians desired for him undisturbed quiet, and advised his mother to leave him in the hands of his friends. She replied, "No, gentlemen, he is my son, and I must be with him; I must converse and pray with him; his soul's salvation to me — to him is of the first importance." She remained by his bedside till the lamp of life flickered out...
>
> ... Three sons and a daughter-in-law had been taken from her in the short spance of one year. She bore these bereavements with a resignation unlooked for by her friends, convincing all that she was graciously aided by the Prince of her salvation, and commending to them the religion of Jesus as "the balm for every wound, the cordial for every fear." She found

relief from the sadness of affliction in the means of grace, in visiting the suffering, and ministering to the wants of the poor, imitating the conduct of her Saviour in going about doing good. [19]

For the remainder of her life Jane would continue reaching out to all those around her. Whether consoling a neighbor, knitting clothing for the poor, or reassuring a friend of God's grace; Jane Trimble was a physical manifestation of the peace God offers to each of us.

Joyfully she welcomed the hour when her redeemed spirit was freed from its earthly tenement, and ascended to its wished-for home in "the better land." She fell asleep in Jesus in 1849, leaving behind her a record of a well-spent life, a life devoted to God and the promotion of human happiness. [20]

Her descendants are many; some of whom became historically noteworthy. Perhaps the most intriguing line is that of Allen Trimble; who if things had gone differently in the Clinch River that day in 1784, would never have had the chance to create a progeny. Allen himself, would go on to serve in the Ohio State legislature and eventually became the Governor for several terms. He was a strong advocate for the canal system, a public education system, the temperance movement, and a bureau of agriculture. Oddly and ironically, he addressed the complaints of some early Ohioans about the growing population of free African Americans by suggesting that they be shipped to Africa. His daughter, Eliza, grand-daughter to Jane, took up the torch for banning liquor as she became a major matriarch of the Temperance Movement in the nineteenth century. Another later descendent from Allen, born in 1943, is Virginia Trimble, a world-renowned astronomer, recipient of numerous prestigious awards, and author of hundreds of acclaimed scientific papers. ♦

ANECDOTE.

A lawyer being sick, made his will, and gave away all his estate to frantic, and mad people; being asked why he did so, he replyed, "From such I had it, and to such I gave it again."

In the Centinel of the North-Western Territory, August 1, 1795 [21]

VI.
O LARD! O LARD!

Daily life on the frontier of the late 1700s had plenty of challenges. Adequate shelter needed to be built without the benefit of power saws and nail guns. Clothing had to be made from raw materials that were either grown in the field or sheared off the backs of animals. And food, the utmost priority, was not at a grocery store just down the path. It had to be either cultivated or hunted. Crops required a full season of tending and of course good weather in order to produce a worthy harvest. Meat was roaming out there somewhere. It needed to be tracked and hunted down nearly every day, but often with limited success.

If a family lived near a stream, the odds of finding fish was reasonable. Otherwise, frisky critters like squirrels might be all that was available. Turkeys, geese, deer, buffalo and even bear were the preferred targets; if they could be found and if you were a good shot. A really fortuitous day was when multiple animals may have been successfully brought down, but then they would need preserving with salt in order to last. Getting hold of sufficient salt to cure the meat was an adventure in its own right.

Over the centuries, salt had been naturally deposited in sparse pockets across the Northwest Territory, especially on either side of the river throughout the Ohio Valley. The Scioto Salt Licks were discovered just southwest of Chillicothe, Ohio. Indians from the nearby tribes were said to occasionally take their white captives there to work. In 1782, at the Blue Licks just southwest of Maysville, Kentucky, salt was already being regularly processed. It was there, in August of that year, that the Americans suffered a tragic defeat at the hands of the Loyalists and their Indian allies. Bullit's Lick, a few miles south of Louisville, Kentucky, was yet another prolific source of salt in the late 1700s.

Because salt was such a highly valued commodity, the U.S. government decided it was best to protect the licks, even those that didn't produce large quantities. A land commissioner of the United States who anticipated the influx of people into the Northwest Territory once wrote: "Salt springs that we now consider not worth working may be found very valuable when the population increases; therefore it is advisable to retain them as public property.[1] And so, many of the salt lick sites were made reserves of the government, not to be sold, but only to be accessible.

The licks themselves were areas where salt had permeated the ground. It might be a spot as small as a puddle or it could cover acres. The animals knew where they were located. The well-worn trails between them bears the proof that herds of buffalo and other animals had frequented these spots for centuries to get their licks in.

Thanks to the memoirs of a good man who worked hard at life in the frontier wilderness, we can get a glimpse of how the salt business evolved on the frontier and how endless the effort to find and preserve meat really was. We may even get a little chuckle along the way. Though this tale is but a snapshot of a few days in one man's life, it none-the-less reflects on the everyday endeavors that a frontiersmen had to undertake; as well as the dangers, nuisances, and amusements that came his direction on an average day during the late 1700s.

The writer was Daniel Trabue, a Huguenot (French protestant) whose family came to America a few generations before him to escape religious persecution from Catholics in France. In 1776, Daniel was a mere sixteen-year-old teenager, yet he signed on for action in the Revolutionary War. His duty for the next three years was as a commissary on the frontier, supplying food to militia and families across the Kentucky wilderness. After his stint in the military he took on a variety of challenges. He was a sutler to the forces at Yorktown, a gristmill owner, a tavern operator, and even a sheriff. In 1802 he founded the city of Columbia in Adair County, Kentucky (not to be confused with the town of Columbia settled on the shores of the Ohio River). When he was sixty-seven years of age, Daniel compiled all he could remember of his colorful life up to that point in time. Thanks to the traveling historian, writer, and archivist Lyman Draper these recollections are still preserved as a narrative in the Wisconsin Historical Society.

Daniel's hunting tale begins at Logan's Fort in the heart of the Kentucky wilderness. It's the winter of 1779-80 and it's been a severe one. As his duty required, the now nineteen year-old Daniel was to find food for the inhabitants of the garrison named after its builder Colonel Benjamin Logan. This fortress was only a hard days ride away from similar communities in the midsection of Kentucky like Harrodsburg and Boonesboro. In fact, more and more stations or fortresses were being built each year as the influx of settlers continued.

At Fort Logan there was an immediate need for food, specifically, protein in the form of meat. By January of 1780, the supply at the fort had dwindled significantly and it was decided that a hunting party needed to be raised to bring in enough game to last Logan's inhabitants through the remaining months of the winter. Daniel relates:

> The conclusion was that we must try to git some salt and kill wild meet. We understood that a company of men was to start on a certain day from Herrodsburgh [Harrodsburg] to go to Bullits lick to boyle and make salt. The conclusion was that I would go.

Thomas Bullit discovered the salt lick that bore his name just a few years earlier while he was surveying Kentucky lands for the Virginia government. The site was the best source of salt to date that anyone had found in the Ohio Valley. To get there it would be a twenty mile jaunt from Fort Logan to Harrodsburg and then another sixty miles once they joined up with the other group leaving from Harrod's site.

Five or six young men from the area were sent to Daniel by relatives and other militia leaders to join him on this journey, but some of them were not all that keen about going.

> All set out. We had good guns and ammonition. When we got to herodsburgh their was nobody going from their. I told these men with me that we would go on, so we set out. We went on some Distance and stoped to eat, and let the horses Eat some Grass. We ate all the provision we had.
>
> These young men said they was afraid to go with me. They was afraid of Indians, was also afraid as their was no road or path that I would not find the way, and another thing was we had nothing to eat we might starve to Death.
>
> I told them they ought to have brought provision with them and as

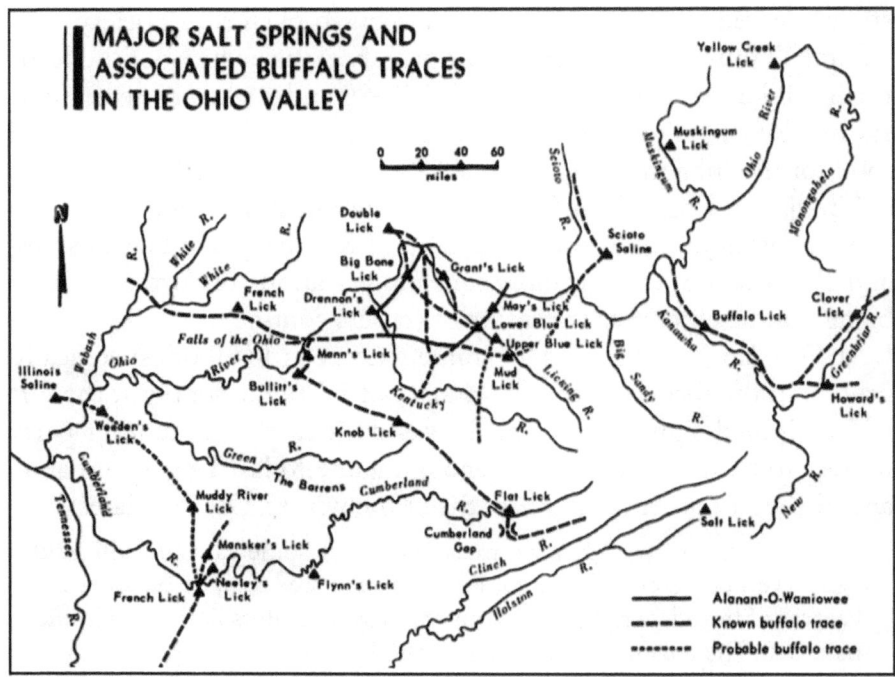

Map showing prominent salt licks in the Ohio Valley and beyond. Note how the buffalo traces run from one location to another. Map found in book: *Salt on the Ohio Valley Frontier*, 1770 - 1820, by John A. Jakle.

to the Indians we had to run that risk. As to finding the way I was not uneasy about that as I knew about steering in the woods. I could find the way as I had been their. At any rates, whther they went or not I would go on with negro Jo.

Though a bit unsettled, the boys moved on under Daniel's lead. Negro Jo was a man who had been sent to go on this trip by an uncle of Daniel's. It's impossible to determine for sure, but it is likely that "negro Jo" was the uncle's slave. At this point in time, "Kentucky" was still western Virginia and many of the new settlers coming into this land were eastern Virginians who brought their slaves with them. Daniel continues:

> We went on our Jurney and at a little before sun set we stopt and took up camp. Told negro boy to hopple out the horses, and all the men as quick as they could to go out a hunting and try their best to kill something.

Hopple is a misspelling of the term "hobble" which is a technique for keeping a horse calm and in place without having to tie it off to a post or tree. A strap called a hobble is secured around the horse's legs restraining their movement. By this means the horses could graze, while hobbling around, without the ability to run off.

When I Returned, I had killed a large fat Rackoon. The men had killed nothing. The negro had a large good fire. The koon was soon prepared for cooking. The men began again their woefull tale. Said they, "We are in a wilderness without any path, nothing to eat but a koon for 6 or 7 Men without Bread or Salt, liable every minute to be Masscreed by the Indians. If we can only be spared until morning we will return to Logan's Fort."

Daniel noted that it was a clear night drenched in moonlight and that they should try their luck again at finding more meat.

I said, "We have 2 good Dogs. I know mine is an exception for game. Let us go out a hunting." All the men refused. I told negro Jo to take his axx. I took my gun and off we went, and in going only about 200 yards wheare some of these men had been out a hunting I saw 5 turkeys on one sycamore tree over the creek. I mooved to a place where I got the turkey between me and the moon, Drawed my sight and killed one, and loaded and fired until I killed all 5 of the largest fatest Turkeys that I had ever seen…

We took our turkeys to the camp and I said, "Now pick and clene them and eate some of the best eating in the government." I soon had one a rosting. The koon was ready for eating.

They asked me to come up and eat some of it.

I Refused saying I would choose Turkey. The turkeys was all cleaned and some of them cooked for the night and the next morning. We all ate heartyly.

The next morning everyone headed out together toward Bullit's Lick, none had turned back as had been threatened. Daniel managed to kill a deer and a couple turkeys which must have allayed any fears the men had of going hungry. Then a buffalo showed up.

One of the men we had with us was a young Irishman who was constant contending and Disputeing with the other young men that was from old Virginia about words and customs, etc. So some time that morning I shot a Buffelo bull and he fell down. We all went up to him. Some of the men had never seen one before this one. I soon Discovered I had shot this buffelo too high and I told the boys to shoot him again.

This young Irishman said, "No"; he would kill him and Jumed at him with his tomerhock and striking him in the forehead.

I told him it would not Do, he could not hurt him, the wool and mud and skin and skull was all so thick it would not Do. But he kept up his licks, a nocking a way.

The buffelo Jumped up. The man run, the buffelo after him. It was opin woods, no bushes, and the way this Irishman run was rather Descending ground and every Jump he cryed out, "O lard! O lard! O lard! O lard!"

The buffelo was close to his heels. The man Jumed behind a beech tree. The bufflo fell Down, his head againt the tree, the tuckeyho boys laughing, "Ha! Ha! Ha!"

These boys certainly had a lot of fun at their friend's expense. Tuckeyho, or tuckahoe, was a slang term of the day used in reference to the more proper English people who came to the Kentucky wilderness from eastern Virginia as opposed to the poorer folk, referred to as the cohee, who did not have British roots.

One of them went up and shot the buffelo again and killed him. The Irishman exclaimed againt them, saying this was no laughing Matter, but that these boys or young [men] (he said) was such fools they would laugh at it if the buffelo had killed him.

These young men would Mimmick him, "O lard! O lard!" etc. and break out in big laughter.

This Irishman said he would go back, that I could not persuid [persuade] him to go further. I advised him to take a load of this buffelo meet as it was very fat and he was welcome to it, to which he agreed to it as we Did not need it. We look [took] a little of it and bid him a Due [adieu], leaving him a butchering his buffelo.

And so the Irishman took no further part in the adventure, having provided his fellows with a hearty respite from the dangers they feared were about. Daniel and the rest carried on and soon reached their destination of Bullit's Lick where they found some folks who had come down from Louisville.

A Mr. T. Phelps - an acquaintence of Mine - was their, had a furnace of small pots and kittles. He wanted to go home and hired his small establishment to us for 2 weeks for which we was to pay him in salt. We fixed up our pots and kettles in addition to Mr, Phelpes' and we went on very well, imediately making salt. The water we had was standing in the lick. Their was a hole or well only about two feet Deep that had been

A massive-headed wild buffalo like those that used to roam the Northwest Territory.

dug out. I was their previous to any Diging and the water stood their in a puddle so that the buffeloes would go their and Drink it. We Did see buffeloes every Day in sight of our works. We killd them when we needed them. [2]

Colonel William Fleming, the head of the land commission, kept a journal of his travels through Kentucky during the same winter that Daniel was on his journey. He explains the technique he saw the men using to render salt from the waters at Bullit's Lick. This account was made just months after the site had begun being worked on a regular basis for profit.

Nov. 13. [1779] Bullets Creek as it is cald is perhaps the best Salt Springs in the Country. The Earth is excavated for twelve or fourteen feet over an area of many acres. By digging ... to any depth of feet, water boils up the deeper, [and] the stronger... they have a trough that holds very

> near 1000 Gallons which they empty thrise in the 24 hours, they have 25 kittles belonging to the Commonwealth [of Kentucky] which they keep constantly boiling and filling them up as the water waistes from the trough... after this management for 24 hours they put the brine into a Cooler and let it stand till cold or near it and draw off the clear brine into the last boilers under which they keep up a brisk fire till they observe it begin to [turn into salt] grain... they slacken the fire and keep them at a simmering boil till it [turns into salt] grains... they then put it to drain... when drained they think it fit for use... the pits will some weeks fill with strong water and then decline... it is noticed that the brine increases in strength as the moon does in Age ... near 3000 Gallons water boil[ed] down yields from three to 4 and 1/2 bushels Salt... [3]

The concentration of salt in these ground waters varied by location and by the depth one dug for it, but it was generally at least five times denser then ocean water. Essentially, this account explains that the men dug long trenches of varying depths and lengths into which the waters would slowly seep, acting much the same way as today's drainage ditches relieve swampy farmland of excess water. When full, the water is scooped into large pots which are heated until the water evaporates and salt crystals are left behind. Other troughs known as furnaces were dug in dry ground. In these trenches constant fires were maintained and over them the pots of water would be boiled.

An early explorer of Ohio lands, Christopher Gist, noted in his journal that

> The Indians and Traders make salt... by boiling it; it has at first a blueish Colour, and somewhat bitter Taste, but upon being dissolved in fair Water and boiled a second Time, it becomes tolerable pure salt. [4]

This explains the use of a second set of boilers at Bullit's Lick. Further drying is done by putting the wet crystals into a cloth and hung over a pot to drain. Finally the dry crystals are poured into bushels which are packed onto horses for travel to wherever it is needed. Depending on the concentration, it took between 250 and 1000 gallons of water to yield one bushel of salt. Techniques varied and were refined in the coming years as salt-making grew into an industry. Numerous licks were in operation around the clock and producing upwards of a hundred bushels a week by 1800.

Curing meat was essential if the kill would not be eaten within a

Old Kettle Furnace in Durant, Ohio shows numerous kettles for processing salt in the mid 1800s; a process only slightly more sophisticated than what the pioneers used. Photo from book: *Salt Deposits and the Salt Industry in Ohio*, by Geological Survey of Ohio, John Adams Bownocker, 1906.

couple days, especially during the warm months of summer. Daniel was hunting in winter, so his meat would freeze on its own once he butchered and packed it.

When the meat reached the fort, it had to be preserved by smoking or salting and sometimes a combination of both. Even though it is written several decades after Daniels adventure, this account from an early cookbook gives a good overview of the beef curing process which had to be similar to what the one the frontier people had to perform.

An experienced housekeeper has furnished the following method for curing and drying beef, which will keep good for two years, without being injured by must or fly, and is much admired. Have the rounds divided, leaving a piece of the sinew to hang up by; lay the pieces in a tub of cold water for an hour; then rub each piece of beef that will weigh fifteen or twenty pounds, with a handful of brown sugar and a tablespoon of saltpetre, pulvrized, and a pint of fine salt; sprinkle fine salt in the bottom of a clean tight barrel, and lay the pieces in, strewing a little coarse salt between each piece; let it lay two days; then make the brine in a clean tub, with cold water and ground alum salt — stir it well; it must be strong enough to bear an egg half up; put in half a pound of best brown sugar and a table-spoon of saltpetre to each gallon of the salt and water; pour it over beef; put a clean large stone on the top of the meat to keep it under the pickle, (which is very important;) put a cover on the barrel; examine it occasionally to see that the pickle does not leak, — and if it should need more, add of the same strength; let it stand six weeks, when hang it up in the smoke-house, and after it has drained, smoke it moderately for ten days; it should then hang in a dry place; before cooking it, let it soak for twenty-four hours: a piece that weighs fifteen or twenty pounds should boil two hours — one half the size, one hour, and a small piece should soak six or twelve hours according to size. [5]

The salting process of the extra meat Daniel and his friends had packed up would take place back at the fort. Once the long and tedious process of boiling down the saline waters produced enough for their needs, Daniel and his companions set out for home. The boys had to have been even more impressed with Daniel's good sense of direction when a group of men who had left Harrodsburg three days before them had finally arrived at Bullit's three days after they had. They too began working at making salt and Daniel and his friends were pleased to have their company and have their numbers increased as a deterrent to any Indian attack.

In about 2 weeks or little more we had got to each hand about 2 bushels of salt and I bought a little more from Mr. Phelps and so we made ready for our return. [6]

All the boys made it safely back to Fort Logan with their stores of salt and meat. Now the curing detail would fall to the women at Fort Logan. Daniel and the boys took a breather from their efforts, but shortly would regroup and go out again "a huntin'." ◆

ANECDOTE.

Milton was asked by a friend, whether he would instruct his daughter in the different languages? To which he replied, "no, sir, one tongue is sufficient for a woman."

In the Centinel of the North-Western Territory, November 9, 1793 [7]

VII.
CAMELS THAT GOT OVER THE HUMP.

Don't Give Up the Ship! We all know those words because of the flag that Oliver Hazard Perry famously flew over his ships the *Lawrence* and then the *Niagara* as he defeated the British in the course of the War of 1812. It was called the Battle of Lake Erie. Nine American ships defeated six British vessels of the Royal Fleet, giving the United States control of this body of water. But before that flag could be hoisted into the warm winds of the lake, the new U.S. ships had to make their way out of the harbor in which they were built. As simple as that may be at most ports, accomplishing it where these ships were built was quite a feat.

The site was Erie, Pennsylvania on the southern shore of Lake Erie. The heroics of Perry and all involved in this engagement have been thoroughly recorded and expounded upon ever since they occurred. The victory was momentous and turned the tide of the war in 1813. But just twelve months earlier, most of the ships engaged in the fight were non-existent. The story of their creation is lesser known, but no less impressive than the battle itself.

War was declared on June 18, 1812. A full month later, the American forces stationed at Fort Mackinaw, an island fortress at the northern tip of Michigan's lower peninsula, were still unaware that they were officially at war with Great Britain. They first learned of it on July 17 from a force of British and Indians who seized their garrison with barely a scuffle. The *Salina*, an American cargo ship owned and captained by Daniel Dobbins, happened to be in port at Mackinaw Island that fateful day.

Captain Dobbins, a merchant, had just delivered one of his usual shipments of salt and other goods to the fort when the surrender occurred. As a private citizen with no military connections, the British allowed Dobbins to leave the island with other residents who had refused to make a promise to them that they would remain neutral should any future conflicts occur between the two nations. "His vessel and one other of the captured, were made cartels to convey the prisoners and non-combatants to Cleveland, Ohio."[1] But Dobbins sailed the *Salina* first to Detroit. There he was surprised to find General Hull in command. Coincidentally, Hull had just arrived at Detroit after abandoning his would-be attack on nearby Fort Malden. Being short-handed, the general made use of Dobbins and his crew around the fortress, but as history notes, he soon surrendered Fort Detroit to the famed British general, Isaac Brock. As a result, Dobbins found himself once again under the thumb of English officers, well at least temporarily.

> Captain Dobbins now obtained a pass for himself… through the influence of Colonel Nichols, of his Majesty's service (an old acquaintance previous to the war), and accompanied [Americans] Colonel Lewis Cass and Captain Saunders, who were in charge of paroled prisoners surrendered at Detroit… to be transported across the head of the lakes in open boats, to Cleveland.[2]

Dobbins made his way along the Lake Erie shoreline from Detroit to Cleveland and then on to his hometown of Erie, Pennsylvania where he was the first to tell the commander of that post, General Mead, the details of the loss of forts Mackinaw and Detroit. The general immediately sent Dobbins on to Washington City to relay this vital news to the highest levels of the government. Colonel Lewis Cass had been continuing on his way from Cleveland to Washington for the same purpose. In fact he had dispatches from General Hull himself, but Cass was detained by an illness so Dobbins ended up arriving in Washington City before him.

President Madison and all his advisors met with Dobbins in an official session. They were incredulous over the devastating news and all agreed that action had to be taken to defend the southern shores of Lake Erie, which to this point had been defenseless. The only American war ships on the lake were with Commodore Chauncey at the far eastern end of the lake. That harbor was Black Rock, just past Buffalo, New York, at the head of the Niagara River. But these forces

Portrait of Daniel Dobbins, a pioneer sailing merchant on the Great Lakes who supervised the buildng of ships used by Oliver Perry in the Battle of Lake Erie. Illustrated by Benson J. Lossing and shown here as it appeared in his *Pictorial Fieldbook of the War of 1812*, 1868.

were focussed on Forts Erie and George on that river, leaving only American merchant ships active on the lake itself.

It was quickly decided that ships needed to be built for Lake Erie's defense as soon as possible. But where? The talks continued for over a week. Numerous locations were discussed with consideration given to the geography of their harbors, population, the type and amount of tree cover, access to roads, etc. On Dobbins' strong recommendation, Erie, Pennsylvania was chosen.

> Immediately upon his [Dobbins] arrival, a Cabinet meeting was held, to whom he gave a full account of matters, including the situation of the frontier, and the most suitable point for a naval depot upon the upper lakes. He recommended Erie, which was adopted. He was then solicited to accept a sailing master's position in the navy, which he accepted, and was at once ordered to Erie with instructions to immediately commence the construction of gun boats, which work he speedily began late in October following. Upon his arrival at Erie, [he] was ordered to report to

Commodore Chauncey at Sackett's Harbor... for further instructions.³

As supervisor of the operation, Dobbins immediately set things in motion at Erie to build the four gunboats decided upon by President Madison. Dobbins, who was now newly enlisted into the military, was ordered by the Secretary of the Navy, Paul Hamilton, to report to Chauncey, then the Commander of Naval Forces on the Upper Lakes, for his next orders. He did so via a letter to Chauncey to which he received a surprising reply. It came through Chauncey's subordinate officer, Lieutenant, J.D. Elliott.

Black Rock, Oct. 2d, 1812

Sir: — Your letter of the 13th ultimo, directed to Commodore Chauncey or the commanding officer on Lake Erie, I have received, together with its enclosed copy of your instructions from the Honorable Secretary of the Navy, each of which, together with a copy of this letter, I have enclosed to him for his consideration.

It appears to me utterly impossible to build gun boats at Presqu'ile. There is not sufficient depth of water on the [sand]bar to get them into the lake. Should there be water, the place is at all times open to the attacks of the enemy, and in all probability when ready for action, ultimately will fall into the hands of the enemy, and be a great annoyance to our forces building and repairing at this place [Black Rock]. From a slight acquaintance I have with our side of the lake, and with what information I have obtained from persons who have long navigated it, I am under the impression Lake Erie has not a single harbor calculated to fit out a naval expedition; and the only one convenient, I am at present at, which is between Squaw Island and the Main, immediately in the mouth of Niagara River. I have no further communication to make upon the subject. Probably in a few days I shall be in possession of Commodore Chauncey's impressions, when you shall again hear from me.

With esteem, yours, &c.,
J. D. Elliott, U.S.N.
Sailing Master Daniel Dobbins. ⁴

Officer Elliott certainly didn't mince words in the giving of his contrary opinion to that of the Secretary of the Navy. But Dobbins would stand his ground. He replied with his rebuttal as soon as he had received Elliott's letter.

Erie, Oct. 11th, 1812

DEAR SIR: — Yours of the second inst., is received. In regard to the idea entertained by you that this place is not a suitable one to build gun boats at, allow me to differ with you. There is sufficiency of water on the [sand]bar to let them into the lake, but not sufficiency to let heavy armed vessels of the enemy into the bay to destroy them. The bay is large and spacious, and completely land-locked, except at the entrance. I have made my arrangements in accordance with my own convictions, for the purpose of procuring the timber and other material for their construction. I believe I have as perfect a knowledge of this lake as any man on it, and I believe you would agree with me were you here, viz: That this is the place for a naval station.

I remain yours very respectfully, &c.,
Daniel Dobbins, U.S.N.
Lieut. J. D. Elliott, U.S.N. [5]

Because he never received further response from Elliott or Chauncey, Dobbins took it upon himself to go to Black Rock in person and explain himself more thoroughly. However, when he arrived, neither Elliott nor Chauncey happened to be there; only a lieutenant with no knowledge or authority to discuss the matter. The trip proved to not be a total waste of time, however, as Dobbins did find a skilled shipbuilder whom he hired on the spot. Experienced shipbuilders were very hard to come by in the region. In fact, many of the men first called upon to build the vessels at Erie were only competent in carpentry work on homes or wagons. Any men who had previously worked on ships were a blessing to the endeavor.

From the beginning, Dobbins sent regular updates to the Secretary of the Navy detailing the progress being made, requesting additional monies, and pointing out that he had yet to receive any communications from Chauncey. These reports undoubtedly triggered Secretary Hamilton to take action. On New Year's Eve, 1812, Chauncey, unannounced, showed up at the shipyard along with a master ship builder named Henry Eckford. The two of them generally approved of Dobbins efforts, but made several suggestions and alterations.

Many of the changes were incidental tweaks, but one that had substance was their order that two of the ships under construction needed to be lengthened by at least ten feet because they were deemed to be ineffective in battle at their current size. Perhaps the most consequential order given was to build two additional ships,

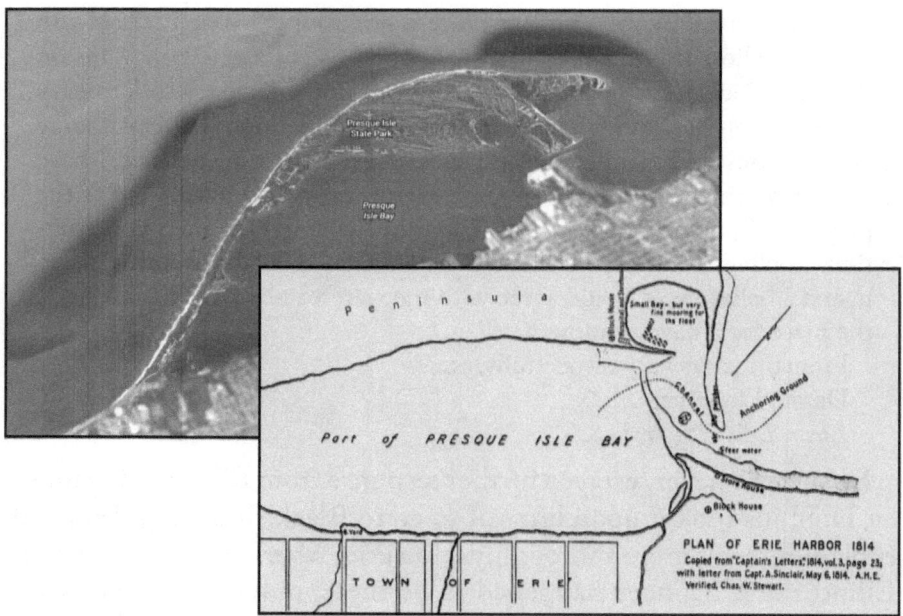

Views of the Presque Isle Bay at Erie, Pennsylvania. Google Earth photo taken in 2020 compared to the 1814 map in book: *Battle of Lake Erie: Building the Fleet in the Wilderness*, by Naval Historical Foundation, Spring 1979. Originally in book: *Seapower in Its Relation to the War of 1812,* by A.T. Mahan, 1905.

which were to be the largest of the fleet. This brought the total number of vessels built at Erie to six.

Soon after his departure on New Year's Day, Chauncey solicited the services of a very accomplished ship designer from New York, Noah Brown, who would draw up the master plans for construction of these two new identical brigs. Brown brought with him over twenty-five skilled New York ship builders as well. Before Chauncey refocused his attention on events along the Niagara River, he recommended that the Secretary of the Navy put Oliver Perry in command of this new fleet being built at Erie. A few weeks later, it was so.

The harbor at Erie had been agreed upon by most of the men involved in the site selection for numerous reasons. One key factor was the geography of the area which Oliver Perry himself described as

> a beautiful natural harbor, consisting of a bay, very narrow at the entrance, but expanding into a spacious sheet of water within. This bay is formed by a peninsula, extending in the form of a crab's claw in a northeasternly

direction along the shore of the lake. From this remarkable point of land, the place had received from the French its previous name of Presquisle. Across the mouth there was a bar, extending lakeward upward of a mile, and varying in depth in the channel from six feet at the shoalest [shallowest] part to ten feet. The shoal being formed of light sand, was liable to be affected by gales of wind, which occasioned it frequently to vary, and sometimes reduced the depth as low as five and even four feet.
This bar, being too shoal for the enemy to cross it with his vessels equipped and armed, had offered great protection to our squadron from attack during its construction and equipment. [6]

Perry arrived in March of 1813 to take command. He worked diligently with Dobbins and others who were in-charge to stay on top of this project. The management task was daunting. All these leaders had to coordinate the procurement of the diverse goods required to build these ships. From Pittsburgh, Buffalo, Washington City, and many other locales, materials such as iron, gunpowder, oil, cannonades, ropes, cannon balls, cloth, and paint had to be hauled in. And it most often arrived after great difficulty and delay; having had to be transported over rough old Indian trails from the eastern locales. Pittsburgh was the closest and most vibrant city at this time and Perry explains how this too influenced the decision to build at Erie.

Its comparative proximity, moreover, to the populous portion of Pennsylvania, and especially the great manufacturing town of Pittsburg, between which and the neighborhood of Erie there was an almost uninterrupted, though tedious, water communication by the Alleghany [River] and its tributaries, gave it great advantages for equipment of a naval force. Besides being situated towards the center of the lake, which became broad at that point, it rendered the squadron less exposed there to a surprise, and destruction by the enemy… [7]

Buffalo too, was able to use water transportation by sailing small ships discreetly along the Lake Erie coast trying to not draw any undo attention from the British.

But it wasn't just materials for shipbuilding that needed constant management. Food had to be brought in regularly. Accommodations had to be built and maintained. Over 300 new workers, many skilled laborers who had come from New York and Philadelphia, were later joined by over 1,000 militia at the site. For a while food had to be rationed.

But there were even more challenges, some causing the builders to employ new techniques that only proved to be successful after-the-fact. For example, though wood was abundant it had to be used while still green leaving each plank vulnerable to change as it aged. And, because they could not find enough oakum, the preferred caulk made from old rope fibers and pitch, lead was used to fill the ships' seams. As it turned out, the lead held even better than oakum against the unseasoned wood. The short supply of iron also meant that the manufacturing of axes and other metal tools was limited. That precipitated the use of "tree nails," wood rather than metal nails, throughout the ships.

Imagine the number of trees that needed to be felled, cut, and fitted together to build six ships ranging from fifty to one hundred and eighteen feet in length. The work was started in late autumn just before a treacherous five or six months of winter arrived. In the midst of bitter-cold, sharp winds and deep snows, that to this day regularly strike the southeastern shores of Lake Erie, the men carried on.

Once downed, the trees were cut in saw pits. This centuries old method of cutting wood was still in use at Erie, as no sawmills had been built anywhere nearby. The pits or trenches were deeper than a man's height. The log to be cut was positioned lengthwise over the pit. Using a long, two-handled saw, one sawyer pulled down from inside the pit while another, straddling the log over the pit, pulled the saw upward. Back and forth they would work the saw blades through the log. It is believed that the slang terms of top-dog and under-dog came from this technique. Usually a rookie or less tenured sawyer was given the under-dog position which was more physical and irritating with sawdust flying in his sweaty face with each stroke. The top-dog still had a tough job, but with a little less strain; and it required a good eye to guide the blade along a straight path to the end. Most likely the grounds were echoing for miles around with the raucous sounds of axes, saws, hammers, and men.

The project progressed quite successfully. The smaller gunboats, the *Ariel*, the *Scorpion*, the *Porcupine*, and the *Tigress* were completed and launched into the harbor at the end of April. Several more ships were sailed to Erie from Black Rock adding to the fleet's numbers. These were the *Caledonia*, the *Somers*, the *Trippe*, the *Ohio*, and the *Amelia*.

A woodcut print of two men working a sawpit.

The *Amelia* was condemned upon inspection at Erie and sunk in the harbor. The *Ohio* acted as a supply boat, skipping the battle, but delivering fresh food and other critical supplies to the survivors who regrouped at Put-in-Bay when it was over. The remainder were the ships that would face off against the British squadron along with the last two sloops-of-war to be built: the *Lawrence*, launched on June 25, and the *Niagara*, launched on the 4th of July.

While the six new vessels were in the harbor, the pressure escalated on Perry to complete his mission.

> Perry was in frequent receipt of communications from the Department [of the Navy] and General Harrison, urging him to a forward movement; and to add still more to Perry's anxiety, Harrison informed him, "The enemy would in a few days launch their new ship Detroit, and had just received a reinforcement of experienced officers and prime seamen." This was truly annoying to Perry, as his vessels were not fully manned; however, those he had were being well disciplined. Everything in the way of completion and preparation was fully attended to…
>
> The enemy made frequent visits near the roadstead [channel] of the harbor, and sometimes the Queen Charlotte would visit alone. At other times the whole [British] squadron would make the menace. On the 21st of July, they made one of these "calls," when the gun boats ran down to the bar at the entrance, and exchanged shots with them, with but little

effect, on our side at least, when they bade adieu, and squared away for Canada, probably to report. [8]

Secretary Hamilton was eager to get Perry in lock step with William Harrison, head of the Northwest forces, who was now based at Sandusky Bay. While the ships from Black Rock guarded the Presquisle harbor, the six new vessels were brought to the channel opening, where they would take their turns crossing the sandbar. Perry chose August 2 to have the ships begin their exit into the channel. It was the beginning of a very tedious effort.

The vessels had been towed to the bar, when, to the great annoyance of Captain Perry, he found that the lake was considerably below its usual level; that there was only four feet water on the bar instead of six, and that it would be necessary to lighten even the small vessels to get them over. Still, the smoothness of the lake and the abscence of the enemy induced him to proceed. [9]

Before the crossings were attempted Perry called together all his officers aboard the *Lawrence*. There he asked a minister of the area to pray for their success.

About to undertake with such slender means an object of so much importance, Perry, who had ever a deep sense of our dependence on a controlling and overruling Providence, now invoked protection and aid from the God of battles. A clergyman, whose ministration he had attended on shore, came off by invitation to the Lawrence; and, the officers of the squadron being assembled, the banner of the cross was raised high above the ensign, and the sacred offices commenced. The man of God plead devoutly for the triumph of our just cause; for our success in wresting the tomahawk and scalping-knife from savage hands, and subduing the ruthless foe who had encouraged and armed them for the slaughter. He then, in an appropriate address, set forth all the motives of humanity, of patriotism, of what depended on them for the rescuing of outraged altars and the diffusion of Christianity, and bade them go forth conquering and to conquer. The feelings of all were affected and elevated by the solemn rites, and the contemplative mind of Perry seemed confirmed in its calm and steadfast enthusiasm. [10]

The smaller ships in the harbor had less draught (depth below the waterline) and so cleared the sandbar after having some of their guns and supplies offloaded until they crossed. The larger ships had a much bigger problem. Both the *Lawrence* and the *Niagara* drew nine feet.

The sandbar allowed only four. But before they could even attempt to get over the bar, they had to get to it.

The winds were blowing against the ships in the harbor, making any movement toward the channel impossible. They would have to be kedged.

> Early in the morning of the 2d, Mr. Dobbins took charge of the Lawrence as pilot. and kedged her to the entrance of the channel, he having sounded and buoyed it out the day before. The water was found to be quite low, in consequence of the east wind. The Niagara was then kedged up near the bar and moored with springs upon her cables, her port broadside facing the roadstead. The smaller vessels were then moored in a somewhat similar manner and preparations made to defend the Lawrence while on the bar.[11]

Kedging is another time-tested means of getting an unmotorized, seagoing vessel to move against the wind. It's a slow maneuver, but is usually successful. A tethered anchor is carried away from the ship by a smaller boat in the direction desired to move. When the line's limit is reached, the anchor is released into the water. Then the men on the ship slowly wind in the line, effectively pulling themselves to the anchor. It's a tedious process that needs to be repeated over and over, and in this case, it was the only means of bringing the *Lawrence* and *Niagara* up to the sandbar.

With the *Lawrence* in position, the first need was to lighten the load by removing as many of the weighty elements as possible. This included the cast iron cannonades, ammunition, and other portable pieces of equipment. These items were loaded onto smaller boats and sailed ahead of the sandbar where they would be reloaded into position after the crossing. But this was still not enough to sufficiently lift the ship. As if they hadn't had enough construction work on their agenda already, a couple of "camels" now would need to be built. Like the humps of the animals of the same name, these man-made camels, basically hollow barges, held large quantities of water. It would be the filling and emptying of these camels' figurative humps that would get them over the real hump of the sandbar.

A ship "camel" was invented in the Netherlands during the seventeenth century to raise ships over the shallow banks around the harbors of Amsterdam. The idea is simple, as explained in a nineteenth

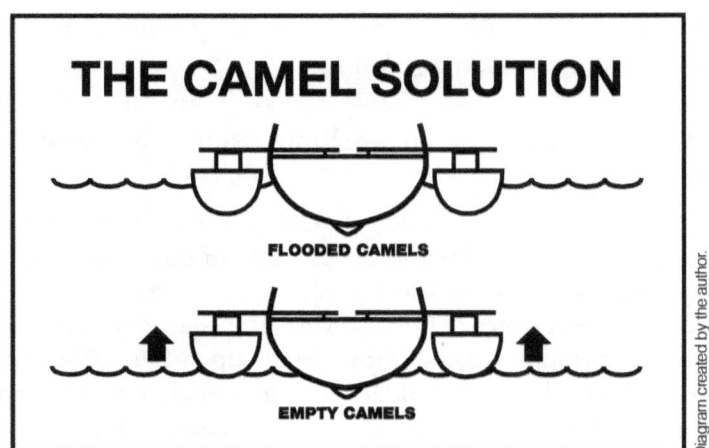

century Cambridge University textbook on hydrostatics (the study of the pressures that resting liquids can produce).

> This is an apparatus for carrying a ship over the bar of a river. It consists of four, or a greater number of watertight chests, which are filled with water, placed in pairs on opposite sides of the ship, and attached to the ship, or attached to each other by chains passing under the keel. If the water be then pumped out, the vessel will be lifted, and may be towed over the bar into deep water. [12]

Dobbins explains how it worked at Presquisle:

> These "camels" were an invention of Mr. Brown; [they] were oblong, with square ends, 90 feet long, 40 feet wide, and six feet depth of hold, with a strong deck. They had two holes cut through the bottom, six inches square, with curbs to guide the long plugs to the holes when required. The "camels" were placed on each side, as before stated, the plugs taken out and the "camels" filled, the heavy timbers thrust through the port-holes, the blocking and lashing secured, when the holes were plugged up, and the pumps set at work. Thus, as the water was discharged, the vessel was lifted. Owing to continued easterly winds, causing low water, the operations with the "camels" had to be repeated before the Lawrence could be floated. After a laborious task, night and day, she got over on the morning of the 4th, and towed out to her anchorage. As a sample of the never-flagging energy of Perry, by two o'clock P.M. everything was replaced, guns mounted, a salute fired, and she was ready for action. [13]

Perry explains the procedure in even more detail:

> The camels were then got alongside, and the water allowed to run into them until their tops were nearly level with the surface. The camels were then lashed together, and solid blocks arranged on top of them, so as to reach the ends of stout spars [poles] which had been laid across the Lawrence through her ports, and securely lashed down to the frame of the vessel. This being arranged, the pumps were set at work in the scows, which raised gradually, lifting the brig with them as the water was discharged. In this way the Lawrence was raised three feet, which, with what she had raised on the removal of her armament, reduced her draught to about four feet. When she got on the shoalest part of the bar, however, it was found that the water had still shoaled, and that it was impossible to force her over, notwithstanding every execution that could be made by heaving on the cables and anchors which had been carried out. The Lawrence had settled a little from the slacking of the lashings and giving way of one of the spars which passed from camel to camel. It became, therefore, indispensable to sink the camels again, get additional blocks between them and the cross-pieces, and replace the broken one. This expedient was resorted to towards nightfall; a few inches diminution of the Lawrence's draught was thus gained, and she was slowly and by main strength hove across the bar in the course of the night and the following day. In this laborious service efficient aid was received from the militia of the neighborhood, under the orders of General David Mead.
>
> Daylight of the 4th of August found the Lawrence's crew, with most of those of the other vessels, still hard at work. She got fairly afloat at eight o'clock, and her guns were quickly mounted, and everything prepared for action...[14]

With the *Lawrence* afloat in deeper waters, the *Niagara* was brought forward to make her attempt at crossing; but more trouble was sailing in from across the lake.

> The Niagara was now towed to the entrance of the channel, and preparations made to lighten her, while the "camels" were being prepared for their work.
>
> In the meantime, early in the morning, the enemy made their appearance in the offing, and hove-to to reconnoitre, when about eight miles out. The smaller vessels having been taken over the bar with but little trouble, were all anchored with the Lawrence; the wind was from the south-east and weather hazy. Perry expecting them to attack, made hasty arrangements to give them as warm a reception as possible; and,

if necessary, to run the Lawrence ashore under the guns of the battery on the bank... [15]

On the brink of a conflict, Perry wondered what the enemy's perception of his situation truly was. He hoped they were far enough away to not notice that the Niagara was still stuck on the bar. In a short time he got his answer as they sailed away without engaging.

The enemy having made off, the work of lightening on board the Niagara went on rapidly — in a few hours everything was on the beach, and the "camels" at work. In the meantime the wind had shifted to the westward, which raised the water, and the next day she was floated, armed, and fully equipped for battle. [16]

With the *Niagara* successfully over the bar, the entire American fleet was now in position to move against the enemy. They did so on September 10, 1813, aboard what just a year previous was wood, alive and growing as trees along the southern shores of Lake Erie; but now transformed into six impressive ships of war, and a couple of camels who gave them a lift. ♦

ANECDOTE.

Justice. — A white trader sold a quantity of powder to an Indian, and imposed upon him by making him believe it was a grain which grew like wheat, by sowing it upon the ground. He was greatly elated by the prospect, not only of raising his own powder, but of being able to supply others, and thereby becoming immensely rich. Having prepared the ground with great care, he sowed his powder with the utmost exactness in the spring. Month after month passed away, but his powder did not even sprout, and winter came before he was satisfied that he had been deceived. He said nothing; but some time after, when the trader had forgotten the trick, the same Indian succeeded in getting credit of him to a large amount. The time set for payment having expired, he sought out the Indian at his residence, and demanded payment for his goods. The Indian heard his demand with great complaisance; then, looking him shrewdly in the eye, said, "Me pay you when my powder grow." This was enough. The guilty white man quickly retraced his steps, satisfied, we apprehend, to balance his account with the chagrin he had received.

In Samuel G. Drake's, Biography and History of the Indians of North America, 1848 [17]

VIII.
WILDCAT McKINNEY.

In 1774, a decade or so before the Northwest Territory was defined, John McKinney was one of the many Virginia riflemen fighting for his right to settle in the Ohio Valley. He had the authority to do so per the Treaty of Stanwix signed six years earlier between the Iroquois and the British. The tribes of the Iroquois confederation occupied lands in the Northeast, yet professed ownership of the lands that would become West Virginia and eastern Kentucky. The Seneca-Cayuga, Shawnee, Delaware, and other Indian tribes who lived in the Ohio Valley disputed their right to sign away these lands, and so disputed any settlements made by the British. As colonists began moving in, several skirmishes broke out between the whites and the resident Indians. In one of these encounters, known as the Battle of Point Pleasant, John McKinney engaged the Indian enemy but he

> was wounded at the first onset. A rifle ball passed through his thighs which so disabled him that he fell. The whites for the moment were compelled to fall back a short distance, leaving the wounded man about halfway between the contending parties, who fought chiefly from behind trees. At length, McKinney, in making an effort to rise to his feet, was discovered by the Indians and another shot shattered his left wrist so badly, that in attempting to hold on to a pawpaw sapling to support himself from falling again, the splintered bone of his arm stuck into the bark of the sapling. The Indians at this juncture made an effort to reach the wounded man with their tomahawks, but the whites discovering the situation of their comrade, advanced to his relief, and shooting two or three Indians gained the ground where he lay, placed him on a blanket, and took him to their encampment. On examination it was found that in addition to the wounds already mentioned, two of his ribs had been cleft

from the backbone by a stroke of the tomahawk. With the exception of losing the use of his left hand in consequence of the wound in his wrist, he entirely recovered. He was also afterward wounded by the Indians in Kentucky while out on a surveying tour. [1]

McKinney was obviously one, resilient fellow. He has been described as stout and well-built, but a bit on the short side. One would think that the tally of wounds he suffered at the hands of Indians would have been enough for a lifetime, but there was more in store for poor John. Such would not be his fate. He would be forced to stir up all his strength and fighting prowess one more time to stave off a most unexpected attack.

On a morning in May of 1783, a traveler happened to ride into Lexington, Kentucky; a community of only a few dozen households and a fort. When the gentleman pulled out an east-coast newspaper from his saddlebag, the information-starved residents converged on him. News took weeks to reach the frontier at this point in time, and the local paper, the *Kentucky Gazette*, wouldn't make its appearance in Lexington for another few years.

There was an exceptionally important report in his edition of the paper. It stated that the American and British negotiators in Paris had put forth articles of peace for their governments' ratification. This news meant that the Revolutionary War may soon truly be over. The people of Lexington wanted to read all the details of this momentous news at their leisure, but the visitor who brought it was leaving town in the morning and his newspaper was going with him. What to do?

The townspeople called on John McKinney. He probably had the best penmanship around, being the schoolmaster, and so he was asked to make a copy of the newspaper stories. He readily agreed, little knowing that this kindness would nearly cost him his life. "For this purpose he rose before daylight and went into the school-house which stood a few rods from the fort on the outside of the picketing." [2]

What happened next has been retold as fact and in fiction, usually embellished to make what is already a good story flow even smoother. Perhaps most famously it was the basis for a scene in a best-selling novel of the late 1800s titled, *The Choir Invisible*. The earliest account comes from the memoirs of a frontiersman, James McBride, whose recollections were posthumously published in 1869. They tell the story quite well.

McBride explains that near to the school, where McKinney was engrossed in copying the stories, three women were tending to their usual chore of feeding and milking the cows. Their names were Mrs. Collins, Mrs. Masterson, and Miss Thompson. As the morning began to brighten

> suddenly a female voice, that of Mrs. Collins, rather above its common pitch, came through a port-hole on the outside of the [Collins'] cabin, saying: "Stephen, run over to the schoolhouse; something is the matter with the master, he hollers like he had a fit." Old Mr. Collins, with young Joel [their ten-year-old son] at his heels, without loss of time obeyed the call. When they reached the school-house door, which was standing open, Mr. Collins stepped in and said: "Why, master, what on earth is the matter?" He replied: "An ugly baste [beast] has been trying here to kill me, but I have got him pretty well conquered." At the same time giving a dig with his lame left hand into the side of the dying animal which he held in his arms, suspended by its teeth fastened in McKinney's breast-bone, a little below the throat.
>
> When the animal had attacked him he seized it in his arms and in the scuffle contrived to get the animal's back against the writing bench or table. Grasping it by the throat with his right hand, he bore on it with all his might, with his body in a doubled-up position against the table, and was not slow in dealing blows with his left fist (over which he always wore a glove, because of its being disfigured by the wound before mentioned). And what with squeezing, choking, and pounding, the breath of the creature was stopped and its life brought to a close.
>
> While matters were in this posture, some one attempted to assist him by taking hold of the dying animal, but he said: "Wait, until I come out of the door, when you can have light to see how to take the teeth out of my breast-bone." He then stepped out to the light, and Mr. Collins, by taking hold of the head of the animal and using some care, at last succeeded in loosening the teeth from the bone, and drew them out, not, however, without considerable pain to the master.
>
> The women who had then gathered around in considerable numbers expressed their fears that it was a rabid or mad cat, and that he would be in danger of hydrophobia. "Never mind," said he with perfect composure, "if it is the will of Providence that I should die in that way, your fretting will not save me." However, if the animal was mad it did not communicate the disease to him. [3]

Illustration by R.M. Brinkerhoff in book: *Stories of Old Kentucky* by Martha Grassham Purcell, Copyright, 1915.

After all of this, and some further tending to his wounds, the unflappable McKinney held his morning session of classes for the children! By midday, however; he finally succumbed to fatigue and went home to recuperate.

McKinney would go on to live a full life: marrying, having several children, moving between Kentucky and Missouri, and working at various civil and political jobs. As Kentucky was vying for statehood, McKinney argued at its convention and then served in the new state's legislature.

But the man-versus-beast fight of that morning in the schoolhouse forever defined John. From that day forward he would be known as Wildcat McKinney. He was often heard to say that he would rather fight two Indians than one wildcat. Based on his performance, it's a sure bet that most men of the day felt likewise; preferring to take on two Indians rather than *Wildcat* McKinney. ♦

ANECDOTE.

The late Earl of Chatham, who bore no good will to a certain Physician, was rallying him one day about the efficacy of his prescriptions. To which the Doctor replied, "He defied any of his patients to find fault with his. – "I believe you," replied the witty Earl, "for they are all dead."

In the Centinel of the North-Western Territory, January 30, 1796 [4]

IX.
OLIVER SWIFT.

In his early years his friends and acquaintances spoke of him as that, "Gentleman from Virginia." He walked many paths in life, literally and figuratively, and always his character and patriotism were readily on display. Even late in life, he was still referred to as "an elegant gentleman." Few remember him today, but he is another perfect example of the courageous, forthright, and intelligent personality that populated much of the Ohio country in its early days. His name was William Oliver.

Little is known about William's early years except that in 1810, prior to his twenty-third birthday, he was already practicing medicine. It was in that year that he made a decision to give up his doctoring and go into business as a sutler, or trader, on the frontier lands of Indiana. The reason for the career change is unknown, but it would prove to become a profound decision affecting many lives in the Northwest Territory.

Will, as his friends called him, had established his business in a dwelling situated just outside the walls of a United States fortress which had been built at the confluence of the St. Mary, St. Joseph, and Maumee Rivers. Named for the hero of Fallen Timbers, General Anthony Wayne, this structure was the second of three incarnations that Fort Wayne would have under the same name. It was a bit larger and better fortified than the original built under the direction of Wayne himself in 1794.

Oliver was the fourth in a line of five men over the years 1802 through 1814 who attempted to make a living of selling his wares to settlers, Indians, and the soldiers of Fort Wayne. Stints at being the primary sutler at the site seemed to last an average of three years or so. Oliver began his in 1810 and was still there in 1812 when war came to the area.

The sutlers on the frontier were a rugged bunch. Some were unscrupulous gents who might sometimes unexpectedly ransack a camp; stealing from the soldiers and then running off to another location. Others were more subtle in the way they preyed upon their customers. They might simply price gouge the products that were most needed. Still others took firm advantage of the popularity of one of their key products — alcohol. Booze had the highest profit margins and was easy enough to supply. Whether it was rum, whiskey, or wine; the soldiers drank up regularly to the chagrin of the officers who were often left with camps of men too drunk to properly serve. These types of self-serving sutlers forced the hand of the officers at most fortresses to lay down regulations. By the early 1800s traders were screened prior to contracting as a sutler of record with a government post. Still, the licensed sutler often had to remain in good favor with the commanders of a garrison. It was not unusual for special favors and kickbacks, perhaps gifts of whiskey, to be given to the officers who controlled the fate of the licensed sutler. Seems that some unscrupulous practices were to be found on both sides of the trading counter!

By no means were all sutlers devious or dishonest in their business endeavors. Oliver, from all accounts, was a very legit and forthright businessman, contracted to honestly supplement the meager foods and supplies being provided at Fort Wayne by the government. In late August of 1812, Oliver happened to be in Cincinnati where he was stocking up with a fresh supply of goods to haul back to his post at Fort Wayne. War had been declared two months earlier, and there was good reason to be weary of potential trouble throughout the Indiana lands that Oliver roamed. Upon his arrival in Cincinnati, he learned some very disturbing news.

First, word came that General Hull, in command of the American Army of the Northwest, had ordered the inhabitants of Fort Dearborn, in what is now downtown Chicago, to abandon that fortress for fear of a massive Indian attack. It was speculated that the capture of the island fortress of Fort Mackinaw by British troops and Indians was going to embolden the Indians to move against smaller, isolated forts like

Fort Dearborn. Unbeknownst to Oliver, while he was heading down to Cincinnati the fifty or so men and their families of Fort Dearborn were beginning their journey toward Fort Wayne. Just a few miles into their trip, they were unexpectedly ambushed by Potawatomie Indians. The result was devastating with most of them being killed or taken captive.

The news of the massacre took several days to reach Cincinnati. When Oliver did hear of it, he feared that the Indian band would move on to attack Fort Wayne next. In fact, it was just a few days later that a large assembly of Indians surrounded Fort Wayne and began a siege. Though Oliver was unaware that the attack was actually underway, he knew he had to at least notify his friends at Fort Wayne about Mackinaw and Dearborn. But, as he was preparing to return, even worse news came riding into town. The unthinkable had happened. Hull had surrendered Fort Detroit to the British. This meant there was little if any protection left against an Indian or British attack at Fort Wayne, or any of the remaining posts and settlements scattered about the Northwest Territory. Fort Wayne had been about equidistant between Forts Dearborn and Detroit. Now, neither would have their back. Luckily, as the siege against them had begun, the eighty or so soldiers of Fort Wayne were still oblivious to their predicament. They put up a sustained fight while hoping for reinforcements. The backup would come, but not from where they had expected it.

William Oliver's whole life was stowed away in his cabin next to that fortress, and even more importantly, he had a kid brother, Peter, serving as a soldier inside the fort. So certainly, he had high stakes in the game.

He left Cincinnati for Fort Wayne, but stopped first at Piqua, a village about ninety miles to the North where Ohio militia troops were encamped. The men there were originally on their way to reinforce Hull's troops in Canada. When Oliver arrived, they too had just learned the fate of Fort Detroit. The mood was sullen and confused. And then word came that Fort Wayne was under attack by the Indians. Oliver, until now a private citizen, decided to sign on to this Ohio militia force as a member of a rifle company. He tried to entice these men to move forward as soon as possible to the aid of Fort Wayne. He even volunteered to lead the effort. But the men were in such disarray they couldn't be mustered to go.

Being extremely disappointed at the lack of support at Piqua, Oliver says:

> I set out for Cincinnati to see Col. Saul Wells of the 17th US Infantry with a view of his marching to [the] relief of Fort Wayne. Governor Harrison as head of [the] Kentucky Volunteers reached Cincinnati [the] same day. I called on him and communicated [the] condition of things [and] informed him I was going for Fort Wayne. He said his troops would continue their march directly for that place.
>
> So that the militia might be so informed, and at the same time asking [that] they might go on [with me] to Fort Wayne, I set out. [I] reached St. Mary's encampment of militia about lunch of 31 August 1812. Found camp in confusion and without organization.[1]

William Harrison was the Governor of the Indiana Territory, and now, as he crossed the Ohio River with two thousand troops from Kentucky, he received word that as a result of Hull's dreadful actions he had been appointed as the new Commander of the Northwest Army. Oliver went right to Harrison to talk. The result was that Oliver's original concern now became his first military mission: to get word to his fellows at Fort Wayne to hold fast through the attacks, because Harrison was on his way with significant reinforcements.

The movement of Harrison's large group of men, on foot, required a lot more time than it would take for a small contingent to proceed on horseback to Fort Wayne. Therefore, Oliver was ordered to first head to St. Mary's (just west of Wapokeneta) where the militia he had visited earlier had advanced to. There he spoke with then Senator Thomas Worthington, soon to be the sixth governor of Ohio. Worthington was also an Indian commissioner sent here with a few other Ohio senators to negotiate a potential agreement with Indians of the region who had not yet allied with the British.

Worthington acknowledged the confusion of the camp and promised Oliver that he would muster as many men as he could to move on for Fort Wayne, himself included. As it turned out, he managed to persuade about eighty men, including several Indian allies, to sign up. The foremost among the Indians were Johnny Logan, Captain Johnny, and Bright Horn. All three of these Shawnee Indians had already proven their loyalty by repeatedly putting their lives on the line for American concerns.

The band set out early on the morning of September 1. Later the next day, still some twenty miles out from the fort, they made their camp and

> feasted most gloriously on venison [that] our Indians had killed during the day. Whilst our company heard report of cannon in the direction of Fort Wayne. [They] Having only howitzers, [we] didn't think they could be heard so far [away]. Rather [we] concluded the British had possession of Fort Wayne. [2]

Oliver thought that they were hearing the much larger cannons of the British who he assumed must have arrived at the fort in support of the Indians. Based on this premise, Worthington wanted to immediately storm the fort with their entire contingent. But Oliver paused and after further discussion the group surmised that if the British and Indians were as large a force as they were imagining, their band of eighty men would not stand a chance against them. They further reasoned that alternatively a handful of men could possibly weave unnoticed through the enemy ranks and gain access to the fort. And so it was decided that Worthington and most of these men would return to St. Mary's. There they would organize the Ohio militia and lead them to Fort Wayne as further reinforcement to Harrison's troops already on their way. Meanwhile, Oliver says:

> Logan with Captain Johnny and Bright Horn, all Shawnees from Waghpockonetta, volunteered to accompany me — away we put in full Indian style without hesitation until within 5 miles of Fort Wayne. Here Logan discovered hostile Indians had been way laying the road to cut off communication. They had excavated the earth on either side of the road alternately at 7 or 8 paces so as to lay the body concealed from view after night — and for their uses between the road and the river [for] day watchings [they] had fallen behind logs and broken branches... [3]

Oliver apparently marked himself in some fashion with paint and dress so as to blend in as an Indian alongside the three true Shawnees. In this way the four of them hoped that they could pass through the enemy Indian lines unnoticed. At this point, Oliver's part in what became known as the Battle of Fort Wayne had an intriguing and some say miraculous twist.

With no Indians present behind those fallen trees along the road, they were clear to proceed. Oliver explains that:

> We then put our horses to their full speed and made thro the woods for a point on the river one mile below the fort. We rode into the bushes between the road and river, dismounted our horses and went on foot to ascertain if the fort was still in our possession — approaching the open [road] I knew a sentinel on post. [4]

That recognition of a guard told Oliver that the Americans still held the fort and was the key to his next move. They re-mounted their horses and then

> taking the main road, moved rapidly to the fort. Upon reaching the gate of the esplanade, they found it locked, and were thus compelled to pass down the river bank, and then ascend it at the northern gate. They were favored in doing so by the withdrawal of the hostile Indians from this point... [5]

For reasons unknown to Oliver at this time, there were no Indians to be seen on this side of the fortress. Little did he know that this was because the enemy was in the midst of executing a devious plot to finally win the day. As Oliver's foursome came around the corner and approached the north gate of the fort, they were shocked to see a contingent of Indian chiefs approaching them with a white flag catching the breeze atop a pole that one of them was carrying.

> Winnemac, Five Medals, and three other hostile chiefs, bearing the flag under which they were to gain admittance to the fort to carry out their treacherous intentions, were surprised by suddenly meeting at the gate, Oliver and his companions. Coming from different directions and screened by the angles of the fort, the parties were not visible to each other until both were near the gate. On meeting, they shook hands, but it was apparent that Winnemac was greatly disconcerted; he immediately wheeled and returned to his camp, satisfied that this accession of strength to the garrison — the forerunner, in all probability, of a much larger force — had defeated his scheme. The others of his party entered the fort, and remained some little time, during which they were given to understand that Logan and his two Indian companions were to remain with the garrison. [6]

The plot of the Indian forces foiled by Oliver's arrival would have been devastating had it been fulfilled. The only reason it had even been

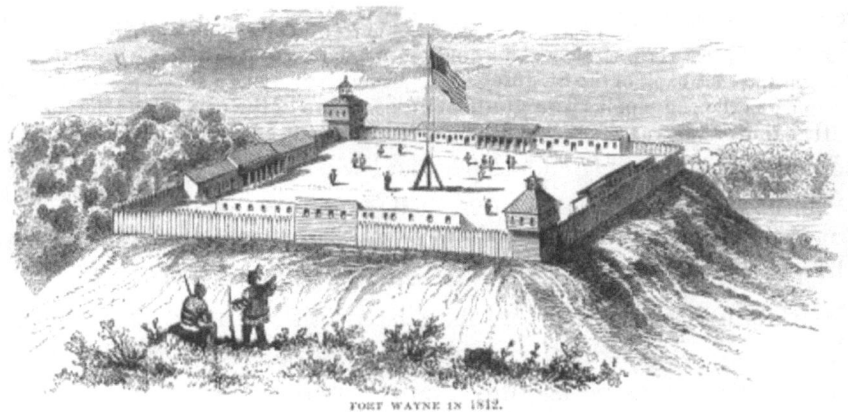

Fort Wayne of 1812. Illustrated by Benson J. Lossing and shown here as it appeared in his *Pictorial Fieldbook of the War of 1812*, 1868.

conceived was due in large part to the behavior of the fortress's incompetent commander, Captain James Rhea, who had heretofore held several meetings with the Indian leaders.

For several days previous to this time, the hostile chiefs under a flag of truce, had been holding intercourse with the garrison; and had, it is supposed, discovered the unsoldier-like condition of the commander. They had accordingly arranged their warriors in a semicircle, on the west and south sides of the fort, and at no great distance from it. Five of the chiefs, under pretence of treating with the officers of the garrison, were to pass into the fort, and when in council were to assasinate the subaltern officers with pistols and knives concealed under their blankets; and then to seize captain Rhea, who in his trepidation, and under a promise of personal safety, would, they anticipated, order the gates of the fort to be thrown open for the admission of the besiegers. The plan, thus arranged, was in the act of being carried into execution at the moment when Oliver and his companions reached the gate. [7]

When the attack on Fort Wayne began days earlier, Captain Rhea's drinking had also begun. Based on many accounts from his subordinate officers, Rhea continued to hold command through the nearly two weeks of the siege fully "under the influence." His orders and actions were disturbing to the men. Real leadership fell to the officers next in line. One of these was Lieutenant Curtis who in a letter to the Inspector-General of the Army testified to the captain's treasonous behavior during one of his meetings with the leader of the Potawatomi Indians, Chief Winnemac.

> Our great captain invited the savage over to his headquarters and after drinking three glasses of wine with him, rose from his seat and observed: 'My good friend, I love you; I will fight for you; I will die by your side. You must save me!' and then gave him a half dollar as a token of friendship, inviting him at the same time to come and breakfast with him the next morning. [8]

Winnemac didn't show for breakfast after that meeting, but instead sent a band of warriors who picked off two of the fort's sentries. Captain Rhea was being fully manipulated by Winnemac, but the timely arrival of Oliver foiled the Potawatomi chief's most daring plot. The news from Oliver that Harrison was on his way gave the men's spirits a great lift. Many were incredulous at the tremendous odds against Oliver saving the day at the precise moment that he did. It has been described as an act of Divine Providence. Lieutenant Curtis again offers his perspective:

> The safe arrival of Mr. Oliver at that particular juncture, may justly be considered most miraculous. One hour sooner or one later, would no doubt have been inevitable destruction both to himself and [his] escort; the parties of Indians who had been detached to guard the roads and passes in different directions, having all at that moment been called in, to aid in carrying the fort. It is generally believed by those acquainted with the circumstances, that not one hour, for eight days and nights preceding or following the hour in which Mr. Oliver arrived, would have afforded an opportunity of any probable safety. [9]

Oliver took some authority within the fort upon his arrival, sending Logan and the other two Shawnees back to Harrison with a message of his success and the state of the fort. After a few days, they successfully survived a renewed siege from the Indians and on September 12 cheered the arrival of Harrison and his reinforcements. The Indians finally dispersed and the fort was revitalized. Captain Rhea was relieved of duty and soon forced to retire as a result of his unacceptable behavior. Oliver continued in service under Harrison.

About a hundred miles down the Maumee River from Fort Wayne, another fort was built during the early winter months of 1813. This was a large structure named after then Governor Return J. Meigs. It is unclear whether he had been part of the crew that built it, but Oliver was stationed there in April.

Through that spring and summer, many critical battles would be fought in northwest Ohio. The British forces led by Brigadier General Henry Proctor aligned with Tecumseh's Indian confederacy to attack Fort Meigs twice in early 1813. The first siege lasted eight days from May 1 through May 8. It was an attack primarily fought with heavy cannon fire from British batteries positioned across the river from the fort. Though they gave quite a pounding to the fortress, Proctor and Tecumseh could not break the Americans and ended up retreating back to Detroit in frustration. Two months later, they made another attempt. This time Tecumseh created a ruse with his warriors on the fort side of the river. The ploy was a mock battle complete with Indian whoops, hollers, and gunfire to make the fort inhabitants think that their reinforcements were being attacked. The goal was to lure the Americans out of the fort and fall into an ambush. The scheme failed.

It was at the beginning of the first siege that William Oliver stepped up once again. Three days before the attack began, the British were spotted by Harrison's spies landing at Fort Miamis; their twenty-year-old, disheveled fortress two miles down river from Fort Meigs. Immediately, Proctor deployed crews to survey the land in what is now downtown Maumee to set up his batteries of artillery. The sight of Proctor's arrival disturbed Harrison who felt he was still inadequately supplied to put up the required defense. Both ammunition and men were in short supply. He knew reinforcements were on their way from Kentucky under the command of General Greene Clay, but Harrison had no idea where they were in their journey north. Would they arrive in time?

With that question unanswered, Harrison called upon William Oliver to make a precarious journey to find General Clay and alert him of the imminent attack and to order him to move ahead with great haste. Clay was coming up from Kentucky, but at this point in time he could have been anywhere between the fort and Cincinnati. That was a lot of land to cover. Luckily, there was a line of forts already established in the region that Oliver could use as stepping stones through the wilderness. Some were recently built by General Harrison as supply depots, some were built by General Hull the year previous as he made his trek northward to Detroit, and others still remained or were rebuilt from the Indian Wars of the 1790s. A close friend of Oliver gives us his recollection of how the adventure began.

> Oliver never hesitated where duty called him. The necessary preparations were made and at the hour of midnight (a dark and dismal night in Apr 1813), a young soldier (Oliver) was seen to issue from one of the gates of Ft. Meigs, then closely besieged by a numerous Army of savages, who environed the Ft and through whose encampment our young friend had to pass; He moved on with slow, steady, but cautious steps. Frequently in his passage through the almost numberless camp fires of his wary foe; — at the breaking of a stick by his horse tread or any, even the slightest noise, Indian warriors would be seen on every side, springing half up, as listening attentively, to learn from whence the noise had come, Intense indeed must have been the feelings of our friend (Oliver); thus surrounded by vigilant and deadly foes; He told me, in conversing lately about this interesting moment 'that his horse seemed to feel the responsibility of the situation in which they were placed — and stopped when a twig would crack' — soon the Indians would become satisfied and again lie down; When suspicion was lulled he would again proceed — & thus by slow cautious movements this miraculous passage through the Indian encampment was effected; and the dispatches, so important to our Garrison delivered to General Clay. [10]

Historian Robert McAfee recorded, just three years after the fact, a somewhat different picture of Oliver's escape from the fort.

> An express was now sent to general Clay, with letters also for the governors of Ohio and Kentucky. This perilous journey was undertaken by Captain Oliver, the commisary to the fort, a brave and intelligent officer, who possessed every necessary qualification for such an enterprise. He was accompanied by a single white man, and an Indian, and was escorted some distance from the camp by Captain Garrard with 80 of his dragoons. [11]

While his friend implies that Oliver was alone on the journey, McAfee says he had a significant entourage to safely get him on his way. Perhaps the dragoons were a decoy, leaving Oliver, and maybe the two others, to weave through the camps as described? The truth is left to speculation, but either way Oliver headed up the mission and did have to maneuver, in some fashion, his way past the Indian camps surrounding the fort. Once he got through, he headed south to the next closest fort hoping to gain some intelligence on Clay's position. That was Fort Findlay which he reached the next day. From there he wrote a letter to Governor Meigs of Ohio explaining the situation at the fort that bore his name. He also stated, "I am now in pursuit of General Clay, and expect to come up with him to-day." [12]

It would take a few more days than hoped before Oliver could track down the general. On May 1, three days into his journey, he found himself back in the region of St. Mary's where he had rounded up his band to rescue Fort Wayne the previous fall. Specifically he was at Fort Amanda, in today's town of Wapokeneta. An ensign stationed there recorded in his journal that:

> This morning Clear & Pleasant... 2 P.M. Mr. Oliver arriv'd from the rapids. Express attended by 2 Men & one Indian. Brought Account that 2000 British & 1000 Indians had made their Appearance in sight of the rapids. Left here at 4 P.M. for Fort Defiance to warn the Kentucky troop of the Approach of the enemy to beware of them in Descending the river. He heard distinctly the noise of Cannon & Beleives That the fort was attacked. General Harrison Commands & has About 2000-troops with Him. [13]

Oliver headed northwestward and finally caught up with one of the two Kentucky regiments he was in search of. Colonel William Dudley's force was on its way to Fort Defiance to reunite there with Colonel William Boswell's regiment and General Clay himself. Oliver found Dudley en route. With the news delivered, Dudley immediately sent a messenger to alert Harrison that the help he needed was on its way. He also requested return orders on how to successfully approach the fort. Leslie Combs, one of the few who knew the lay of the land in this region, volunteered to deliver this message. But he ran into a battle already in progress as he approached the fortress. Combs and his companions were attacked and he had to return to Defiance without getting the message through to Harrison.

On May 3, the fifth full day since Oliver had left Fort Meigs, all the parties had finally coalesced at Fort Defiance and everyone was brought up to speed. Because they had already lost significant time,

Oliver was sent back to Fort Meigs with Major David Trimble in a canoe down the swift currents of the Maumee River. This time the effort was successful. Harrison was relieved to learn that Clay was soon to arrive and indeed he landed along the Maumee River banks the next day in the midst of the on-going attack.

The fort withstood the first siege in no small part due to Oliver's brave 150-mile trek through the wilderness to find and persuade the reinforcements to arrive at the fort sooner than otherwise may have been possible. Two months later as the second siege was made on Fort Meigs, Harrison was at a supply depot known as Fort Seneca near today's Tiffin, Ohio. General Clay had been left in charge. Clay, obviously convinced of Oliver's qualifications, sent him yet again as a courier to ride the sixty miles to Fort Seneca and alert Harrison of the second attack.

Oliver certainly managed to see a lot of the Ohio and Indiana lands during his time in military service, and he obviously liked what he saw because just four years later, when the war was over, he became a significant figure in the land deals and development of what would become Toledo, Ohio and suburbs.

In 1817, Oliver was a principal player in a Cincinnati land speculating firm known as the Baum Company. They began buying lands along and close to the mouth of the Maumee River. One area was the very land on which the British troops and artillery had been set up to fire against him while he was stationed inside Fort Meigs. With a team of surveyors Oliver plotted this ground as the city of Maumee.

Twenty years earlier, as a result of the Greenville Treaty, about three-quarters of what would become Ohio was ceded to the Americans. But the northwest corner of Ohio remained Indian territory. That is except for a twelve by twelve square-mile block that the US had negotiated for in this treaty, because they saw it as a strategic location for potential military use. As it happened, Fort Meigs was built within it.

But four years after the war, in 1817, things were peaceful and Ohio's population was pushing faster than ever into this area regardless of it still belonging to the Indians. A new treaty was negotiated between the Indian tribes of the region and the U.S. government. It became known as the Fort Meigs Treaty. As a result the Maumee River Valley was opened for settlement. The square of land owned by the government was put up for auction. Oliver, through the Baum company, purchased many of the newly surveyed lots within the block.

Over the years, properties frequently changed hands. Oliver and others repeatedly suffered through foreclosures and transfers. The Baum company that Oliver was part of merged with a competitor, the Piatt company, and became the Port Lawrence company. Their holdings covered much of what today is the southern half of downtown Toledo, and the village established took the company name. A short time later, another former officer during the war, B.F. Stickney, thought the area was ripe for another town to take shape and so purchased the lands that would become the northern half of the current downtown. He named his village Vistula. Still later a group of investors from the Buffalo, New York area thought they would form yet another town and named it after their company, Manhattan. Their investment encompassed what today is known as the Point Place area of Toledo.

All of this land speculation was spurred on by its critical location along the Maumee River. From here ships from all over the world that were traversing the Great Lakes could transport goods inland to the heart of the country. And, at this time there was serious talk about the creation of the Miami-Erie canal which would connect Toledo with Cincinnati. When that was completed, shipments would be floated straight to the Ohio River and on to the Mississippi River. Each of the villages near the mouth of the Maumee River felt that they had the most strategically located land to serve as the port of landing at what would become the canal's point of origination.

As it happened, the Manhattan village dissipated and the villages of Port Lawrence and Vistula merged to become the Toledo of today, and from their docks passage to the canal would begin. But is that Toledo, Ohio or Toledo, Michigan? William Oliver would again become involved, at least on the fringes, in yet another war. This one was to determine Toledo's fate.

The first several decades of the 1800s saw both Ohio and Michigan claiming ownership of the roughly eight-mile wide strip of land that runs from the current eastern border of Indiana to the western shores of Lake Erie; forming the northern-most border of Ohio where it

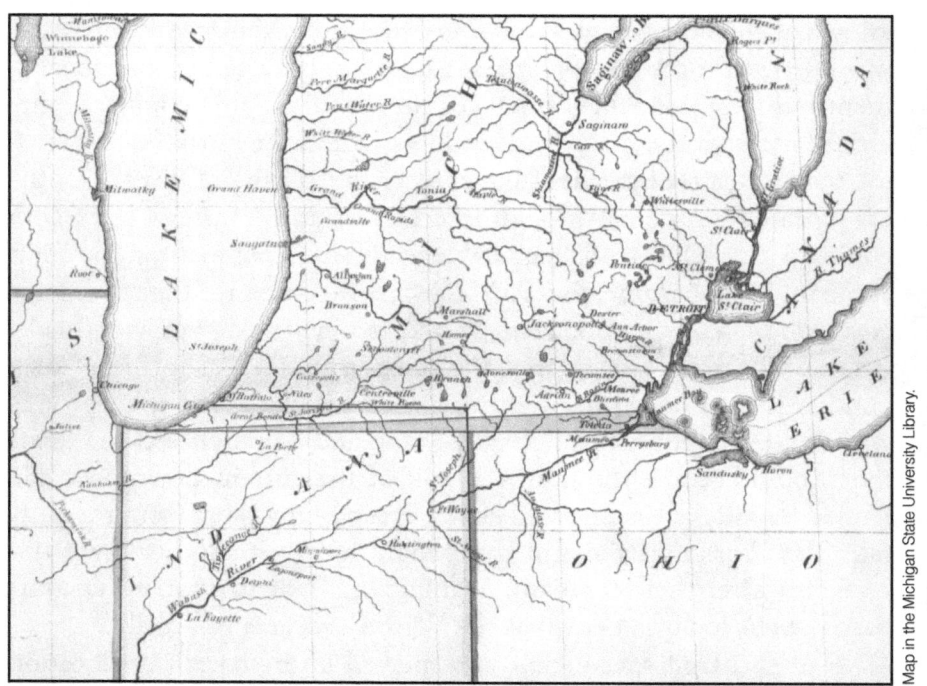

Portion of an official government map drawn by David Burr which was part of U.S. House Report 380 presented to the 24th Congress highlighting the contested land area between the territory of Michigan and the State of Ohio, 1836.

abuts Michigan. Two survey lines were drawn over the years and the correctness of one over the other was in constant dispute. This resulted in a contested territory which included Toledo and so was referred to as the Toledo Strip. When the issue of ownership finally came to a head in 1835, as Michigan was applying for statehood, it likewise became known as the Toledo War.

This war also determined the fate of what today is a premier university. Going into the Treaty of Fort Meigs, the Indians of the region expressed a fondness for a Catholic priest named Father Gabriel Richard of St. Anne's parish in Detroit. Father Richard spearheaded the education of the populace of the Michigan Territory. The Indians specifically allotted a few tracts of land on what is today the downtown riverfront of Toledo to the good father for the purpose of establishing a school. Teaming up with Augustus Woodward and several other influential religious and political leaders around Detroit, Father Richard, et al, planned to establish the "University of Michigainia" on these gifted tracts of land.

Though the parcels changed hands and were exchanged for others many times over the years, in the end, it was William Oliver who bought them from the University trustees. That fact eventually led to Ann Arbor, Michigan becoming the home of the University of Michigan, instead of Toledo; thus creating one of the longest churning sports rivalries in the nation with the Ohio State University.

Though more a war of words than bullets, the Toledo War had its share of taunts, fights, arrests, and chases. In both 1835 and 1836 there were several occasions when hundreds of militia from both sides were poised for attack. The only real blood drawn was when the son of the former officer, Major Benjamin Stickney, stabbed an arresting sheriff from Michigan with a small dirk; the wound not being serious. It was the frequent arrests by Michigan authorities of people professing to be Ohioans, while doing business within the disputed strip, that kept the fires of war burning. The legal battle went on for decades and even pitted former president John Quincy Adams, who favored Michigan's ownership rights, against the sitting president, Andrew Jackson, whenever Congress argued the issue.

In a brash maneuver in the summer of 1835, Ohio's legislature created a new county of the lands lying within the strip. They named it Lucas, after then Governor Robert Lucas, and further declared Toledo to be its new seat of government. Resolutions were also passed stating that Toledo would be attached to the second circuit of courts and that a court of common pleas would hold session there on September 7, 1835. This action would legally bear witness to the fact that Toledo was in the state of Ohio.

Governor Mason of the Michigan Territory, a young, impetuous man who was not going to back down from a fight, learned of the planned court session and sent a thousand militiamen to guard against it taking place. Not to be out-smarted, Lucas ordered his own militia, under the charge of Colonel Vanfleet, to accompany the team of judges and clerks into Toledo on the date specified. But the governor took some unexpected liberties with the timing of the proceedings. Willard Way, a prominent figure living in the area in question that day, gave this account years later:

> Colonel Vanfleet told the judges that Sept. 7 would commence immediately after midnight, and that there was no hour specified in the law when the court should be opened. 'Governor Lucas wants the court held, so that by its record he can show to the world that he has extended the laws of Ohio over the disputed territory, in spite of the vaporing threats of Governor Mason. If we furnish him the record, we shall accomplish all that is required. Be prepared to mount your horses to start for Toledo precisely 1 o'clock a.m. I will be ready with an escort to protect you.' [14]

The party of court officials and their guards made it to a small schoolhouse in what is now downtown Toledo and there the session began at three o'clock in the morning.

> The proceedings were hastily written on loose paper and deposited in the clerk's hat. When the court adjourned, the officers and escort went to the tavern… registered their names and took a drink all around; while filling their glasses for a second drink, a mischievous wag [prankster] ran into the tavern and reported that a strong force of michigan men was close by, coming to arrest them. They dropped their glasses, spilling the liquor they intended to have drunk, and sprang for their horses with all possible haste, leaving bills to be settled at a more leisure time. [15]

As they raced south toward the state line, the one that was not disputed by Michigan, a most unfortunate discovery was made.

> They took the trail that led to Maumee, by way of the route nearest the river. They went at such furious speed that, if their charge had been made in the opposite direction towards the enemy, they would have pierced the most solid columns. When arrived at the top of the hill… not discovering the enemy in pursuit, they came to a halt and faced about. It was then discovered that the clerk had lost his hat, and with it the papers containing the proceedings of the court, from which the record was to be made up. The clerk wore one of those high bell-crowned hats, fashionable in those days, and which he used for carrying his papers as well as covering his head. It was then the custom in traveling to carry everything in the top of hats, from spare collar and dickey to court papers. The hat of the clerk, reaching high above his head, burdened with its load of papers and other incumbrances, was steadied on with the left hand for greater safety, while the right held the reins. But in spite of this precaution, it struck against an overhanging limb of a tree with such violence, that it was knocked off and fell to the ground. Having

Illustration by L.J. Bridgman in 1881 of what has been called the "Sunrise Court" that was held by Ohio officials in the wee hours of the morning of September 7, 1835 within the disputed Toledo Strip of land. The action would soon lead to Toledo becoming part of Ohio instead of Michigan. Drawing found in book: *The Story of Ohio*, by Alexander Black, 1888.

succeeded in holding court without molestation, or bloodshed, and now losing the papers, would leave them in as bad condition, or worse, then if they had done nothing, in case they should fall into the hands of the enemy. Notwithstanding, they all believed they had been discovered and pursued, and might be surrounded by superior numbers and taken, if they delayed; yet the importance of recovering the papers was such as to nerve them to the boldest daring. Colonel Vanfleet's courage and tact did not desert him in this emergency. He had succeeded in accomplishing what he had contemplated; and now their labor would be lost, and the expedition an entire failure, without the recovery of the papers. With him, to will was to do. He directed the clerk and two of the guards to dismount, and feel their way back carefully in search of the papers, while the balance of the posse kept watch, to cover retreat. He cautioned them to move with as little noise as possible, and if likely to be discovered by the enemy, to conceal themselves and watch their movements, so that they could use the best possible advantage to accomplish their object. The orders were that nothing but utter impossibility would excuse a failure to recover them. The search proved successful; the hat was found and the papers recovered. The party reported no enemy in sight. [16]

With papers in hat, the men re-grouped and seeing no one in pursuit proceeded leisurely to the border that would assure their safety. The ruse of being chased nearly ruined the entire effort, and could have cost lives, but luckily for Ohio this event would lead to a satisfactory and final resolution. In January 1837, the territory of Michigan became the state of Michigan. Ohio was given the Toledo Strip in exchange for Michigan receiving its upper peninsula.

While William Oliver was not physically involved in the Toledo War, his land holdings were. Besides some of them playing a role in the University of Michigan's eventual location, other parcels of Oliver's property were crossed over as the court entourage made their retreat. In fact, the hill on which the group paused and discovered that the papers were lost, was owned by Oliver. Ironically, in just a few years, Oliver would build a house on that hilltop which would become a prominent Toledo landmark to this day.

By 1853, the county seat of Lucas, which had been moved to Maumee, was returned to Toledo and from that terminus the Miami-Erie canal was in full operation. The railroad had also arrived and one hotel, the *Island House*, took advantage of it by serving as a train station and a house of lodging. Business was booming, as they say, and Oliver decided to put his entrepreneurial vision to work again. He had already built a steam mill, and operated a wholesale flour enterprise for years. Now he hired a nationally renowned architect, Isaiah Rogers, to design a grand hotel that would rival any in the country. In a bold marketing move, the new roadhouse began rising just a block away from the ever-popular *Island House*, giving guests a choice of accommodations and ready access to other services.

Unfortunately, William Oliver would not see his hotel come to fruition as he passed away later that year. His son-in-law and others carried his dream to its completion in 1859, with an opening of great pomp and fanfare according to an article in the *Toledo Blade* newspaper.

> There was a very fashionable assembly convened in this new institution of our growing city, last night, but although the affair is deserving of more than a mere local item we feel ourselves incapable of doing justice to the splendor and truly magnificent appearance presented by the scene... on about the highest ground in the city, overlooking and conveniently near the immense Union Railroad Depot,

The Oliver House circa 1880. Upon opening in 1859 it immediately rivaled the best hotels in the country; flaunting elegance in every one of its 170 guest rooms. Beyond the fine furnishings, gas lights and running water were featured.

commanding a complete view of the river and the bay, the city also and the surrounding country, and yet within four or five squares of the business centre of the city, the Oliver House has one of the best, airiest, and most commanding positions of any hotel in the country: and its plan designed by ISAIAH ROGERS, of Cincinnati with especial reference to the spot is pronounced the most convenient and perfect of any ever made by that distinguished architect, who is well known as designer of the Burnet House, and many of the best Hotels in America... The Opening Festival was indeed a splendid affair. The dining room was thronged with merry dancers, and the fine promenades and attractive rooms of the house were filled with the gay crowd. The supper was appropriately the crowning glory of the occasion, possessing every imaginable dainty and achievement of the modern cuisine. It was not until daylight that the music was hushed, and the party broke up. [17]

Over the years the *Oliver House* has been reincarnated several times for multiple purposes and as of this writing it is a fine restaurant and brewery.

Oliver had married Elizabeth Ruffin, daughter of the renowned Major William Ruffin who served under Generals St. Clair and

Wayne in the Indian wars of the late 1700s. They raised two children. Oliver resided for periods of time in both Toledo and Cincinnati. He gave politics a try by serving as a senator in the Ohio State legislature from 1837 to 1839. Then he followed in the footsteps of his father-in-law by serving almost three years as Postmaster of Cincinnati. This position was reserved for him by his former commander and later President William H. Harrison. It seems fitting that the man who swiftly delivered messages against all kinds of treacherous odds would be in charge of the government office that tried to emulate his dedication to getting the message through, albeit against the less deadly elements of rain, snow, sleet, and hail. ♦

ANECDOTE.

Near the city of St. Joseph's, a few years since, the rite of baptism was performed on a number of females by immersion in the river. As it was winter, it was necessary to cut a hole in the ice; and the novelty of the scene attracted a large crowd, among whom were several Indians, who looked on in wondering silence. They retired without understanding the nature or object of the ceremony they had seen; but observing that all the subjects of immersion were females, and getting a vague idea that it was to make them good, the Indians came back a few days afterward, bringing their squaws with them, and cutting another hole in the ice, near the same place, immersed each and all of them, in spite of their remonstrances, being very sure, if it was good for the whites, it was quite as well for the reds.

In Harper Magazine's Book: American Wit and Humor, 1859 [18]

X.

THE BROTHERS CLAIRVOYANT.

Much of the notoriety that the Shawnee tribe of Native Americans has received, and still garners today, is due in large part to its two preeminent historic leaders, Tecumseh and the Prophet. These two brothers couldn't have been more different in appearance and personality; yet through the early years of the nineteenth century they joined together in a most creative effort to unite Native American tribes.

Books abound with the stories of each of these men. Their influence on the history of early America has been thoroughly documented and repeatedly analyzed by both their contemporaries and dozens of historians since. What has frequently been glossed over in these narratives, however; or at least not pursued in depth, is the apparent awareness and contact with the supernatural that these brothers had experienced. There is little in the historical record to question that they had a true faith in God, but they also claimed some extraordinary communication with Him, especially during the years of their tribal unification effort.

Of course all cultures have a religious undergirding. Whether the belief system is in one god, multiple gods, or self; each society in the world has a spiritual aspect to it. In most Native American tribes there is a special appreciation of Nature and for the Creator who put it all into motion. In the most simplistic terms they all believed in a singular benevolent Great Spirit; but each tribe also acknowledged many other spiritual beings. In the case of the Shawnee, the good and most powerful Great Spirit was known as *Waashaa Monetoo* while the primary, but lesser, evil spirit was named *Motshee Monetoo*. In a very general sense this mirrored the Christian "God the Father" and "Satan".

In the days of Tecumseh and the Prophet, many signs and messages had been attributed to the Great Spirit, the validity of which can be argued to no end among theologians and historians alike. Such debate is not so dissimilar to a miracle in our day being believed to be the work of God or a mere coincidence. There is no doubt, however, that the attention of the common Indian would be aroused at the mere suggestion that the will of Waashaa Monetoo had been made known to one of his religious leaders. It may be going too far to say that the Native Americans had a superstitious bent, but almost all had a spiritual one. Faith ran deep. If the Great Spirit sent a message, they were certainly inclined to listen.

To the amazement of their peers, and many of us since, the two Shawnee brothers appeared to have had a deep relationship with the Great Spirit; so much so that they were able to foretell the occurrence of rare heavenly displays and profound acts of Nature. Further, one or the other brother could explain the significance of these events per the personal insights they had received from the Great Spirit. Keeping in mind that one brother has gone down in history as an iconic hero of his people, while the other is still considered a fool and a fraud by most, it is hard to reconcile these differences in their character when trying to distill the legitimacy of their close connection to the supernatural. In fact, because of Tecumseh's extensively documented virtue, courage, and honesty it may sound scandalous to even raise the question of anything unseemly in his behavior. But a look at the circumstances and culture of the Shawnee and their neighboring tribes in the decades immediately following the American Revolution triggers a desire to resolve whether the predictions and messages of the brothers were of God, of man, or a combination of both?

As they grew to adulthood, the personality gap between these two men continued to widen. Tecumseh was the charming, persuasive, and certainly rough-and-tumble sibling. Lalawethika, the name that the Prophet was given at birth, was unfortunately the clumsy, babbling, homely boy who shied away from physical conflicts. Yet, as the 1700s rolled into the 1800s, and the boys reached their prime, they used their talents in tandem to bring together scattered tribes from across the Northwest Territory and beyond into an

Indian confederation, albeit a short-lived one. It was Tecumseh's charisma and logical reasoning that attracted warriors to the fold; while Lalawethika drew them in on spiritual grounds after he had experienced a purported divine transformation.

The link to celestial events was immediate for Tecumseh. His very birth occurred at the moment that a brilliant comet happened to streak across the night skies over his Chilicothe village in the Ohio Valley. Such occurrences were considered to be of great significance to the Native Americans who believed that they were direct signs from the Great Spirit. In this mindset, the name Tecumseh, meaning, "Panther shooting across the sky," was bestowed on the babe who was born under this heavenly wonder. The supernatural connection had been made.

In manhood Tecumseh had grown to become a beloved leader and a fierce warrior. He was regarded as a man of integrity, despising cowardice and always true to his word. He was also a diplomat. Rather than recklessly running headstrong into the many conflicts he had encountered with the British, Americans, and even his fellow Indian leaders; he had always first sought to hold meetings of negotiation. The self-determined purpose of his life was to save the Indian culture from obliteration. Perhaps better stated, this appears to have been the Great Spirit's ordained purpose for his life.

Tecumseh believed that land could never be owned, and therefore it followed that he believed it could never be sold. Yet many of the chiefs and leaders of various tribes around him were doing just that; selling land through treaties with the United States. Ironically, just as the British had not consulted the Indians when they gave the lands between the Appalachians and the Mississippi River to the Americans as settlement terms of the Revolution; so now, twenty years later, Indian chiefs from various tribes began selling lands they didn't own, or even live upon in most cases, without the consultation of the tribes who in fact did reside upon them.

Just a few years after the United States was born, former Indian lands in the Northwest Territory were being occupied by its citizens. This was justified in the Americans' view because of the terms of the Treaty of Paris; but it was strongly objected to by the Indians. Skirmishes between the two cultures became more and more frequent and

Portrait of Tecumseh. Illustrated by Benson J. Lossing and shown here as it appeared in his *Pictorial Fieldbook of the War of 1812*, 1868. This is the image most frequently cited to be the most accurate depiction of Tecumseh. However it was created some fifty years after his death and admitted to by Lossing to be somewhat speculative - based on two purported sketches he had viewed.

escalated to major battles by the early 1790s. An alliance of twelve tribes in 1794 was defeated by Anthony Wayne's forces in the Battle of Fallen Timbers. As a result, one of the most important treaties in early American history was signed at Fort Greenville. This document ceded much of what would become the state of Ohio to the Americans. It was a huge step in frontier settlement because the long held southern boundary line of Indian territory, the Ohio River, had now been officially breached. Tecumseh refused to sign the treaty. But by the authority of the chiefs who did sign it, the property transferred hands.

Over the next ten years the Indians sold many more tracts of land to the Americans. Tecumseh remained steadfast against all of them. The years leading up to 1805, which marked Lalawethika's transformation, saw many cultural, natural, and political upheavals among the Indians.

The Americans had driven a wedge into the heart of Indian society. A move was on to civilize these so-called savage people. Young warriors,

Portrait of Tens-Kwau-Ta-Waw (the Prophet), whose birth name was Lalawethica. One of numerous portraits of Native Americans that were commissioned by Thomas McKenney in the mid-1800s. Drawn, printed and coloured at L.T. Bowens Lithographic Establishment. Published by F. W. Greenough.

primed by Tecumseh and Lalewethicka, resisted the idea of blending into the American culture. They were eager to do anything possible to retain possession of their lands, but this put them at odds with the older chiefs who were seemingly willing to give up and assimilate into the American way of life. So deep ran the feelings that like-minded bands from within the tribes moved away to settle their own villages. Further disruption to their normal way of life came through disease. Influenza and small pox were rampaging the Shawnee and numerous other tribes throughout the Indiana and Ohio territories; bringing fear and death with it. Starvation also became a stark reality because the land had been over-hunted, leaving less wildlife to meet their needs. The very fabric of Shawnee society was being ripped apart by these conditions and the antagonistic opinions about how to deal with them. In most Indian minds their plight was attributed to the presence of the Americans on their land.

These tragic dynamics worked to create a quite depressed society. There was little hope that things would improve on any front. It was a time ripe for the holy men of the affected tribes to step up. The professed prophets began preaching about remedies to these problems. They proclaimed in agreement that the outbreak of disease, and all the disruption brought on by the white mans' presence, was punishment sent from the Great Spirit for their sins. Specifically, it was the Indians' increasing acceptance of white mens' ways that had given rise to all this discomfiture. Through repeated visions, or dreams, the prophets claimed that the Great Spirit had explicitly demanded that the Indians needed to return to their roots, lest they become extinct. The prophets' sentiments carried a lot of weight with the general population of the tribes. These holy men were trusted and so many Indians were influenced by them to examine their lives and see just how far they had drifted from their ancestral truths.

The American government was preaching too. Their message was the complete opposite of the one suggested by the prophets. They proposed a plan of assimilation into the American culture and a rejection of most of the old Indian ways. Acceptance of this option would be a cultural and spiritual hurdle too high for most Indians to clear; but some did. In practical terms it meant that they would get a plot of land and take up the farming of crops and livestock in order to sustain themselves. Those who decided that this was their best opportunity did so because they had already witnessed the ever increasing influx of Americans and they had accepted the inevitability that sooner or later their hunting grounds would no longer be accessible. It was not necessarily that they had given up, but that they had viewed assimilation as a way to keep at least a portion of their lands, some of their culture, and to live in a spirit of peace, rather than one of conflict with a neighbor proven to be extremely powerful and growing even more so.

Most Indians, however, could not accept such a radical departure from their traditional lifestyle. In Native American societies, men were the hunters and women the farmers. And many tribes were transient, establishing a village for a number of years and then moving to a new location. The Americans' suggestion would confine each Indian family to a limited amount of land, dilute their sense of tribal family, and turn on their heads the roles each member played within these social units.

The Quakers at this time were aligned with the "civilization" philosophy of the U.S. government, and so they frequently encouraged it when they sent missionaries to Indian tribes. One of these Friends, as members of the Quakers were called, who was working with the tribes living along the Wabash River in 1805 observed that

> the Indians were very industrious, and attended to his directions; the young women wished to work in preparing the ground and in tending the corn; from this he dissuaded them; and as some spinning wheels had just arrived at Fort Wayne, which had been sent on by government, he encouraged them to go there, and learn to spin and knit, [being taught] of a white woman who happened to be at that place; this they did, and soon learned both to spin and knit; and he left them knitting yarn of their own spinning, when he came away. [1]

Though there are multiple reports similar to this which detail how some Indians began adapting to the American way of life, most Native Americans felt it was much too costly both culturally and spiritually. Young Indian men took extreme offense to what they perceived to be a very demeaning proposal. How dare the Americans suggest that warriors and hunters do women's work? And the women themselves admittedly had a hard time giving up the farming duties at which they were quite expert. It was a true clash of cultures and Tecumseh and Lalawethika wanted no part of such a change to theirs.

The same Quaker Friend went on to explain his impression of the Indian condition:

> When we reflect on the gradual, but continued decrease of these people, from the time the Europeans first visited this continent, until the present, and the many whole tribes, of which not any trace now remains, except their names, there is every reason to believe, that, should the Indians continue to pursue their former mode of life, a few centuries more, many other whole nations of them will become entirely extinct.
> Impressed with this melancholy consideration, it must be a prospect truly gladdening to the enlightened christian mind, to survey the hastening of that day, when this part of the human family, weaned from the savage habits and allured by the superior advantages of civil life, shall exchange the tomahawk and scalping knife for the plough and the hoe; and instead of ranging the forests in seeming affinity to the wild beasts of the desert, shall peacefully and rationally enjoy the productions of the fruitful field! [2]

It was against this somewhat frenzied backdrop that Lalawethika dramatically rose to prominence in a very uncanny way. Up to this time he had very little influence over anyone. His quirky behaviors, babblings, and frequent drunkenness made him the butt of many a Shawnee joke. He had matured enough, however; to have learned the art of healing with herbal formulations. Knowledge of such remedies enabled him to act in the capacity of a man of medicine in his tribe; but he was restricted to providing only fundamental medical attention due to the mistrust he garnered. So starved was he for respect that he often just rambled on and on about anything and everything hoping all the while for some sort of positive attention. The admiration that was showered upon Tecumseh simply accentuated Lalawethika's inadequacies. To rejuvenate his squashed ego, Lalawethika turned more and more frequently to alcohol, which proved to worsen his persona amongst his peers. But in November of 1805, something happened.

The accounts vary in their eccentricity. Some say that he fell into a trance that lasted three days. So deep was this stupor that he was taken for dead. While funeral preparations were being made, he suddenly awoke. Other accounts say that he was smoking a pipe when he fell into a dream-like state of unknown duration. What was burning in that pipe is never mentioned. Yet others, relate that he simply had a dream. Benjamin Drake, one of the earliest biographers of Tecumseh and the Prophet, states the change as a simple matter of fact, occurring at a time when factions of the Shawnee tribe were trying to meet and reconcile differences with each other. Drake also gives us one of our first hints that Lalawethika may have been a bit deceptive toward his new followers.

> In the early part of the year 1805, a portion of the Shawanoe nation, residing at the Tawa towns on the head waters of the Auglaize river [Defiance, OH], wishing to re-assemble their scattered people, sent a deputation to Tecumseh and his party, (then living on White river), and also to a body of the same tribe upon the Mississiniway, another tributary of the Wabash, inviting them to remove to the Tawa towns, and join their bretheren at that place. To this proposition both parties assented; and the two bands met at Greenville, on their way thither. There, through the influence of Laulewasikaw [Lalawethika], they concluded to establish themselves; and accordingly the project of going to

the Auglaize was abandoned. Very soon afterwards, Laulewasikaw assumed the office of a prophet; and forthwith commenced the career of cunning and pretended sorcery, which enabled him to sway the Indian mind in a wonderful degree, and win for himself a name on the page of history.[3]

However it unfolded, Lalawethika had become the prophet of the Shawnee and his personality had taken an immediate turn of one hundred and eighty degrees. Some sort of dream or vision was quickly reported by Lalawethika, who now became known not simply as a prophet, but as *The Prophet*. His vision supposedly involved an oft-used "fork in the road" scene. In this case it presented the Indians as a whole with a choice of one path leading to heaven, which few were taking, and the other leading to an eternity of torment. The message of the Great Spirit given through his vision was a dire need of repentance by the Indians. Lalawethika, himself, exhibited a profound change; giving up the bottle and many other ways of the white man that he had adopted. Per the Great Spirit, he preached that all the Indians needed to show their repentance by refusing to engage in the behaviors of the whites and by no longer using their material goods. Over the years the use of American clothing, cookware, and foods had increased. The promise of the Great Spirit was that if the Indians returned to their roots they would be led along the road to heaven while their temporal problems in the present would be removed as well. In simplest terms, relief from the encroachment of the Americans and their diseases would be forthcoming if they repented.

Another early historian of the mid-1800s, Thomas McKenney, offers an insightful opinion which infers that Tecumseh and Lalawethika may have seen the value of putting this spiritual appeal in play to unify the tribes. It could be argued that the brothers were following a determined plan to not only rally the tribes around a mutual desire to keep their land, but also to bind them even more tightly in a spiritual embrace.

> Tecumthe was not only bold and eloquent, but segacious and subtle; and he determined to appeal to the prejudices, as well as the reason, of his race. The Indians are very superstitious; vague as their notions are respecting the Deity, they believe in the existence of a Great Spirit, to whom they look up with great fear and reverence; and artful men have, from time to time, appeared among them, who have swayed their

credulous minds, by means of pretended revelations from Heaven. Seizing upon this trait of the Indian character, the crafty projector of this great revolution prepared his brother, Tenskwautawaw, or Ellsquatawa, (for the name is pronounced both ways), to assume the character of a Prophet; and, about the year 1806, the latter began to have dreams, and to deliver predictions.[4]

The visions actually began in 1805 and to cement his change in everyone's mind, as noted, Lalawethika shortly thereafter wanted to be called Tenkswatawa or Elkswatana (spellings vary) which translates to the English, *The Open Door.* Already known as *The Prophet* this new moniker suggested that he was the metaphysical gate through which the other Indians could learn from the Great Spirit.

The transformation was real, at least for a while, and for the first time in his life the now thirty-something Shawnee medicine man was getting the attention and real respect he always wanted. The visions continued and he would explain each one to the growing number of warriors who were now following him and settling in his village. It was the younger Indians who were inclined toward this new way of life, and it attracted not only fellow Shawnee, but men from numerous tribes living across the Northwest Territory. It was a spiritual movement that measured up in its own right to the Christian revivals occurring across the frontier at this same time. Just as Ottawas, Wyandots, and many others had begun flocking to hear the Prophet preach; on one occasion in 1802, 20,000 frontier settlers congregated at Cane Ridge in Kentucky to hear ministers sermonize on how God wanted them to live their lives. The second Great Awakening, as it became known at this time, was not a phenomenon exclusive to the white man.

Was the spirit of God truly changing hearts throughout the wilderness of the Northwest Territory? If one is inclined to believe stories like those of the grand meeting at Cane Ridge, where the spirit of God made converts of thousands and urged the already faithful participants to repent; is it so much of a stretch to believe that the Great Spirit was moving through the souls of Native Americans as well?

That said, some of the circumstances surrounding Lalawethika's visions, especially his first one, do generate some suspicion. The timing, for instance, is significant. Benjamin Drake explains:

It happened about this time that an old Shawanoe, named Penagashega, or Change of Feathers, who had for some years been engaged in the respectable calling of a prophet, fell sick and died. Laulewasikaw, who had marked the old man's influence with the Indians, adroitly caught up the mantle of the dying prophet, and assumed his sacred office.[5]

As you can gather, the life-changing vision of Lalawethika, or simply his decision to take on the challenge of being a prophet, came just a short time after a void in that profession had developed as a result of Penagashega's death. Coincidence?

A deeper look into Indian history reveals a little-discussed similarity between the tandem of Tecumseh and the Prophet with earlier pairings of men representing the Indian heart and the Indian soul, so to speak. Such teamwork was not unheard of. In fact, the great Ottawa leader, Pontiac, similarly had a spiritual influence from the Delaware prophet, Neolin, forty years earlier. The preachings of Neolin had an uncanny resemblance to what the Prophet was now advocating. Both spoke of rejecting the white mans' vices of materialism, alcohol, and other sinful behaviors which were contrary to traditional Indian ways. With these spiritual principles instilled in his warriors through Neolin, Pontiac led a coalition of tribes, against the British in what has become known as Pontiac's War. This effort points to yet another little spoken-of reality: the Shawnee brothers were not the first to raise a confederation of tribes for the purpose of securing their lands. Pontiac was one of the first to do so in the Northwest Territory, and later Blue Jacket with Little Turtle, would re-introduce the idea through the battles of the 1790s. Even while Tecumseh and the Prophet were gaining followers, so to, tribes much farther west were beginning to unite in opposition to problems they were having with the white men along the Mississippi River. Tecumseh was simply on the cusp of taking a tried and true strategy to a new level.

For several years before Lalawethika had his vision, there was an elderly woman named Beate who was a prominent prophetess living with the Delaware on the White River. She too, had many visions given to her by the Great Spirit. As the diseases continued to ravage her tribe and many others in the region, she preached the same message that had been prescribed by Neolin and other prophets before her. The Indians' misfortunes were the result of their abandonment of their old ways. Her warnings and prophecies spread throughout the region, including the nearby Shawnee village where Lalawethika resided. Beate was also said to have had the power to recognize those who were deceptively living amongst them while practicing witchcraft. These supposed witches were believed to have had ancient medicine bags with serums taken from sea monsters who lived very long ago. Using this arsenal, they were accused of poisoning both bodies and minds. Hence, it was believed that they were using their dark powers to spread the killer diseases raging through the villages.

In the diary of a Moravian missionary named Abraham Luckenbach, who was working to convert the Delaware to Christianity at this time, we can learn a little more about the emotions and beliefs churning in the minds of these Indians.

> The dances of the Indians are generally held in honor of their protecting deities, concerning whom they declared that they once upon a time appeared unto them in a dream, in one or another form, for example, in that of a large bird; that they talked with them, told them their future fate for better or worse; that they either would be great Chiefs or Warriors who would do great deeds, great witch-doctors who would deal in supernatural things, or that they would possess great riches and many relatives, or the contrary. If the latter was the case, however, they did not sing their dreams, but sadly related them...
>
> ... On such occasions, the Chiefs addressed their people, both the men and the women, and, although they themselves did not abstain, [they] strictly prohibited the use of strong drink, fornication, adultery, stealing, lying, cheating, [and] murder and urged hospitality, love, unity; as things well-pleasing to God, which is proof that even the heathen is not without knowledge of good and evil and therefore has a conscience which accuses or excuses him, and which will also judge him. It was customary among them on these occasions to erect tents around the Council House. After the ceremonies were over, they went, in companies, from one tent to the other to visit and to greet one another with a mutual handshake. In connection with this, they assumed a solemn mien and used courtly language according to the age or circumstances of the family addressed. All this makes a good outward show to one who does not know them or their circumstances. But, after one has made a closer acquaintance with them, one learns, unfortunately, how they distrust one another, even their nearest relatives, because of poisoning, witchcraft and

the black art, so that really not one confides in another. When one of their relatives dies, whether old or young it is not unusual for one or the other relatives, or even someone else, to be suspected of having brought about the death either by poisoning or witchcraft. The fellowship of love is therefore unknown among them, and on such occasions they merely make a pretense, because they are really afraid of one another. One sees from this how far imagination, stimulated by fear, causes people, who are still in the grip of superstition, to go. Because their hearts are evil they cannot think well of one another. [6]

Luckenbach also shares his observations of Beate and parts of her visions that had a powerful effect on the Indians experiencing this revival along the White River. This story was passed down by Buckongahelas the Chief of the Delaware:

There had appeared unto her [Beate] one evening while she was alone in front of her house, two men, whom she could not recognize, and whose voice she alone could hear. These told her "Stand still, because we have something to tell you." And when she stood still, the two spoke unto her and said: "We came to tell you that God is not satisfied with you Indians, because at your sacrifices you do many strange things with wampum and all sorts of all juggling, and also do not keep separate spoons with which to stir the sacrificial meal and to dip it out." Having said this, they threw down seven wooden spoons, and continued: "You Indians will have to live again as in olden times, and love one another sincerely. If you do not do this, a terrible storm will arise and break down all the trees in the woods and all Indians shall lose their lives in it." [7]

The story continues with the two men arguing over the proper sign to send to the Indians so they would believe this warning. It was decided that a recently deceased hero by the name of Schaponque would be resurrected as the necessary proof. For the record, Schaponque is still resting comfortably where he was originally laid. A month later, with the Indians showing little improvement in their behavior, Beate had another vision. This time it was a visit from a devil who warned again, "it will go badly with you, unless you turn about at once and do even as the first two spirits told you…" [8]

A third vision was related to the missionaries by an Indian who heard it from Beate. It further explains the confliction the Indians were having with her prophesies. This Indian states that

he had heard her [Beate's] words; that she also forbade all evil, drinking,

Portrait of William Henry Harrison
drawn on stone by Chas. Fenderich from a painting by Mr. Franquinet.

fornication, stealing, murder, and the like. She had also told him everything about himself, what he was and what he thought as he came to her, and that she had been right in everything she told him; that she knew everything the Indians do and think even though she does not see it. He thought to himself: "This is strange! We hear that all evil is forbidden us and also believe that this woman received her words through an appearance of God; we sacrifice and worship for a long time in accordance with her words, and still I notice that the Indians continue to do what they are commanded not to do, and are unable to give up what she forbids..."[9]

Certainly the details of these prophesies, visions, and convictions of Beate of the Delaware, Pengahshega of the Shawnee, and many prophets of other tribes, were also known to Lalawethika. It seems reasonable to assume that he was deeply affected by the preachings of these prophets just as were most of the Indians. Evidence of this comes in hindsight as Lalawethica did take up the challenge to turn from his sins, especially his excessive alcohol consumption. This was a period during which the collective Indian conscience was being examined and their behaviors challenged. And genuine or not, exploited or not, the dictates received from the Great Spirit were a key factor in the

Shawnee brothers' successful recruitment of a resistance force against the Americans.

It shouldn't go unnoticed that the fear of witches, and the witch hunts that followed, originated by prophets like Beate years before the Prophet came on the scene to accelerate them. Was the marking of individuals as witches and their termination part of a sincere effort to purge the society of evil? Or were there ulterior motives to these actions? There is no way to know for sure, however; it is curious that most of the targeted witches were the older, more passive tribal leaders who had assimilated or desired to blend into American society. These so-called witches had no plans to return to their Indian roots, and so were seen as an evil and an obstacle to the resistance effort.

The older civil chief of the Shawnee, Black Hoof, and many of his community were among those of this contrary mindset. They saw the increasing influx of Americans as the inevitable end of their way of life. They had already fought wars against the whitemen with limited success, and saw no need for further bloodshed and certain defeat. Tecumseh viewed things differently. He would fight, if necessary, to keep as much Indian land as he could. Shortly after the Greenville Treaty signing, he broke off from the main Shawnee unit and formed his own village. The physical location changed a number of times from Greenville in Ohio, to the White River in Indiana, and eventually to the Tippecanoe River region where it was named after his brother — Prophetstown. Though he was considered a chief by the members of his band, Tecumseh was not officially recognized as such by the governing body of his Shawnee tribe.

The number of followers who came to live in the village of the Prophet continued to increase following his initial vision in 1805. This centralization of Indian population did not escape the notice of William Harrison, who was then the Governor of the Indiana Territory. The fear was that this growing band might be planning to attack the American frontiersmen or worse; dare to declare a general war on the Americans, perhaps with help. News of the Prophet's targeting of people as witches and promoting their execution set off more alarms. Logan Esarey, an early Indiana historian and writer noted that

> Harrison thought this was a carefully laid plan of Tecumseh and the Prophet to get rid of the Indian chiefs and reorganize the tribes. Joseph

Renard's son had been deposed among the Kickapoos and Winnemac was marked. Little Turtle was ignored and the old chief Teteboxti of the Delawares murdered. He usurped the power of the Shawnee chiefs so much that they applied to Harrison for protection. They had followers in every tribe within a hundred miles and it seems they insisted on their converts acknowledging the chieftainship of the Prophet.[10]

Early in 1806, the situation prompted Harrison to send a letter to the Delaware who were one of the tribes swept up in the frenzy of sorcery now being promulgated by the Prophet in their village.

My Children —

My heart is filled with grief, and my eyes are dissolved in tears, at the news which has reached me. You have been celebrated for your wisdom above all the tribes of red people who inhabit this great island. Your fame as warriors has extended to the remotest nations, and the wisdom of your chiefs has gained for you the appelation of grand-fathers from all the neighboring tribes. From what cause, then, does it proceed, that you have departed from the wise councils of your fathers, and covered yourselves with guilt.

My children, tread back the steps you have taken, and endeavor to regain the straight road which you have abandoned. The dark, crooked and thorny one which you are now pursuing will certainly lead to endless woe and misery. But who is this pretend prophet who dares to speak in the name of the Great Creator? Examine him. Is he more wise or virtuous than you are yourselves, that he should be selected to convey to you the orders of your God? Demand of him some proofs at least of his being the messenger of the Deity. If God has really employed him he has doubtless authorized him to perform some miracles, that he may be known and received as a prophet. If he is really a prophet, ask of him to cause the sun to stand still — the moon to alter its course — the rivers to cease to flow — or the dead to rise from their graves. If he does these things, you may then believe that he has been sent from God. He tells you that the Great Spirit commands you to punish with death those who deal in magic, and that he is authorized to point them out. Wretched delusion! Is, then, the Master of Life obliged to employ mortal man to punish those who offend Him? Has he not the thunder and all the powers of nature at his command? — and could he not sweep away from the earth a whole nation with one motion of his arm?

My children! do not believe that the great and good Creator of mankind has directed you to destroy your own flesh; and do not doubt but that, if you pursue this abominable wickedness, his vengeance will overtake and crush you.

The above is addressed to you in the name of the Seventeen Fires. I now speak to you from myself, as a friend who wishes nothing more sincerely than to see you prosperous and happy. Clear your eyes, I beseech you, from the moisture which surrounds them. No longer be imposed upon by the arts of an imposter. Drive him from your town, and let peace and harmony once more prevail amongst you. Let your poor old men and women sleep in quietness, and banish from their minds the dreadful idea of being burnt alive by their friends and countrymen. I charge you to stop your bloody career; and if you wish the friendship of your great father the President if you wish to preserve the good opinion of the Seventeen Fires, let me hear, by return of the bearer, (Capt. William Prince) that you have determined to follow my advice. [11]

The Prophet was not pleased with Harrison's move to stir doubt in the minds of his followers. He decided to take up Harrison's challenge. One account from an early edition of the *Indiana Magazine of History* states that the Prophet

told his followers that on a certain day, and at a fixed time when the sun was at the height of its powers, he would place the same under his feet, and cause darkness to come on the face of the earth. On the day announced, the Prophet stood among his fearful band awaiting the hour. The day was wholly clear and without clouds, but at the appointed time the terrified savages saw a disc of blackness gradually pass over the face of the sun; the birds became agitated and flew to cover; the skulking dogs drew near their masters; almost absolute darkness fell on all about; the stars of heaven appeared in the zenith, and in the midst of it all, the Prophet exclaimed: "Did I not testify truly? Behold! Darkness has shrouded the sun." The account of that day, faithfully set forth by J. Fenimore Cooper, then a youth, is filled with strange relations of the unnatural appearance of all earthly things; of the sudden awe and fear that came into the minds of all; how women stood near their husbands in silence and children clung to their mothers in terror, and if these were the emotions experienced in a civilized community, made fully aware of the coming event, what must have been the impression produced on the superstitious mind of the savage, wholly unenlightened in the ways of science? From that day, the power of the savage Prophet was secure until the spell of his magic was forever broken by the whistling bullets of Harrison's regulars and Yellow Jackets at the Battle of Tippecanoe. [12]

The Prophet had called Harrison's bluff, at least in the eyes of his believers. The truth is that it simply was a poor choice of words by Harrison who should have known, as many of his day did, that a total eclipse of the sun was predicted by scientists in the East to occur just weeks after he wrote his letter to the Delaware. It is very likely that word of this upcoming event had reached Tecumseh or the Prophet through their contact with white traders and other acquaintances. And they used it for all the magic it was worth. The average warrior had little contact with the whites and so when the eclipse was seen as the Prophet predicted, their superstitious nature left them convinced of his power and his connection to the Almighty.

Proof that the eclipse, which the Prophet had seemingly caused, was actually common knowledge to the general American public beforehand is evident in a thirty-four page booklet titled, "Darkness at Noon or the Great Solar Eclipse of the 16th of June 1806." The publication date was May 1806; a full month before the event. If anyone needed specificity, and Tecumseh and the Prophet did, page seven explains:

> This remarkable eclipse will happen on Monday, June 16th, in the forenoon: the times and appearances of which will be as follows: Beginning of the eclipse, 9:58:45...
> ...The duration of this eclipse will be 2 hours and 48 minutes, and the time of total obscurity will be 3 minutes and 30 seconds, as seen from Boston. [13]

The details go on and on, giving anyone of that day, who was interested, a definitive explanation of what to expect. Records show that the eclipse did occur on the predicted date and at the predicted time. Modern maps detailing the prime viewing areas of all eclipses, historical and those yet to come, show that the Shawnee village along the White River in the Indiana Territory would have been in a prime viewing area for the 1806 eclipse. The best scientific analysis suggests that the Prophet's followers would have seen a 99.6 percent eclipse of the sun. [14]

Over the next several years, with this heavenly confirmation of his authority, the Prophet continued to preach and teach. The followers multiplied. The village moved a few more times between 1805 and 1809 and the population grew. The village was genuinely peaceful and spiritually based, not yet wanting a confrontation with the Americans,

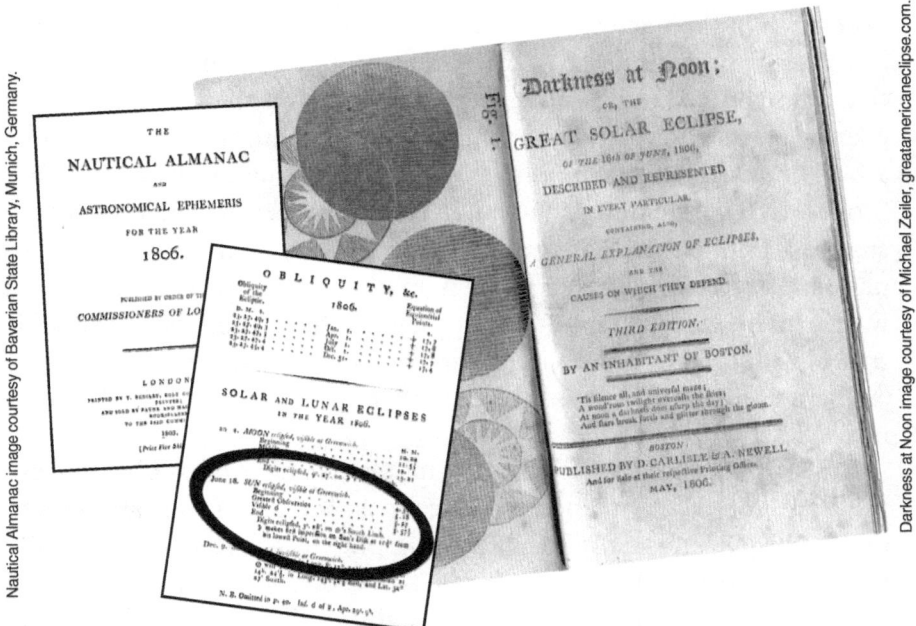

The 1806 *Nautical Almanac*, published three years previous in 1803, forecasts the Eclipse of June 16, 1806. Likewise, the booklet *Darkness at Noon*, was published in Boston in May 1806, one month before the event.
Both publications show that in-depth information and predictions of astronomical events was readily available to anyone looking for it. Farmers in the Northwest territory were known to frequently refer to the almanacs.

just coexistence. However, bands of tribes in the West were forming their own union with overtones of war. Harrison had to be wary that the Prophet was strictly promoting a spiritual endeavor and that he was not a party to the far western movement.

Witch hunts continued. At one point the Prophet overstepped common sense, perhaps his first major blunder since his vision, when he accused several Shawnee leaders, including Black Hoof, of being witches. Wisely, he backed off and never made a real effort to murder the chief, however actions like this did nothing to reunite the Shawnee villages and attitudes.

In 1809, Harrison had finally gone too far. The Treaty of Fort Wayne was signed. Tecumseh could not abide another sale of Indian lands. This one gave the Americans a huge portion of the Indiana Territory, over three million acres! Much of it was being used by the Shawnee.

Just as Pontiac and Blue Jacket before him, Tecumseh understood that an organized opposition force was required if the Indians had any chance of resisting the Americans. Only by being tied together like a bundle of sticks, he preached, could the Indian bands avoid being broken by the greater American force. Alone, each would be easily snapped, until one by one they no longer existed. With this illustrative philosophy, Tecumseh sought the help of any tribe, or even individual warrior, who was willing to join his new confederation. Eventually his travels would take him far in all directions as he sought the Creeks of Alabama, the Sioux west of the Mississippi, and some of the Iroquois in the East.

The Prophet, and later Tecumseh, met with Harrison at Grouseland, the home of the Governor in Vincennes, Indiana, in an attempt to resolve disputes over the treaty signing practices. They were generally not productive as Tecumseh insisted that all treaties were null and void; while Harrison flaunted the signatures of numerous chiefs who said that they were indeed in effect. They were at a stalemate.

Tecumseh's continuing effort to recruit every tribe on the continent to his confederation eventually took him to Tuckabatchee, near present-day Montgomery, Alabama, in September of 1811. This was Creek country and Tecumseh arrived in time for a council of various tribes who were addressing the American problem. The job of persuading the Creeks to join the war effort that he and his brother had begun along the Wabash River was a daunting one. Tecumseh gave it all he had; speaking and even dancing with extraordinary flair. However, he met with very limited success. A longtime resident of the Creek villages who served as a public interpreter refers to the poor reaction Tecumseh received in a letter written and published in a Georgia newspaper just a few months after Tecumseh's visit.

> The deputation said to have come from him [the Prophet], arrived in September, and on the 20th of that month for the first time entered the public square at Tookaubatchee. A War pipe preceded them the same day, which was rejected unanimously by the chiefs... One of the most respectable chiefs of the Upper Creeks reported that the Shawnee deputation spent a whole day in the public square at Tookaubatchee, talked much of conversations with God on Indian affairs... But their opinion

was, the leader [Tecumseh] was a mad man or a great liar, in fact both, and as they could not understand him, they would take no notice of his foolish talks. [15]

This seemingly complete negative response could have been a deceptive move on Tecumseh's part. It's believed that for obvious reasons he did not want any Americans, the writer of this opinion being one, to hear his true message which was war against the United States. He ended up presenting his real purpose in a separate meeting with the Creeks when no Americans were present and at that time received some positive reaction though not nearly what he hoped for.

To convince his listeners that he was truly speaking on behalf of the Great Spirit, he pointed to the appearance of a great comet in the sky. Throughout Tecumseh's visit, this comet was at its peak brightness. What perfect timing to have this celestial event occur in conjunction with the visit of a persuasive speaker who not only invokes the Great Spirit as the source of his war message, but bears the name of the heavenly body again shining above him? This was a potent sign, and Tecumseh did not let it go unnoticed.

The interpreter among the Creek spoke of the comet's appearance in very different terms in his letter, pointing only to a scoffing comment by an American colonel who saw it as a warning to the Indians that trouble was coming their way from the Americans living east of the mountains.

> As to the lamp in the West, all that I heard of it was a remark of col. Hawkins on the comet then in the North West; speaking of some of the fanatic Indians, [do] you see that comet, says he, and that its tail points to the NE; towards the comet [head] there is mischief brewing, and the tail points towards that part of the United States, from whence a force is coming to stifle it. [16]

Tecumseh explained that the comet's appearance was no accident. The Great Spirit, he said, provided this sign so that they would join the effort of the Shawnee brothers. The fact that the comet gradually faded as Tecumseh made his way northward, added an even further ominous effect and convinced many more of the truth of Tecumseh's words and his connection to the Great Spirit.

But Tecumseh was still very disappointed with the number of Creek recruits he had gained. In anger, he is said to have promised yet another sign which would prove the Great Spirit's displeasure with their obstinance.

On his return from Florida, he went among the Creeks, in Alabama, at Tuckhabatchee, a Creek town on the Tallapoosa river, he made his way to the lodge of the chief called the Big Warrior. He explained his object; delivered his war-talk — presented a bundle of sticks — gave a piece of wampum and a war-hatchet; all which the Big Warrior took. But Tecumthe, reading the spirit and intentions of the Big Warrior, looked him in the eye, and pointing his finger towards his face, said, — "Your blood is white. You have taken my talk, and the sticks, and the wampum, and the hatchet, but you do not mean to fight. I know the reason. You do not believe the Great Spirit has sent me. You shall know. I leave Tuckhabatchee directly — and shall go straight to Detroit. When I arrive there, I will stamp the ground with my foot, and shake down every house in Tuckhabatchee." So saying, he turned, and left the Big Warrior in utter amazement, both at his manner and his threat, and pursued his journey. The Indians were struck no less with his conduct than was the Big Warrior, and began to dread the arrival of the day when the threatened calamity would befall them. They met often, and talked over this matter — and counted the days carefully, to know the day when Tecumthe would reach Detroit. The morning they had fixed upon as the day of his arrival at last came. A mighty rumbling was heard — the Indians all ran out of their houses — the earth began to shake; when, at last, sure enough, every house in Tuckhabatchee was shaken down! The exclamation was in every mouth, "Tecumthe has got to Detroit!" The effect was electric. The message he had delivered to the Big Warrior was believed, and many of the Indians took their rifles and prepared for war.

The reader will not be surprised to learn that an earthquake had produced all this; but he will be doubtless, that it should happen on the very day on which Tecumthe arrived at Detroit, and in exact fulfillment of his threat. It was the famous earthquake of New Madrid, on the Mississippi. We [Thomas McKenney, the writer of this history] received the foregoing from the lips of the Indians, when we were at Tuckhabatchee, in 1827, and near the residence of the Big Warrior. The anecdote may, therefore, be relied on. Tecumthe's object, doubtless, was, on seeing that he had failed, by the usual appeal to the passions, and hopes, and war spirit of the Indians, to alarm their fears, little dreaming, himself, that on the day named, his threat would be executed with such punctuality and terrible fidelity. [17]

How do we explain Tecumseh's supposed prediction of an earthquake? Did he have a true vision or message from the Great Spirit? It's possible. Could he have had foreknowledge of the earthquake, much as he probably had of the eclipse? This too is possible, though much less likely. The scientific community to this day has trouble predicting earthquakes with any real specificity. They can only suggest areas that are prone toward them or measure their strength after the fact. There are reports of strange things happening in Nature anywhere from minutes to weeks before an earthquake occurs. Animals are known to scatter or act oddly. Sightings of a colorful mist seeming to rise from the ground and lingering in the air have been reported. It is true that like all Indians, Tecumseh, was very much in tune with Nature and so there is some reason to believe he may have picked up on some natural sign that gave him the confidence to make such a bold prediction. But the most plausible yet disappointing explanation is that Tecumseh's earthquake prediction may never have been made at all.

The earliest report of it is stated above, and as noted by the author himself, was made in 1827. That means that for sixteen years no one talked about such a phenomenal prediction! Communication was slow in that day, but word of other significant events travelled the continent in a reasonable amount of time. If the prediction was made, how much more would its fulfillment have strengthened the case that Tecumseh and the Prophet had serious inroads with the Great Spirit? How many more Indian tribes would have signed on with the brothers? It is just too long a stretch of time for the story of such a historically successful prediction to have rested dormant.

It is much more believable that the story is no more than lore that grew after the fact. The New Madrid earthquakes, as they came to be known, did occur a couple months after Tecumseh was noted to have left the Creek village of Tuckabatchee. They came in three major waves, each with multiple aftershocks. The first occurred on December 16, 1811, followed by a second in January and a third in February of 1812.

A Kentucky newspaper published a letter written by a man who was in New Madrid, the epicenter, on the day the first series of quakes had struck:

The Great Earthquake at New Madrid,
in book: *The Great West*, by Henry Howe, 1851.

About two o'clock this morning we were awakened by a most tremendous noise, while the house danced about and seemed as if it would fall on our heads. I soon conjectured the cause of our trouble, and cried out it was an earthquake, and for the family to leave the house; which we found very difficult to do, owing to its rolling and jostling about: the shock was soon over, and no injury was sustained except the loss of the chimney, and the exposure of my family to the cold of the night. At the time of this shock the heavens were very clear and serene, not a breath of air stirring, but in five minutes it became very dark, and a vapour which seemed to impregnate the atmosphere, had a disagreeable smell and produced a difficulty of respiration. I knew not how to account for this at the time, but when I saw in the morning the situation of my neighbors' houses all of them more or less injured, I attributed it to the dust and soot, &c which arose from their fall. The darkness continued till day break; during this time we had eight more shocks, but none of them so violent as the first. Fifteen minutes after seven o'clock, we had another shock. This was the most severe one we have yet had

— the darkness returned and the noise was remarkably loud. The first motions of the earth were similar to the preceding shocks, but before it ceased we rebounded up and down, and it was with difficulty we kept our seats. At this instant I expected a dreadful catastrophe—the uproar of the people heightened the colouring of the picture— the screams and yells were heard at a great distance.

Tuesday Dec. 24. —The shocks continue: we have had eight since Saturday—some of them very severe, but not sufficiently so to do much additional injury: I have heard of no lives being lost—several persons are wounded. This day I have heard from the Little Prairie, a settlement on the bank of the river Mississippi, about 30 miles below this place. — There the scene has been dreadful indeed— the face of the country has been entirely changed— Large lakes have been raised and become dry land and many fields have been converted into pools of water. Capt. George Ruddell, a worthy & respectable old gentleman, and who has been the father of that neighborhood, made good his retreat to this place with about 200 souls, informs me that no material injury was received from the first shocks; when the 10th shock occurred he was standing in his own yard, situated on the bank of the Bayou of the Big Lake; the bank gave way and sunk down about 30 yards from the water's edge, and as far as he could see up and down the stream— It upset his mill and one end of his dwelling house, sunk down considerably; the surface on the opposite side of the Bayou, which before was swamp, became dry land; the side he was on became lower.— His family at this time were running away from the house towards the woods; a large crack in the ground prevented their retreat into the open field. They had just assembled together, when the 11th shock came on, after which there was not perhaps a square acre of ground unbroken in the neighborhood, and in about 15 minutes after this shock the water rose round them waist deep. The old gentleman leading his family, endeavouring to find higher land, would sometimes be precipitated headlong into one of those cracks in the earth, which were concealed from the eye by the muddy water through which they were wading. As they procceded the earth continued to burst open & muddy water, and stone coal were thrown up the distance of thirty yards; frequently trees— of a large size were split open 15 or 20 feet up. After wading eight miles he came to dry land. "I have heard of no white person being lost as yet. Seven Indians, were swallowed up & one of them escaped; he says he was taken into the ground the depth of two trees in length that the water came under him and threw him out again— he had to wade and swim 4 miles before he reached dry land"— The Indian says the Shawanoe Prophet has caused the Earthquake, to destroy the whites. [18]

The description speaks to the strangeness and duration of the earthquake, but it's the last line that raises eyebrows even higher. It suggests that just a few months after the fact, an Indian living in the New Madrid region believed that the earthquake was the work of the Prophet! It not only shows that the reputation of the Prophet had reached these Indians of Missouri, some four hundred miles away from Prophetstown, but it means that they had attributed profound supernatural powers to him. Could this lead one to conclude that Tecumseh was assured his prediction would come true because his brother had told him the day on which he was going to cause it? Hmmm.

The bottom line is that whether Tecumseh predicted the New Madrid earthquakes or not, they had absolutely convinced the Creeks of Tuckabatchee that he was right about one thing — the Great Spirit was displeased that they had not joined his war effort. After their village lay in shambles, a good number of them signed on to the fight. In this newspaper report, as in others, no one was saying Tecumseh predicted it, only that the Prophet had caused it. Perhaps testimonies yet to be discovered in other newspapers, diaries, journals, etc., will someday shed more light on whether Tecumseh indeed had dared to make this phenomenal prediction.

When Tecumseh returned from Tuckabatchee to Prophetstown, he discovered what a fool his brother truly was. The Prophet had been warned to not stir up any trouble with the Americans while Tecumseh was on his mission in the South. None-the-less, he brazenly attacked Harrison's encampment of troops just outside of the village in the early hours of a November morning. His message to the warriors on the eve of the battle would prove to be the beginning of the end of his credibility.

> Prior to the assault, the Prophet had given assurances to his followers, that in the coming contest, the Great Spirit would render the arms of the Americans unavailing; that their bullets would fall harmless at the feet of the Indians; that the latter should have light in abundance, while

the former would be involved in thick darkness. Availing himself of the privilege conferred by his peculiar office, and perhaps, unwilling in his own person to attest at once the rival powers of a sham prophecy and a real American bullet, he prudently took a position on an adjacent eminence; and, when the action began, he entered upon the performance of certain mystic rites, at the same time singing a war-song.[19]

As it played out, the Prophet watched from a hilltop while reciting incantations over his troops below. The fires in the American camp did provide abundant light as the Indians charged into it. And, looking out from the lit ground the Americans were surprised to see the warriors spring from the darkness of the woods. However, the faux promise, the big one stating that the enemy bullets would have no effect on the Indians, was dead wrong.

This defeat had serious consequences. The alliance was nearly dissolved as many dispirited warriors returned to their home tribes; disillusioned over their prophet. The mystique of Tenskatawa would never be regained. His bluster had gotten the best of him and he was exposed as a fraud. He would go back to living a rather obscure life of little influence or consequence.

In spite of his brother's antics, Tecumseh was able to regroup and gain the support of additional warriors before war was officially declared by the United States on Great Britain in June of 1812. His confederation allied with the British and several battles ensued over the next year and a half. At first the victories went their way, but as 1813 unfolded the tide kept turning in favor of the Americans. On October 5, 1813, while the Prophet yet again remained distant from the action on the battlefield, his brother, Tecumseh, was killed at what became known as the Battle of the Thames.

Before his death, Tecumseh would have one more encounter with the spirit world. In fact, it was concerning his own demise. The incident is told by historian Lyman Draper who learned the details of it from William Caldwell, an aid to Tecumseh who was with him the day of his final battle. It seems that

> Col. Matthew Elliot, [and] Capt. Thomas McKee [both British Indian officers and agents], and a few other whites were present some twenty minutes before the firing commenced. While the men were getting their places, & awaiting the approach of the Americans, [and] while Elliot,

Tecumseh, McKee, Wm. Caldwell & several others were sitting on a log, & [also] a young Shawonoe runner or aid of Tecumseh's — all of a sudden, a noise came, like the sharp whizzing of a bullet. Elliot, Caldwell, & all heard it distinctly — no enemy in sight — no report of a gun — & Tecumseh jumped, & instantly placed one hand on his back & the other on his breast, as though wounded & in pain; presenting a strange & ghastly appearance. Capt. Caldwell asked Tecumseh, "What was the matter?" He said, "he could not exactly tell, but it is an Evil Spirit which betokens no good." Elliot said, "Capt. Caldwell, a precisely similar occurrence happened to your father — he fell, supposing a shaot had passed through both legs just below the knees, but he found himself unharmed; the next day in a fight (about the last battle he was engaged in during the Revolution, & perhaps the year before peace), he was shot precisely as the singular presentiment & pain indicated the previous day — & that Tecumseh would surely be killed. [20]

As the battle began, Tecumseh was positioned with William Caldwell somewhere in the midst of the British lines. Many of these soldiers gave up the fight immediately and retreated as the mounted Kentucky militia charged toward them. As told again by Draper, per Caldwell,

> While Tecumseh + Capt. Caldwell were three or four yards apart, in the rear of these runaways, watching the Americans + and retreating British regulars. Tecumseh exclaimed "Waugh!" clasping one hand behind + the other before. indicating a wound through his body, but clasping his rifle in his hand. Caldwell asked him if he was wounded, he said "yes" + at the same time pointing to the flying British regulars as having shot him in the back + out at his heart. Caldwell asked if he could walk — he replied he could. "You had better go on, if you can, + I'll walk behind," said Caldwell. Tecumseh at once started, + only went about a rod, when stepping over a large fallen oak, apparently weak + attempting to sit down as though he could go no further, he fell his back upon the tree — dead. [21]

Even the end of Tecumseh came with supernatural effect as dramatic as had occurred at his birth.

The Shawnee brothers had teamed up to successfully raise the largest coalition of Indian tribes ever to fight in unison against the encroachment of white men onto their lands. In the end, their fight was lost, but the process was a study of the grit and planning that was necessary to make a firm stand for what they believed in. Though the Prophet eventually let his ego become his undoing, for a brief critical period of time he was a spiritual superstar. Tecumseh was a star all his life, being born under a shooting one, after all. It is obvious that both were genuinely spiritual men. It is left to the reader, however, to decide how much of their life experience was of God and how much was of their own cunning. Perhaps it was a little of both. ♦

ANECDOTE.

James Galloway lived in Xenia, Ohio and was a close personal friend of Tecumseh. In fact, tales abound that Tecumseh had fallen for his young daughter at one point in time. In a letter to Lyman Draper, the definitive historian of the frontier era, Galloway related an anecdote that shows Tecumseh's lighter side as well as his self-confidence and ability to read people.

A large Kentuckian had come to Ohio to see the country in 1802 or 3, and explored Mad river and some of its branches in order to select land to purchase, or settle on, and put up one night at the house of Capt. Abner Barrett, on the head of Buck creek, in what is now Champaign County [Ohio]. Here he learned with some alarm, that there were Indians encamped a short distance off. About dark, the door of the worthy captain's house, was suddenly opened without any previous knocking, according to Indian custom, and Tecumthe entered with his usual stately air: he paused without saying a word and looked around him, when at length his gaze was fixed upon the stranger, whom he discovered to be much alarmed, and could not look the stern savage in the face. After a pause of some seconds, he addressed the Captain, pointing at the same time to the agonized Kentuckian — a big baby! a big baby! He then stept up to him, and gently slapped him on the shoulder several times, repeating, big baby, big baby! to the great alarm of the astonished man, and the amusement of the Captain and the others present. This anecdote shows that the haughty chief at once discovered in the countenance of the poor fellow, the cause of his turning pale, and the apprehension he manifested. He no doubt expected his scalp to be taken off in short order.

In letter of James Galloway to Lyman Draper, January 29, 1841 [22]

XI.
THE RACE TO PARIS – HARMAR'S VICTORY.

For all practical purposes, the Battle of Yorktown, in October 1781, marked the end of the United States' War for Independence. The defeat of General Cornwallis and the capture of over 9,000 British troops by George Washington and his ally the French General Comte de Rochambeau got the attention of the British government and triggered serious discussions of how to finally end the conflict. As talks began, however, it was the recognition of the colonies as a new nation, the primary American purpose of the war, that proved to be the major stumbling block to progress. That was until a new Parliament, as well as a new Prime Minister, Lord Shelburne, took office; ironically on the Fourth of July, 1782.

Money is usually at the root of most decision making, and this new body of English leaders saw it that way as well. They determined that the cost of defending, controlling, and financing the colonies and all the bureaucracy that went along with it had become just too massive. On the other hand, the idea of establishing a flourishing system of trade with a new country, well; that seemed much more practical and lucrative. It would still take another year of negotiations before all parties could reach an agreement on all the terms, but ultimately on September 3, 1783, American delegates John Adams, Benjamin Franklin, and John Jay, along with British envoy and member of Parliament, David Hartley, put their names to the Treaty of Paris that birthed the United States of America.

Though it took nearly two years for him to get the words out and onto paper, in this treaty King George officially stated:

His Brittanic Majesty acknowledges the said United States, viz, New Hampshire, Massachusetts Bay, Rhode Island and Providence Plantations [the official name of this state referencing the original Puritan colony established in 1636], Connecticut, New York, New Jersey, Pennsylvania, Delaware, Maryland, Virginia, North Carolina, South Carolina and Georgia, to be *free sovereign and Independent States*; that he treats with them as such, and as for himself his Heirs & Successors, relinquishes all claims to the Government, Propriety, and Territorial Rights of the same and every Part thereof. [1]

On September 5 in a letter to the President of the Continental Congress, John Adams wrote:

Sir: On Wednesday, the 3d day of this month, the American ministers met the British minister at his lodgings at the Hôtel de York, and signed, sealed, and delivered the definitive treaty of peace between the United States of America and the King of Great Britain. [2]

A little aside to this historic moment is the fact that Adams' phraseology of, "Signed, sealed, and delivered" may have been one of the first times that this popular idiom appeared in print. In England, and hence the colonies, it was a matter of serious importance to transfer the ownership of land, and so a strict protocol was established. It became a regular practice to have any document that dealt with real estate transfers to be signed by the parties involved, impressed with a seal, usually a hot wax stamp exclusive to the signer, and then delivered to the new property owners. This momentous cession of land would be no different.

However, after the many months of croissants and conversation in Paris, there was still one more act to be played out in this historic performance. The treaty called for several more signatures: the King's and the appropriate members of the Continental Congress. No one doubted that all parties involved were eager to sign the document; it was the time required to get it to them and back to Paris that raised concern. King George III was at the ready just across the Channel in nearby London. No problem. The United States signers, however, were on the other side of the Atlantic ocean. Getting to them would be a long and treacherous jaunt. Crossings typically lasted a month or more in each direction at this point in time.

With this concern in mind, but in an effort to keep things moving,

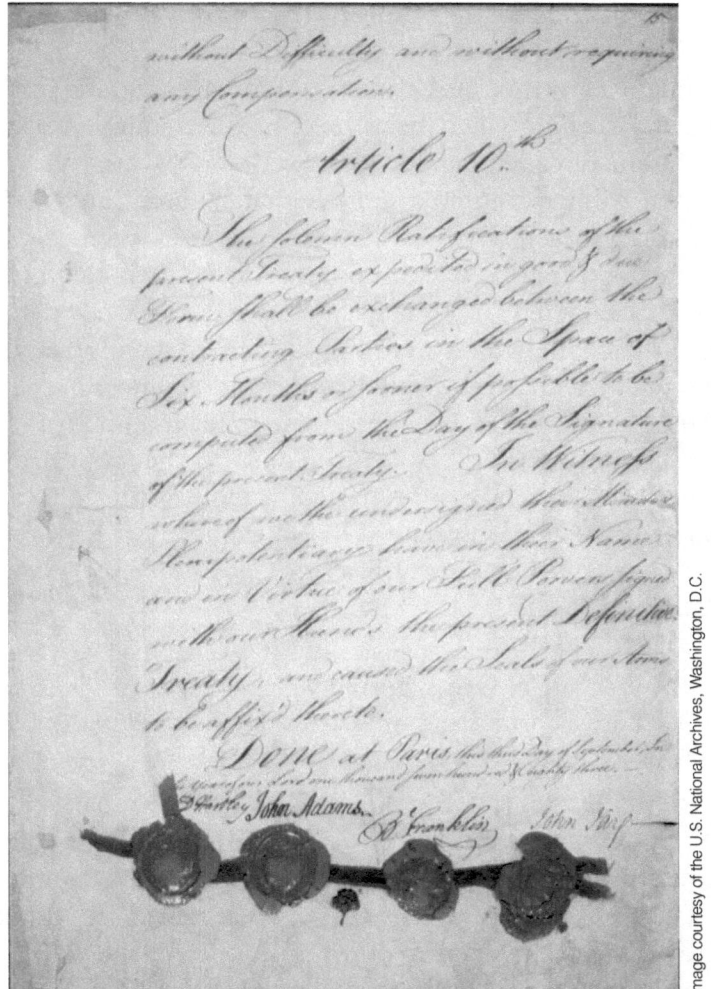

The final page of the Treaty of Paris, 1783, showing the signatures and stamps of the four diplomats: David Hartley, John Adams, Benjamin Franklin, and John Jay.

a six month deadline for its ratification was written into the treaty itself. This meant that the British copy, signed by the King; and the Americans', signed by the Congressmen; needed to be exchanged by March 3, 1784. Otherwise? Who knew; but the Americans felt that missing the due date could have serious repercussions, including a possible return to the battlefield. It seemed that six months was more than sufficient time for all of this to transpire even with two months lost to ocean travel; but fate would prove otherwise.

Let's begin a few months before the September signing in Paris. The Continental Congress had been meeting that summer at Independence Hall in Philadelphia. However, on June 21, disgruntled former continental soldiers gathered around that building and vociferously taunted the representatives as they exited. These veterans of the war were quite upset that they had still not received their pay for the military services rendered far too long ago. Even the local law enforcement endorsed their complaint by refusing to disperse them. So shaken were the congressmen that they opted to move their meeting place. They reconvened in Princeton, New Jersey the following month.

From July through early November of 1783 the Continental Congress met in Nassau Hall, a prominent building still standing on the campus of Princeton University. On November 1, in his waning days as president of this Congress, Elias Boudinot addressed a letter to the U.S. diplomats in Paris.

> Yesterday we gave public audience to Mr. Van Berckel. Just before the Ceremony began Col Ogden arrived with the News of the completion of the Definitive Treaty, this gave a large addition to the general Joy that was already great on the occasion of the Day.[3]

Mr. Pieter Johan van Berckel was the first ambassador to the United States from the Netherlands, an ally in the Revolution. There was much pomp and ceremony planned to welcome his visit when Colonel Ogden arrived with even bigger news. Soon letters were going out in every direction announcing the Paris signing. One example follows as the delegates of Maryland in attendance alerted their governor.

> We have the pleasure to inform yr. Excellency and Honors that the definitive Treaty was signed on the 3d of Sepr. This intelligence was brought by a Col. Ogden who left Paris the 10th of Sepr., and says the official account of this event may be expected every day by Mr. Thaxter, private Secretary to Mr. Adams, who saild from L'Orient in a packet on the 20th of Sepr.[4]

And so it became widespread knowledge that peace was officially at hand and the physical treaty was on its way to America in the hands of John Adams' personal secretary. Before Congress adjourned early in

November, they needed to elect a new president to replace the resigning Mr. Boudinot. Thomas Mifflin was chosen and just a few days into his term, on November 22, Mr. Thaxter arrived with the treaty.

At this time, there was an ardent and ongoing contest between cities to win for themselves the privilege of being the permanent seat of Congress. Annapolis, Maryland was a contender and so it was the site chosen to begin the next session on November 26. Thomas Jefferson, who was elected to Congress as a representative from Virginia in June, was now put in charge of the ratification process and noted that

> Congress had now become a very small body, and the members very remiss in their attendance on it's duties insomuch that a majority of the states, necessary by the Confederation to constitute a house even for minor business did not assemble until the 13th. of December. [5]

So nearly three weeks were lost before an official session of Congress could be opened because it wasn't until then that representatives from seven states had arrived. Even so, Jefferson noted in his autobiography that

> the definitive treaty of peace which had been signed at Paris on the 3d. of Sep. 1783. and received here, could not be ratified without a House of 9. states.
>
> On the 23d. of Dec. therefore we addressed letters to the several governors, stating the receipt of the definitive treaty, that 7 states only were in attendance, while 9. were necessary to its ratification, and urging them to press on their delegates the necessity of their immediate attendance. And on the 26th. to save time I moved that the Agent of Marine (Robert Morris) should be instructed to have ready a vessel at this place, at N. York, & at some Eastern port, to carry over the ratification of the treaty when agreed to. It met the general sense of the house, but was opposed by Dr. Lee on the ground of expense which it would authorize the agent to incur for us; and he said it would be better to ratify at once & send on the ratification. [6]

Now we see that several more issues are being raised and the situation is getting more confused. Jefferson knows that nine, not seven, votes are required to get this done, yet several delegates will soon argue that seven are sufficient. Jefferson also prudently suggests that Congress's Superintendent of Marine and of Finance, the powerful financier, Robert Morris, secure ships in readiness to transport the

Portrait of Josiah Harmar. A photographic reproduction of an engraving by John Sartain and based on a painting by Raphael Peale circa 1790-1799.

treaty back to France. However, Dr. Arthur Lee, physician and diplomat from Virginia, squabbles about the cost of doing so. Arguments ensued on these and several other fronts while the clock kept ticking.

The law had stated that each state had one vote. However, two representatives of each state had to be present for that one vote to be counted. On December 13, a session was begun because a majority, seven, of the states were finally present. Seven was sufficient for routine affairs, however the law also stated that nine states must be present in order to approve a treaty, which was the prime order of business now before them.

December 23 dawned and proved to be a very busy and eventful day. With the war complete and peace looming, General George Washington appeared before Congress to resign his military commission and his authority as Commander in Chief to the President of Congress, Thomas Mifflin. The chamber was packed with citizens, delegates, and special guests for the momentous event. However, of all the people who found a way to get to Annapolis this day, the missing delegates were still not among them. Another ten days had now been lost and so, as Jefferson noted, desperate letters were sent to the governors of each state who did not have adequate representation at Annapolis.

By January 3, with only the same seven states represented, Jefferson proposed an alternative course of action. He hoped it would appease both the arguing Congressional parties as well as the King of England.

The essence of his proposal was this: The seven states who were present would sign the treaty and send it off immediately to Franklin and his fellow delegates. Instructions would also be sent to Franklin explaining that he should hold this copy of the treaty in reserve, with the hope that a duplicate, with the required nine signatures, would arrive before the deadline. If the nine signature version had not arrived in time, Franklin was to approach the British for an extension of the deadline. If granted, no problem. If denied, the seven signature treaty was to be presented on the day of the deadline along with an explanation of it representing a good faith gesture under the circumstances; those circumstances being the horrible weather conditions that had prohibited travel on many fronts that season. The British were to be reassured that a nine vote version would be in their hands as soon as possible. This plan was adopted. A treaty vote would be taken on January 14.

With tension lingering about the viability of this approach, Thomas Mifflin decided to make a last ditch effort to get more representatives to Annapolis before the vote in order to reach the nine state requirement. He sent his chief aide and friend, Colonel Josiah Harmar on a mission. Harmar was to travel to Trenton, New Jersey to plead for that state's delegates to get to Congress as soon as possible. Then Harmar was to go to Philadelphia to try to convince Richard Beresford, South Carolina's missing representative, to make the trip to Annapolis in spite of his being bedridden with a debilitating illness.

Mifflin wrote a personal letter to William Livingston, Governor of New Jersey, imploring him to send delegates to Annapolis. Josiah carried the message.

> I have already addressed three separate dispatches to your Excellency of the 23d of November & of the 23d & 24th of December stating to you the arrival of the Definitive Treaty and the necessity, by an Article thereof, of its ratification and Exchange at Paris by the 3d of March

next: I have also stated in those dispatches the particular situation of Congress. Nine States being necessary to a Ratification & Seven only being present. Apprehending that these Letters may have miscarried & having Reason to believe that the Representation from South Carolina will be compleat in a day or two, I have dispatched Col. Harmar my private Secretary with this Letter to your Excellency, informing you that if the Delegation of New Jersey attends in Congress without further delay we may yet ratify the Treaty in time. A Representation of Nine States to ratify the Definitive Treaty before the Time limited for its Exchange expires must appear to your Excellency too important to be longer delayed. [7]

And so, Josiah Harmar was seen galloping away from Annapolis on January 4. He would cover nearly four hundred miles in nine days. As a result, on January 13 the day before the final vote, two delegates from Connecticut, who may have been alerted at one of Harmar's stops, had arrived. This assured one more state's vote. A delegate from New Jersey also arrived, but being only one of the two needed, New Jersey was still lacking. Then on the morning of the vote, Richard Beresford of South Carolina made his way into the chamber, having been personally transported to Annapolis by Josiah Harmar the night before.

On January 14, 1784, Thomas Mifflin could finally write to our diplomats in Paris:

> GENTLEMEN: This day, nine States being represented — viz., Massachusetts, Rhode Island, Connecticut, Pennsylvania, Delaware, Maryland, Virginia, North Carolina, and South Carolina, together with one member from New Hampshire and one member from New Jersey — the treaty of peace was ratified by the unanimous vote of the members. This being done, Congress, by an unanimous vote, ordered a proclamation to be issued, enjoining the strict and faithful observance thereof, and published an earnest recommendation to the several States in the very words of the fifth article.
>
> They have likewise resolved, that the ratification of the treaty of peace shall be sent by a proper person to our commissioners at Paris to be exchanged, and have appointed Colonel Josiah Harmar to that service. He will have the honor of delivering to you the ratification, together with copies of the proclamation of Congress, and of their recommendation to the States, conformably to the 5th article.
>
> I take the liberty of recommending Colonel Harmar as a brave and deserving officer, and am with the highest respect and esteem, gentlemen,

your most obedient, &c., Thomas Mifflin. [8]

Finally! The treaty was ratified and would soon be on its voyage back to Paris. But the six month window had already dissipated to six weeks. And there were still complications. It was now winter, and what a winter it was; so severe that it garnered special note in the annals of meteorological history.

> The winter of 1783-84 was known as the Long Winter in New England in the United States. The first snowfall of the season blanketed the eastern seaboard from New Jersey to Maine on 12-13 November 1783. Morristown, New Jersey… records showed 7 additional snowstorms struck in November and December and then followed by a major snowstorm on 30-31 December. About 20 inches… of snow accumulated in this late December storm. Three more snowstorms struck in January and then a strong one occurred on 26-27 January piling up 18 inches… of snow in 24 hours. The total snow accumulation at Morristown [New Jersey] during those 3 months was 83.5 inches… of snow. Snowstorms continued into March and April. Philadelphia, Pennsylvania recorded a temperature -11° F… on 9 February. Hartford, Connecticut recorded a temperature of -20° F… on 14 February. [9]

Other reports point to just how cold and snowy it really was. The Delaware River, which defines the boundaries of Pennsylvania, New Jersey, and Delaware, became ice-bound and was closed to travel from late November until the middle of March. Maine reported that it was horrifically cold, snowy, and stormy compared to what people had ever experienced before. The Susquehanna River, which weaves through Pennsylvania, flooded to record heights of ten to twenty feet above normal due to the heavy melting snows and torrential rains of the long winter. At several points, huge boulders of ice and raging waters swept livestock, horses, and personal property down river. Ice closed the harbors at Philadelphia and Baltimore for extended periods. It was so cold and roads unpassable, that one report tells of a prominent gentleman who ice-skated some thirty-plus miles from Baltimore to Annapolis; presumably along the frozen shoreline of the Chesapeake Bay. Too bad the absent delegates hadn't considered that.

All of this highlights that it was indeed a horrible winter that impeded delegates from getting to Congress by land or by water routes all across New England. And, in the midst of this weather, the treaty needed to successfully get back across the ocean. With so many factors working against them, Congress approved sending three copies, in possession of three different people, to Paris. They hoped one would make it before the deadline arrived. Jefferson explained:

> Jan. 14. Delegates from Connecticut having attended yesterday, and another from S. Carolina coming in this day, the treaty was ratified without a dissenting voice, and three instruments of ratification were ordered to be made out, one of which was sent by Colo. Harmer, another by Colo. Franks, and the 3d. transmitted to the agent of Marine [Morris] to be forwarded by any good opportunity.[10]

Colonel Harmar was the key runner in this race. Mifflin wrote this letter to him on the day of the signing explaining the immediate course of action he was to take.

> Sir,
>
> Congress having this day appointed you to carry the Ratification of the Definitive Treaty to our Ministers at Paris it is necessary that I should give you private Instructions how to proceed in the Business allotted to you.
>
> You will with all possible Expedition go to Philadelphia. Upon your arrival there wait upon the Honble. Mr. Robert Morris & produce to him the Act of Congress of this date, herewith delivered to you, directing him to supply you with money to defray the necessary expenses of your appointment. Mr. Morris will inform you at what time the french Packet will sail from New-York and will give you, at your request, every assistance in his Power to facilitate your Journey.
>
> By a Letter I have just received from the Minister of France [Chevalier de la Luzerne] it is probable you will meet him on your Road to Philadelphia. Enquire for His Excellancy at every Stage, and be particularly careful that you do not suffer him to pass you before you have delivered my Letter to him and have requested his Commands to Europe, intreat him to give you a Letter of Recommendation to the Captain of the Pacquet Boat at New York, on which Subject I have written to him; If he should desire you to wait three or four Hours for his dispatches, you are to comply with his Excellency's request.
>
> The moment you are on shore in France endeavor to procure Horses or a Carriage for your journey to Paris and be as expeditious as possible in that Journey. At Paris enquire for Mr. LeGrand, banker there and inform him that you have public dispatches for our Ministers & request him to

inform you where you may find Mr. Adams, Mr. Franklin, Mr. Jay or Mr. Laurens, follow his directions in this point and deliver your dispatches to the first of those Gentlemen you may meet. Rake a Receipt for the dispatches when delivered specifying the several Papers delivered by you and the time of delivery.

This Service being performed you are at Liberty to return to America recollecting that the Act of Congress of this date provides only for your necessary Expenses on the particular Business assigned by them to you.

You will deliver my Letter to the Marquis de la Fayette with my warmest Wishes for his Welfare.

Should you go to London, deliver my Letter to Mr. Robert Barcley, who will be your friend in all things. God bless you my dear Harmar. I am Your Friend. [11]

That same day, Mifflin sent a letter to La Luzerne, the French diplomat spoken of to Harmar, explaining how he had planned for them to cross paths as Harmar headed north to New York while La Luzerne headed south to Annapolis.

Congress have appointed Colonel Josiah Harmar my private Secretary to carry the ratification to our Ministers at Paris; and I have instructed him to pursue the rout marked by your Excellency's Letter of the 10th Inst. and upon meeting you to wait for such commands as you may be pleased to honor him with. Let me entreat your Excellency to give Colonel Harmar a recommendatory letter to the Captain of the Packet Boat at New York, that he may upon his arrival in France the most expeditious means provided for his Journey to Paris. [12]

Charles Thomson, the Secretary of Congress, wrote individual letters to each of the diplomats in Paris. In this excerpt from one to Franklin, he re-enumerates the threesome involved in the race to Paris.

And that it might reach you with the greatest dispatch they immediately sent off col J Harmar with the ratification by the way of New York, there being no vessel sailing from this bay [Annapolis]. They also sent a duplicate to be forwarded by Mr. [Robert] Morris, and this day from an earnest desire that it may if possible arrive in due time they have determined to send lieut col D.S. Franks with a triplicate to take the chance of a vessel from some of the eastern ports. [13]

As it played out, Robert Morris explained to Mifflin that he was unsuccessful in finding a ship sailing earlier than Harmar's or Franks's.

Sir: I have delayed answering your excellency's favor of the 4th of last month, in hope that I might have been able to announce to you the having sent off the duplicate of the definitive treaty. Hitherto no opportunity has offered. But as Colonel Harmar has sailed and probably Lieutenant-Colonel Franks, I am not so anxious on that subject as I have been. [14]

Lieutenant-Colonel David Franks was the primary back-up courier to Harmar. He was a successful businessman, diplomat, and former aide-de-camp to Benedict Arnold. For that service he was penalized for life. Although officially acquitted of any treasonous activities in connection with Arnold, Franks faced the politics of his day and fought a lifelong battle to clear his name in some circles. In good standing with the founding fathers as of January 1784, he was readily entrusted with getting the treaty to Paris.

In a letter to Mifflin, Franks explains that he booked passage out of New York to London instead of a direct route to Paris, and considered it

> particularly lucky in finding this vessel so ready to sail and the more especially as after the strictest inquiry there appeared to be none further to the Eastward in so much readiness; but unfortunately ever since that time to this moment the Harbor of New York has been so full of Ice that all kind of navigation is impassable. I am very much embarrassed on the manner in which I ought to act so as not to incur the displeasure of Congress; were I to follow the Letter of the Resolution I should immediately give up all thought of going to Europe and return to Annapolis, but as Col' Harman [Harmar] is not yet sailed, or the duplicate not yet sent from Philadelphia [Morris's], I humbly conceive that the spirit of that Resolution would justify my going on with my dispatches... We shall sail as soon as the Ice will permit us, which I hope will be in a day or two; Col. Harman [Harmar] will go out at the same time, when I shall do myself the Honor of writing again. [15]

The "Letter of the Resolution" Franks alluded to was that of the specific deadline, which it was obvious he could not meet. After further delays, Franks set sail and reported from London on April 8, thirty-six days past the deadline:

> I do myself the Honor of informing you that I arrived here yesterday after a very long and disagreeable Passage of Six Weeks and four days from N. York. On my arrival at Dover I was told that Mr. Franklin and Mr. Jay both were in London, but found on my coming here that

they had sett out some time since for Paris to which place I mean to follow them as I am informed by the English ministry that they have had no official accts. of the arrival of the Packet in which Col. Harman [Harmar] sailed. [16]

So Franks continued on to Paris not knowing the true status of Harmar's efforts. Harmar had much of the same trouble getting out of the New York harbor as Franks had. In a letter of February 13, a Pennsylvania delegate, Cadwalader Morris, alerted a fellow Congressional delegate from South Carolina, Jacob Read, that he was at

> this Moment informed by a Gentleman from New York, that the packet, on board of which Col. Harmar Embarked the 21st Ultimo, had returned into that port, having run ashore in the Neighborhood of the Hook, and received so much damage, as to make it Necessary to refit. Colo. Franks is also at N York. [17]

A few weeks later, Mr. Read in-turn re-iterated this troubling situation to the Governor of South Carolina:

> I am sorry to inform you that Colonels Harmer and Franks were prevented from sailing with the ratification of the Treaty till the 19th Ultimo, so that 'tis impossible those instruments Can be in time for Exchange, however as the greatest good faith has been observed on our part and nought but the Act of God has prevented the ratification getting to Europe in Time. I trust no ill will result to the union from the delay. [18]

But it wasn't just a simple matter of waiting for better sailing conditions. Harmar had boarded his ship, christened *Le Courier de l'Amerique*, on January 19. There he remained until the twenty-fifth. On that day he watched as other vessels finally began making their way out of the harbor. However, the captain of his ship was not onboard. He was at Long Island helping to rescue another French ship that had wrecked there on its way into port. Another ten days would pass before Harmar's captain was back at the helm and everything was in order for safe sailing; or so they thought. Only briefly underway, the *L'Amerique* ran aground on Governor's Island off the New York coast. In a very precarious position the ship sat as it was repeatedly pounded by waves and large blocks of floating ice. In this frightful pose it had to remain for several hours until the tide rose and they were dislodged. However, rather than venture out to sea, they were forced to return to the dock. In a letter to Mifflin on February 21, after another seventeen days of waiting, Harmar exclaimed, "Off the hook, On board the French Pacquet Le Courier de l'Amerique... with fine weather & a fine wind." [19] Now it was simply a matter of how fast those "fine winds" could propel Harmar's vessel to France even though the March 3 deadline was certainly lost.

Harmar was on the water for thirty-three days before his ship docked at the coastal town of L'Orient in France. But it would still be an excursion of four days over land to get to the residence of Benjamin Franklin in Passy, a village of Paris, where he had been living throughout much of the Revolution. At last, on March 29, Harmar handed over the ratified treaty to Franklin, albeit, twenty-six days late. Franklin and John Jay immediately wrote to David Hartley, the British diplomat and key negotiator of the treaty.

> Sir,
> We have the Pleasure of acquainting you, that the Ratification of the Definitive Treaty is arrived here by an Express from Congress. You have already been informed that the Severity of the Winter in America, which hindered Traveling had occasioned a delay in the assembling of the States As soon as a sufficient Number were got together, the Treaty was taken into Consideration, and the Ratification passed unanimously. Inclosed you have Copies of the Proclamation issued on the Occasion, and of the Recommendatory Resolution. The Messenger [Harmar] was detained at New York near a Month, by the Ice which prevented the Packet Boats sailing, otherwise he would probably have been here in February. We are now ready to exchange the Ratifications with you whenever it shall be convenient to you. With great & sincere Esteem we have the honor to be Sir, your Excellency's most obedient & most humble Servants. [20]

Now the ball was in England's court and the Americans waited for any possible repercussions for having missed the deadline. Hartley responded directly to Franklin's fellow diplomat, Henry Laurens.

> Dear Sir: It is with great satisfaction that I am able to inform you that it is not thought necessary, on the part of Great Britain, to enter into any formal convention for the prolongation of the term in which the ratifications of the definitive treaty were to be exchanged, as the

Illustration of a packet ship similar to *Le Courier de l'Amerique* upon which Harmar sailed to France. Depiction in book: *The French Royal Packets of the New York Line – Analysis of Letters Carried, 1783-1793.*

The French moved quickly to establish a Royal packet line between France and the United States after the Revolution, and a decree establishing a state-sponsored transatlantic mail service was issued on June 28, 1783.

delay in America appears to have arisen merely in consequence of the inclemency of the season. I took care to express, on your part, the motives of candor and attention to this country which were the ground of your offer; and it gives me pleasure to assure you that they were received with equal candor and attention on the part of the British ministers.[21]

The worry was all for naught. The British would incur no offense from the delay. In a few days, the King would sign his copy of the treaty and on May 12, 1784, the copies would officially be exchanged.

Perhaps the reason there was no fallout over the deadline was that Europe had also experienced the same frightful winter. There was general distress throughout London with travel impeded after a twenty-seven day stretch of snowfall. In Paris, the wines were chilled to freezing in cellars. Even the migration of birds was affected. A large flock of merganser ducks, known as sawbills because of their serrated beaks, who are indigenous to Louisiana were seen for the first time in France. In addition to all the weather issues, the King also had his political hands full as Parliament was in a flux at this time with an election and changes in leadership. All things considered, it is easy to understand why they were so understanding.

Harmar would stay in Europe for over two months exploring Paris and traveling to London as well. Some time was spent on government business, some was seeing the sites and imbibing the culture. But by August he was back where he started, in America; mission accomplished. Little did he know that while he was gone Congress had made a decision that would change his life. They voted to resurrect a military force to protect and preserve the "West" which was now owned by the United States as result of the treaty just signed. This First American Regiment, as it was known, needed a leader. Whether it was for his noble service as an officer in the Revolution or for his most recent successful race to Paris, or both, Harmar was made lieutenant-colonel commandant of the new force. The appointment would set events in motion which, in just six years, resulted in a military rout that would embed Harmar in the history books forever, unfortunately in a very negative light.

Just two months after his return from France, Harmar was heading west in command of his new troops. But, beforehand, he did make time for one very important personal move. About a year previous he had become smitten with a young lady named Sarah Jenkins. In October 1784 they were married.

Harmar was a highly respected officer throughout the Revolution, fighting in several key battles and serving under General Washington at Valley Forge. He had gained the respect of most of his peers; even Washington is said to have regarded him as one of the best officers in the Army. That seems to have been the general sentiment toward him throughout his career and continued now with this appointment as Commander. When the Revolution had ended, he took a less dangerous position as personal aide to Thomas Mifflin while he led Congress. It was thought that Mifflin's influence helped Harmar receive his new command in 1784.

Harmar had learned military skills from the best, Baron von Steuben, who was Washington's Chief of Staff while he was at Valley Forge. The techniques and disciplines of warfare that Steuben instilled in the Continental Army are often cited as the prime reason the Revolution was won. Harmar spent much of the first six years of his command teaching his meager army of a few hundred men in the ways Steuben had taught him. What Harmar didn't seem to realize was that Steuben's formal method of battle would not work against his new enemy, the Native Americans. This would prove to be a contributing factor to Harmar's downfall.

Harmar would work on treaties with the Indians and locate his forces at several posts over the first few years. One fortress would bear his name. Then in 1787, the Northwest Ordinance opened the lands west of the Appalachians and north of the Ohio River to settlement by any frontiersman who dared to do so; daring because of the treacherous wilderness and the under-appreciated presence of the Indians. Because money was in such short supply, the government planned to make profits by selling this vast wilderness in small parcels. This was a huge organizational step for the government and one that curbed the illegal squatting that had been going on previously. Deeds were sold and treaties were signed to acquire both money and land.

From the beginning of his first term as President in 1789, Washington saw the trouble at hand. Indians were refusing to sell land and were attacking settlers. He knew the situation would require prompt action because the income from land sales was critically needed to pay off the country's Revolutionary debts. Because he had little money to work with, Washington wanted to spend as little as possible on the military action he was about to propose. The fiscal restrictions, at least in part, contributed to the disaster Harmar incurred in late 1790.

Washington only provided a few hundred regular soldiers for Harmar's use, keeping the number down because they would be at the top of the list to be paid. The remainder of Harmar's troops, approximately a thousand, were militia who at this point in time were less than reliable. Not only were they reluctant to fight beyond their state borders, but they had no military training and were primarily composed of young boys and old men who were definitely out of their league in a fight with the cunning Indians.

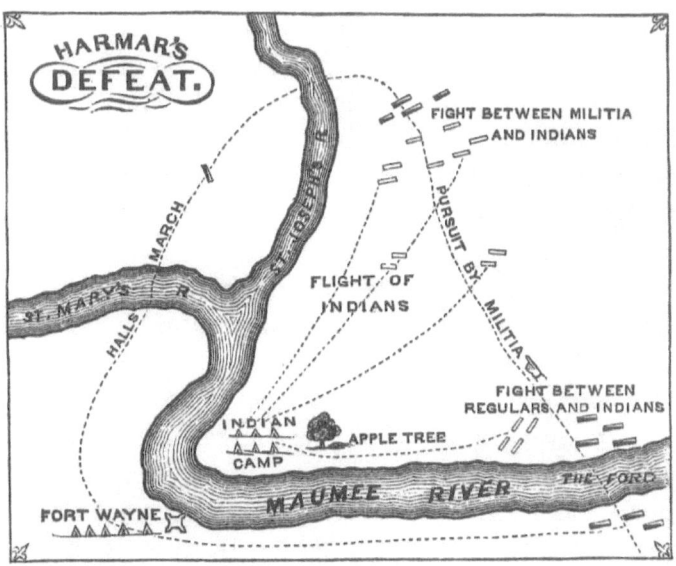

Map of area where General Harmar was defeated. Illustrated by Benson J. Lossing and shown here as it appeared in his *Pictorial Fieldbook of the War of 1812*, 1868.

None-the-less, in late September 1790, Josiah Harmar was ordered to march his force from the fortress that he had built and named Fort Washington, in present-day Cincinnati, to the area of today's Fort Wayne, Indiana. His mission was to take out the Indians of that region who had refused to leave. These Indians were being well supplied with arms and ammunition to fight the Americans by British traders who viewed the Americans as a threat to their lucrative trading business. These British merchants shouldn't have been on American soil in the first place.

The short version of what transpired is as follows. Little Turtle, as head of the Miami and other allied tribes, allowed the Americans to burn several of their vacated villages along the Wabash River. The men feeling a bit cocky that they had caused the Indians to abandon a fight, started roaming the grounds for any booty they might find. Harmar, as well, became somewhat arrogant boasting that he had won the war without firing a shot. He decided to send a contingent of men into the woods to take out the Indians that he had erroneously assumed were cowering nearby in fear. One thing led to another until the American detachment was suddenly surrounded by a superior force of Indians.

Most of the militia men ran for their lives, some all the way back to Kentucky, while the thirty or so regulars were killed and scalped.

When the report came back to Harmar, who was several miles away from the fight, he was shocked by the bold attack from the Indians, the cowardice of the militia, and by the number of his men who lost their lives. He proceeded to burn anything and everything of potential use to the Indians. That included all vegetation in and around the Indian villages. Feeling he somehow could still claim a victory for leaving the tribes without sustenance, he ordered the troops to return to Fort Washington. Just a short stretch into their journey home, Harmar was coerced by one of his top officers, Colonel Hardin, who had led the previous debacle, to return and spring a surprise attack of their own on the Indians as they returned to their burned out village.

The plan might have worked, but for a series of bad moves. In a ruse, small groups of Indians repeatedly appeared along the troops' route and successfully drew off handfuls of militia men in pursuit of them. Making it worse, the Americans attacked these bands of Indians with gunfire instead of knives or bayonets; thus alerting the Indians in the village of their presence. Eventually the main bodies of the American troops were ambushed again and numerous lives were lost. Some reports say that it was only the occurrence of a lunar eclipse that kept them from thoroughly decimating the Americans. The Indians viewed it as a bad omen and backed off. Through all of this, Harmar was again at the base camp unengaged.

When the magnitude of the disaster was made clear to him, Harmar again turned his troops back toward Fort Washington; but now nearly a hundred of them were wounded. Even worse was the fact that he had left the bodies of another hundred dead men on the battlefield, unburied, in his haste to retreat. Being the commander, Harmar bore the brunt of President Washington's anger as well as that of the entire country for this act of disrespect.

An honest look at the event of that October would allow for an argument to be made that a number of people, besides Harmar, were also at fault. There were anxious officers trying to prove themselves with rash military strikes. Farmers and trappers newly settled on the frontier had reluctantly signed on to fight with no prior experience. Politicians had cut financial corners in the effort and so supplied Harmar with a force short of the necessary able-bodied soldiers and weapons. And, there was an overall naive dismissal of the fortitude and fighting capabilities of the Native Americans by all the leaders.

But of course, Harmar made his share of bad decisions that cannot be dismissed. He used formal battle maneuvers against an enemy employing guerrilla warfare tactics. He assented to unsound ideas of lesser officers. He kept himself distant from the heat of the fight. He left his dead men behind. And, he was accused of using alcohol in excess throughout the campaign. It is suspected that some of the accusations of incompetence and drunkenness may have been manifested as payback by the bitter Kentuckians who didn't want their own reputation impugned for their own obvious cowardice.

Until this battle took place, praise had been showered on Harmar from far and wide. He served boldly in the Revolution, acted as Thomas Mifflin's personal aide in the Continental Congress, braved the elements to desperately and successfully bring representatives back to Congress for the timely vote, and withstood numerous impediments in a focussed drive to deliver the treaty of peace to Benjamin Franklin. But after the defeat in the Northwest Territory, even George Washington turned on him. Perhaps it was in a moment of deep frustration, having just learned of the disaster and hearing potentially slanderous reports from the AWOL Kentucky militia, that the President vented in a private correspondence to the Secretary of War.

> MY DEAR SIR, I have received your letter of the 10th inst, and will declare to you without reserve, that my forebodings with respect to the Expedition against the Wabash Indians are of disappointment; and a disgraceful termination under the conduct of B. Gen. Harmar.
>
> I expected little from the moment I heard he was a drunkard. I expected less as soon as I heard that on this account no confidence was reposed in him by the people of the Western Country, — and I gave up all hope of success, as soon as I heard that there were disputes with him about command. [22]

The criticisms of this event are still being studied and give a clearer picture of the truth of the matter each time they are reviewed. Although there is legitimate fault to be found in some of Harmar's actions, he did go through a court martial and was cleared of any wrongdoing in the conflict. None-the-less, the whole affair has forever become known as

Harmar's Defeat. Funny how human nature often tends to remember the worst about people rather than their best. Perhaps added to the historical record should be his steadfast excursion across the Atlantic to carry the birth certificate of our nation to our forefathers. That indeed deserves to be forever known as Harmar's Victory! ♦

ANECDOTE.

In a letter of January 1784, Cadwalader Morris a representative of Pennsylvania in the Continental Congress, is found a brief account of a Philadelphia fireworks celebration marking the Ratification of the Treaty of Paris that had gone awry.

"Most horrible Mistake was made last Night in Exhibiting the Fire Works," Morris wrote on the 23rd. "About 1/2 past 6. the Rockets were began, and one, in its fall took part of the Oiled Canvass, and the whole went off in One glorious, though horrible Explosion. The Rockets, which were on the Scaffolding, flew off in a hundred different directions — killed One Man on the Spot, and Wounded Many others. I was at One of the president's Windows. The Women Screaming, fainting and Crying. The Scene was distressing Enough, though I must Confess, the Explosion, had a glorious Effect." [23]

XII.
THE FORGOTTEN COLONY OF CLARK.

It was in the spring of 1780, at the spot where the Ohio River pours itself into the Mississippi, that Fort Jefferson was erected. On an elevated flood plain, flanked by rolling hills, it was thought that this fortress would provide the additional protection needed for the Americans who were pushing further and further to the West. At this point in time, the Revolution was going into its fifth year. And though often glossed over in traditional history books, the war was being fought in the wilderness of the "West" as well as in the former colonies. Though there may have been fewer frontier battles, with smaller numbers of combatants fighting against each other, the contests were just as intense and just as fatal as any along the Atlantic coast.

The British were using most of their men in the eastern engagements and so had solicited the Indians to do much of their fighting for them in the West. Many of the attacks on frontiers settlements by Indians were prompted, if not at least funded, by the British. They supplied the Indians with the goods they and their families needed, as well as arms and ammunition for battle against the Americans.

Use of the Mississippi and Ohio Rivers was crucial to all parties involved in the Revolution; Americans, British, and Indians alike. Although it was just another in an existing line of garrisons in the area, Fort Jefferson was being raised at a strategic point along these water routes. With all their goods in tow, traders, Indians, and military forces would have to pass this new fortress as they turned toward Pittsburgh in the East, St. Louis in the North, or New Orleans in the South. On paper, Fort Jefferson looked like an extremely wise and strategic move for the Americans to make, but it would prove to be an ill-fated and now long-forgotten endeavor.

As we delve into its history, it will become evident that the story of Fort Jefferson is remarkable, not so much for its physical structure or where it was built; but rather for the diverse souls who inhabited it for but a brief period of time in our nation's infancy. A look at just some of these people and the circumstances they endured can't help but evoke an appreciation for their acts of heroism and their heartache.

George Rogers Clark is a name most Americans recognize, though some may confuse it with his younger brother, William, of Lewis and Clark fame. George was a bold and daring patriot. He garnered several nicknames in his life; "Hannibal of the West" being one of the most appropriate. He spent most of his life in service to his country in the lands that became the Northwest Territory. Battles he led during the Revolution proved to be pivotal successes. For several years, the idea of building a fortress at the mouth of the Ohio River had been on the minds of both Clark and Patrick Henry, who had served as the Governor of Virginia. But it wasn't until Thomas Jefferson succeeded Henry as governor in June of 1779, that their idea took root.

> It was in pursuance of the policy of Thomas Jefferson, then Governor of Virginia, who deemed it a matter of vital moment to maintain a watch at that point [present Wickliffe, Kentucky] and vindicate the authority of the Commonwealth [of Virginia] upon her farthest border. It was the object of the settlement, which was called Clark's Colony, to raise supplies for the garrison and give strength and support to the post.[1]

Clark had not only drawn up the engineering plans for the fortress's physical appearance, but he specified the personnel required as well. He insisted on a minimum of two hundred troops to defend the site. And, to make this distant post almost self-sufficient, he wanted at least a hundred families to settle around the fort. His idea was that these frontiersmen and women would grow the crops, raise livestock, and provide others services for the soldiers as well as for their neighbors. It was reasoned that as the community flourished it would become less vulnerable to attacks from either Indian or British forces.

Construction began in April 1780. The structure stretched for one hundred feet on each of its four sides. A ten-foot deep trench was dug along its outside perimeter with the dirt thrown up as an eight foot wide and ten foot tall embankment. Atop this ground wall posts were sunk, adding another ten feet to the height of the facade. Squared bastions projected from each of the four corners. It was a simple and functional fortification.

George Rogers Clark was ever-antsy to take care of business. For several years prior to the building of Fort Jefferson, he had been defending rural settlements in the West from British and Indian attacks. He was often successful and gained the respect of his fellow Kentuckians and the nation as a whole for his accomplishments; though some have been critical of the blatant hatred he held toward his enemies. His most renowned achievement came in 1779, when he had secured the West for the Americans by capturing Forts Kaskaskia and Vincennes. These outposts were located at strategic points along major rivers of the frontier. To have them under the command of the Americans was vital. Although Clark went on to defend and protect more and more lands for settlement, nothing ever compared to these two victories.

It was about a year after Vincennes had been won that Clark was found supervising the construction of Fort Jefferson; but he would spend very little time within its walls thereafter. By May of 1780, just a month after the fort was completed, Clark was already off on another exploit. This time he had gone to the defense of Cahokia, an outpost of the Americans that was situated near Fort Kaskaskia, just across the Mississippi River from St. Louis. The British and Indian forces were repulsed yet again and Clark gained even more acclaim for persuading several tribes to turn from the British and ally themselves with the Americans from that point on.

In June, he returned to Fort Jefferson, but only to recruit as many men as he could to defend another fort from British attack, this time it was at Louisville. As it turned out, Clark's timely arrival just ahead of the enemy's appearance at the site had prevented an attack. Clark's next move was to go to Harrodsburg in Kentucky where he mustered additional men to march with him into the Ohio Valley. The force ended up decimating the abandoned Indian villages at Chillicothe and Piqua.

And so it went on for Clark as he seemed to be continuously engaged in one conflict or another. He even found himself back in the eastern end of Virginia in a skirmish that he lost against Benedict Arnold who was then commanding British troops at a site called Hood's Point.

A long held dream of Clark's was to capture Fort Detroit from the British. He spent a good deal of time planning and preparing to be at the ready for such an adventure if and when it should ever be called for. That day seemed to have come late in the Revolution but the government scratched the plan at the last minute. As a testimony to his dedication, Clark had often put up much of his own wealth to recruit men into his service. Most of these monies were never repaid by the government leaving him in poor standing late in life. As the years passed, Clark suffered disappointments on several fronts, and accusations of alcoholism took a toll on his reputation and his health.

Part of Clark's frustration and diminished approval had come from the very Kentuckians he had associated himself with. For its first three years of existence, Kentucky was merely a county of Virginia. The residents of this "county" were concerned about themselves. While Clark's heart was with them, he always felt a need to act in the interest of the entire nation as well. In 1780, when he had sought settlers and soldiers to build and man Fort Jefferson, which was far to the West, the settlers of eastern and central Kentucky wavered because they had wanted protection from their local enemy. Attacks had been frequent on their homesteads by the Shawnee and several other northern tribes. In their view, Clark had gone too far, in all senses of that word, by seeking to take on Indians who had allied with the British in the distant Illinois country. Though his previous victories there were generally appreciated, and considered great in the national view, they did little to make the average Kentuckian feel safe on his own back porch. Most felt that these faraway fights and fortresses simply drew men away from defending their own homes and families.

This sentiment was just one of the deterrents to Fort Jefferson's survival. Many of the men who were stationed in the stockade had often been diverted to fight at other locations in the Illinois, Ohio, and Kentucky countries, leaving Fort Jefferson short-handed. Additionally, the inhabitants were frequently hungry, making do with very meager supplies of food. Captain Robert George, who was in command of the fortress, penned a letter to one of Clark's key officer's, Lieutenant Colonel George Slaughter, explaining the dire food situation at

Painting of George Rogers Clark by James B. Longacre, 1825.

the fort as of February 1781. The problem stemmed in part from the spoiled food that Slaughter had just sent them.

> ... the Small Supplies you have sent us, have been of infinate Service... but the supplies I beg may be of a better Quality than what is yet come to hand. The Beef is really of the poorest kind — ill-cured, and not half salted — the Barrels being bad, the pickle became wasted, if ever any had been put in, and tho' the Meat does not absolutely stink, it wants little of it. The approaching Season being warm, more especially require[s] that the Troops should be victualled [fed] with the Wholesomest diet... 'Twere well if all that you send was first inspected. [2]

Smack! But Captain George further noted concerns about the supplies of alcohol stating, "Send us as much Whisky as you please as we are forced to expend our Taffia for Provisions." [3] Taffia was a Caribbean blend of rum distilled from cheap molasses and sugar cane scraps. Though this statement implies that alcohol was in regular use, which it certainly was, it also brings to light another problem: the lack of cash in hand.

The government was delinquent on sending money as well as the food and spirits promised. As a result, goods were being bought from traders in the region on credit. And the credit of the government proved to be bad. Food merchants who had agreed to the credit tact were eventually duped one too many times and finally refused to sell anything unless it was a cash transaction. As a last resort the officers turned to bartering away their booze to get food.

Even earlier, when Fort Jefferson was merely four months old, John Dodge, the Virginia Indian agent to the region, had sounded an alarm about the fort's dire food situation. Dodge adroitly alerted Governor Jefferson that

> the troops and Inhabitants at this place, not having received the expected supplies from Government, and being well assured that without some timely relief, the post and settlement must be evacuated, I was also constrained at divers times to issue quantities of the goods intended to be disposed of to our indian allies, in order to furnish them with the means of subsistence... I see no other alternative, from the present appearance of our affairs, but that the few goods I have left, after supplying the troops, must all go for the purchase of provisions to keep this settlement from breaking up: and how I shall ever support my credit, or acquit myself of the obligations I have bound myself under, to those of whom I have made purchases for the troops before the arrival of the Goods, I know not — Our Credit is become so weak among the French inhabitants, our own, and the spaniards on the opposite side of the Mississippi, that one dollars' worth of provision or other supplies cannot be had from them without prompt payment, were it to save the whole Country. [4]

Clearly John Dodge is peeved. He was not shy in telling his governor that the government was extremely negligent on multiple levels. Though Dodge had managed to acquire food, it was on the horribly bad credit of the government. That meant the merchants would sell nothing further to him. And, the food he had secured was originally ear-marked to placate their Native American allies. Now it was going to the starving soldiers and settlers of Fort Jefferson. The Indians would not appreciate that move. Even further, Dodge makes clear that all these factors had made the residents at Fort Jefferson so desperate that they were close to abandoning the fortress altogether.

In the governments's defense, some of the food shipments they had sent were delayed or sabotaged by enemies along their route. Also, the intensity of the Revolution had accelerated and had centered itself in Virginia at this point in time. Fighting in Virginia proper had demanded the full attention of the men and monies that the new state government had at its disposal. The western situation took second place.

By mid-summer of 1780 the inhabitants of Fort Jefferson were not only ill-fed, they were seriously ill.

> The garrison not exceeding thirty men under Captain George, two-thirds of whom were sick with the ague and fever were reduced to the lowest extremity. Pumpkins with the blossom yet on them, afforded their principal food. 5

As if the starvation, disease, and the general lack of attention from the government wasn't enough, perhaps the most intimidating factor causing some inhabitants to abandon the fortress was the persistent assaults of some very angry Indians. Specifically, the Chickasaws. This tribe had deemed that a broad area of land along the Mississippi, stretching through Kentucky, Tennessee, and Illinois, was theirs. Fort Jefferson was built right in the heart of it without their permission. That move was more than frowned upon by the Chickasaws.

Letters between Governor Jefferson and Clark point to the fact that they were cognizant of the importance of signing a treaty with the Chickasaws before they acted. They could have acquired the land amicably, yet the fort was built without any negotiations. Theories as to why it went down in this fashion vary. Some say it was simply an act of defiance against the Indians. Others say that Clark was impatient, knowing that negotiations could take months before reaching an agreement, so he decided to forego them and build the fort immediately. It is also speculated by some historians that Fort Jefferson was influential in swaying the British to cede what became the Northwest Territory to the Americans during the Paris peace talks. Its presence, along with other fortresses positioned on the banks of the Mississippi, demonstrated that the Americans were already deeply embedded in the western lands.

Regardless of why the fort was built without the consent of the Chickasaws, this tribe had considered it an invasion by the Americans. They didn't need a lot of encouragement to attack, but this certainly gave them the perfect excuse. The Chickasaw were already dependent on the British for goods and weaponry, so confronting Fort Jefferson was a friendly "thank you" to the Brits as well as a personal action to defend their own land.

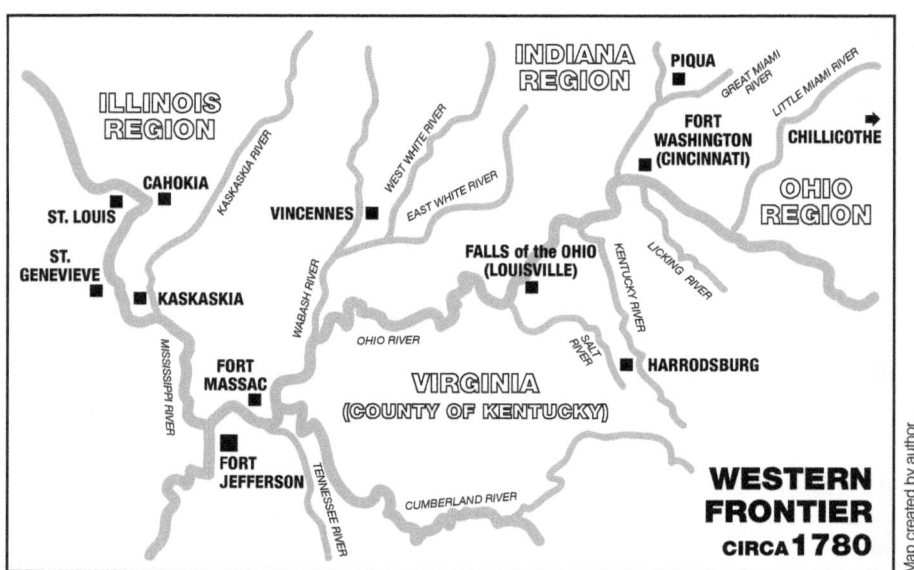

Map created by author.

The Indian attacks were quick and frequent. Usually small bands harassed and killed the settlers who were trying to establish their farms around the fort. Such raids were enough to drive most residents into the fort instead of working their farms around it. These Indians were also responsible for ambushing several of those already few shipments of food that were sent by the government. Their attacks intensified through the summer of 1780 until a full-scale assault was made on Fort Jefferson in July. In alliance with the Choctaws of the region, the Chickasaws presented a combined force of somewhere between five hundred and a thousand Indians. It shouldn't have taken much to overpower the fortress as ill and short-handed as they were, but the Americans within managed to put up a stoic defense.

The Indians were being led by James Colbert, a Scotsman who found favor with the Chickasaws. His descendants would become leaders of the Chickasaw nation for generations to come. The siege lasted six days and a description of its conclusion comes from a man named Patton who was a mere boy inside the fort when the event transpired.

> On the sixth day Colbert and George met under a flag of truce to agree upon terms of capitulation; but they were unable to effect it. As Colbert was retiring, he received a wound from some of the Indians who were

THE FORGOTTEN COLONY OF CLARK

with our men in the blockhouses, and fell [wounded]. This treachery according to our own usages, enraged the Indians to the utmost pitch of exasperation: at night they collected all their forces, and made a furious assault upon the fort, endeavoring to take it by storm. [6]

At this point, a man named Owen decided to take matters into his own hands.

> When the Indians had advanced in very close order, Captain George Owen, who commanded one of the block-houses, had the swivels [cannons] loaded with rifle and musket balls, and fired them in the crowd. The consequent carnage was excessive, and dispersed the enemy. At the same time, General Clark, who was stationed at Kaskaskia, and had been sent for, arrived with provisions and a reinforcement, which effectually raised the siege to the great relief of the garrison. [7]

This action of Owen preserved the lives of those in Fort Jefferson that day, but it made him a marked man among the Indians. Just a few years later, according to his family's friend and historian, William Hayden English,

> they captured him [Owen] near the falls of the Ohio [Louisville], in what is now Indiana, as he was hunting, or attempting to pass between the falls and Vincennes, and, after torturing him in the most frightful manner, finally burned him to death at the stake at or near the Wea towns (Ouiatanon) [Lafayette, IN]. It is said he himself had some Indian blood in his veins. His descendants settled in Scott county, Indiana. The author [English] knew them intimately, and when a young man heard Captain Owens's sons, George and Thomas, then old men, speak of these events. Their hatred of the Indian race was so vehement that the people of Lexington, then the county seat of Scott county, had difficulty in keeping them from killing two friendly Indians who happened at that place half a century after Captain Owens's death. The author [English] was present and remembers the circumstances distinctly. [8]

In the course of the siege another hero had stepped up. Her name was Nancy Ann Hunter.

> On one occasion, when the savages that had beleaguered the settlement seemed to have gone away and it looked safe and quiet all around, a favorite cow was permitted, with her calf, to stroll outside the gate. But shortly, Indians were seen prowling among the thickets. In this emergency, as the

men were parleying what to do, hesitating to expose themselves, Nancy Ann Hunter ran out into the open space, and taking up the calf brought it within the enclosure, the cow following, while the arrows of the savages whistled by and cut her clothing, herself unharmed. [9]

A bold move indeed for a young girl that most records show was all of eleven years old (though some accounts say she was a few years older). Her action was prompted by her concern for the many infants within the fortress who were desperate for milk. That unflappable character must have come from her father who was known to venture across the river from the fort to hunt buffalo for the often starving inhabitants. After Fort Jefferson was abandoned, Nancy is presumed to have been with the portion of her family that moved to Kaskaskia. There she met, Israel Dodge, the son of John Dodge the Indian agent of Virginia cited earlier. They were married when Nancy was a mere thirteen years old.

Nancy's father-in-law, John Dodge, had a perilous, and let's call it slippery, life. He was a trader in the Great Lakes region before the Revolution began, but was captured and taken to Detroit by the notorious British Governor of Quebec, Henry "The Hair-buyer" Hamilton. This moniker was given Hamilton because of his eagerness to make payments to Indians who had brought him the scalps of American frontiersmen. No such payments were given for Americans brought in alive as prisoners. Hamilton wanted them dead. In an executive session of the state's council it was reported to Governor Jefferson just what Hamilton had done to John Dodge

> ... he [Hamilton] loaded him into a dungeon, without bedding, without straw, without fire, in the dead of winter and severe climate of Detroit; that, in that state, he wasted him with incessant expectations of death; that when the rigors of his situation had brought him so low that death seemed likely to withdraw him from their power, he was taken out and somewhat attended to, until a little mended, and before he had recovered ability to walk was again returned to his dungeon, in which a hole was cut seven inches square only, for the admission of air, and the same load of irons again put on him; that appearing, a second time, in imminent danger of being lost to them, he was again taken from his dungeon, in which he had lain from January till June, with the intermission of a few weeks only, before mentioned. [10]

John Dodge shortly thereafter won his freedom, but perhaps it was this grueling, near-death experience and the broken promises of the Virginia government, that affected his outlook on life. A short time after his captivity, he was acting, as noted, as an Indian agent and was in charge of providing goods to the people of Fort Jefferson. However, accusations of some underhanded dealings for personal gain surfaced. One report to Governor Jefferson said:

> With respect to Capt Dodge the complaints against him are so general & have so good authority for his having misapplied the publick goods, and apprehending that he may possibly be collecting a cargo of Peltry[furs] for the new Orleans market that I have given Capt George Orders to make enquiry as to his conduct & if any thing of this sort appears, to seize his person & what goods he may be possessed of & secure them 'till further Orders. [11]

And so John was considered a less-than-honest character that one needed to be wary of. His son, Israel, may not have been as unscrupulous a figure as his father had been accused of being, but he was never-the-less a restless, entrepreneurial spirit; and a renegade. After a couple years of marriage he moved Nancy and their first child, Henry, from the Louisville region to what would become Bardstown, Kentucky. There he built the first stone house of that town, which not only served as the family home, but also as a tavern to generate income. Soon, Nancy bore a second child, a daughter that was named after herself. Then, after nine years of marriage, Israel left Nancy with their two children and sought adventure three hundred miles away near a Spanish settlement called St. Genevieve on the western banks of the Mississippi.

Henry, their first child, was born in the first year of their marriage when Nancy was barely a teenager. Intriguing circumstances encountered at the time of his birth prompted the choice of Henry as his name. As it happened:

> In the fall of that year [1782] while upon a journey from this place [Kaskaskia] to her parents in Kentucky, Mrs. Israel Dodge stopped over for rest and refreshment at "Post Vincennes," where Henry Dodge was born, October 12, 1782, under the hospitable roof of Moses and Ann Henry; the first American child born in what now constitutes the state of Indiana. The earlier white inhabitants were Canadian French…

> ... A few days after the birth of the child, a Piankeshaw chief came in, and said that it [the baby] could not be allowed to live in their country, and he would dash out its brains. The mother [Nancy] plead for the life of her first born. Moses Henry explained that it was the "papoose" of a friend of his, whose "squaw" was sojourning in his house—that the child was born out of due time while the young mother was on her way to her people, and that they would soon go on their journey. These expostulations prevailed, the chief at the same time remarking, "nits make lice; this little nit may grow to be a big louse and bite us;" a prophecy which came true. In gratitude to her benefactor, Mrs. Dodge gave his full name [Moses Henry] to the child, which he retained until he was grown, when he adopted the single name, Henry. [12]

And so Moses Henry Dodge survived the precarious first few days of his life on earth. But there was more trouble ahead. Indians were still attacking settlers throughout Kentucky, and the Dodge and Hunter families could not escape their aggression. Henry would often tell of his earliest childhood memory; seeing the bloodied, dead body of one of his uncles being carried on horseback in the arms of another uncle after one such Indian attack. In fact several brothers and sisters of both Nancy and Israel were killed in a similar fashion. Henry himself was captured by the Indians when a young boy, but was returned under circumstances that are unknown.

Then, one day in his fourteenth year, Henry's life changed forever when he

> saw a brawny savage bending over the prostrate form of a woman with one hand in her tresses, the other brandishing a butcher knife, as if to take her scalp. As she screamed for help he seized a stone and felled the Indian to the ground, apparently dead. He at once informed his people of what he had done. His mother [Nancy], apprehending that the Indians would seek revenge, told him that he must flee for his life. He spent the night in a graveyard, the next day joining a company of pioneers going west, and reached St. Genevieve in safety. [13]

This was the same region his father had moved to about six years earlier. Whether they had any contact is unknown. None-the-less, his survival of at least three near-death episodes in his young life bode well for him and for the United States. Henry Dodge went on to a stellar career in service to his country.

When the War of 1812 was declared Henry enlisted. Years later as a colonel, he led a militia force into a fierce confrontation with a band of warriors led by the Sauk Chief, Black Hawk. It became known as the Battle of Wisconsin Heights and was a key victory in the war named after that Chief. It also fulfilled the Piankeshaw Chief's "nit to lice" prophecy about Henry. Finally, having attained the rank of Major-General, Henry led the United States dragoon regiment on an important expedition into the Oklahoma Territory through which he moderated the first ever meetings between the Americans and the Plains Indians. It became known as the Dodge-Leavenworth Expedition. At age fifty-four he turned to politics and became the first Governor of the Wisconsin Territory. That was followed by a stint as a representative of that territory to the U.S. Congress, then another term as Governor; and finally when Wisconsin became a state in 1848 Henry would be elected one of its first two Senators. After serving for nine years he finally retired at age seventy-five.

All of this is only part of Nancy Hunter's legacy. She re-married shortly after she had been abandoned by Israel Dodge. Her new husband was Asael Linn whose life and genealogy was filled with plenty of its own intrigue.

Asael was the son of a famed Revolutionary hero, Colonel William Linn, who had several notable adventures in the West. William had served with Clark in the capture of Kaskaskia, but is perhaps most remembered for a mission assigned him by Governor Jefferson. He journeyed to New Orleans in order to secure military goods and ammunition that was desperately needed for the war effort in the East. The cargo he bore back from Louisiana by boat included one hundred and fifty-six kegs of gunpowder. At one point, William and others had to portage the kegs in order to circumvent the Falls of the Ohio at Louisville; each man shouldering one barrel at a time and making multiple cumbersome trips. The powder arrived, dry and ready for use, at its intended destination of Fort Pitt, where it was then dispersed to American forces. Unfortunately, just a few months after Fort Jefferson had been abandoned, William Linn was killed. His death scene is noteworthy as it displays his resolve to fight to the end. It is recalled by his loving granddaughter-in-law with a bit of familial romanticism.

> A few years after the United States had gained their independence from the yoke of England, Col. [William] Linn set out at the head of

sixty men on a march against a body of hostile Indians who had foraged the White settlements and taken many lives. At a point near what was called Linn's Station, not far from Louisville, his party was met by a force of three hundred Indian warriors, who had received full intelligence of his approach and mustered in strength to receive him… The Indians were inspired with furious animosity against Col. Linn — his knowledge of their character and stratagems, his superior sagacity and dauntless intrepedity, his genius in border warfare, and the frequency with which they had been defeated by him; the dread inseparable from his name; the confidence and courage with which his protection inspired the weak and isolated societies of his partisans; added to the frightful chastisements with which he had repeatedly visited their common enemy, combined to render him, for long years, an object of deadly hatred and hereditary revenge.

This was the era of Indian combination and preconcerted movements; his destruction appeared inevitable, and would open the way to sweep every stranger from the land; but in order to glut every horrid passion of their swarthy race, they determined to take him alive; his death could have been easily effected as he led on and encouraged his men. Suddenly a cry arose in the English tongue, "Take him! take him alive! take him alive! we want to eat his heart!" Instead of aiming at the vital parts of his person, they fired volley after volley below his knees, until his feet were shot to pieces and the bones of his legs broken. When he fell the braves rushed in to disarm and bear him off alive; but they found him in his last hour the same avenging implacable foe they had dreaded through life. Gaining his knees, the dying hero grappled with his enemies, giving and receiving many a death wound before he expired. Of them he slew, hand to hand, seven, before his arm was rendered nerveless by death. [14]

Asael, like his father William before him, would have a most precarious Indian adventure of his own. Just a few years before he met and married Nancy, twelve-year-old Asael was kidnapped by Indians, giving him something in common, as well, with his future step-son Henry Dodge. Asael's event, like the one just related about his father, was attested to by his daughter-in-law years later.

Mr. Asael Linn, the father of Dr. Linn, accompanied four young gentlemen from his father's residence near Louisville, on the Ohio River, in pursuit of wild game. Carried away with the ardor of the chase, they had gone some distance from home before they were aware of it, when they suddenly found themselves surrounded by a number of hostile Indians.

Resistance was vain. After one of their party was wounded in the leg they were secured as captives by the savages, and forced across the Ohio River. The Indians travelled at a rapid pace, fearing pursuit from the white settlements. [15]

It was a boy named Lewis Fields who had been shot in his leg, making it extremely difficult for him to run as fast as the Indians had demanded. Asael feared the looks of annoyance cast by the Indians upon Fields who repeatedly forced the group to slow down. Every effort was made by Asael to assist his friend in the hope that he would not be dispatched by one of the impatient Indians.

After three days of near constant retreat from the Ohio River, the Indians determined it safe to make a camp. To keep their captives in check, the older boys were lashed to trees. Asael was not considered a threat to run because of his age. He was allowed to move freely under the watchful eyes of the elder Indian guards who had remained in the camp while the rest went hunting for food. Asael had convinced himself that he would be killed once they reached the village of these Indians because he was the son of the man who had wreaked so much havoc upon them in years previous.

When the shade of the night had desended, young Linn was made to lie down flat upon the ground; the two old Indians spread a blanket over him, placing themselves on the edge of it on both sides of the brave boy, wedging him in between them, compressed by the blanket with their weight upon it. In a short time the old men, overpowered with fatigue, fell into a deep sleep. Linn watched their movements with intense anxiety, and when convinced his captors were asleep, commenced with great dexterity and presence of mind to draw his person from under the blanket without disturbing those upon it; for if awakened, his death would not have been delayed one moment. When liberated from his painful situation, the first object Linn beheld was one of his companions, Mr. Wells, bound to a tree near him; and seeing from the gleams of light sent forth from the watch-fire, a tomahawk near to his hand, he seized it, and soon cut the cords that bound his friend. Mr. Wells made him a sign to retain the weapon, and arming himself with another, they drew near to their blood-thirsty foes and in an instant buried their tomahawks in the heads of the Indians.

Weakened in frame, and of the most humane disposition, in spite of the justice and necessity of the act, Linn's heart recoiled from putting a sleeping enemy to death, and the wound he inflicted, although completely stunning in its effect, did not produce death, but left a hideous and distorting mutilation on the face of the savage. In a few moments the captives were liberated from the cords that were cutting into their flesh. Collecting in great haste a few fragments of food, securing all the hatchets and knives they could find for their defense, and concealing the guns, (as the Indians might at any instant be so near their path as to hear a report from them, and the weight of them would retard their flight,) before the light of day (a bitter cold morning in the month of November) these five boys, not one of them out of his teens (Linn not twelve years old), commenced their flight through the wilderness towards the Ohio River, half-starved, almost naked, and bearing with them one of their number, wounded, sore and crippled.

Poor Lewis Fields suffered so much from his inflamed wound in consequence of the great exertions he was compelled to make, that he frequently stopped and implored his friends to leave him to his fate, and save themselves by retreating more rapidly than it was possible to do while he continued with them; but the faithful little band of friends, deaf to his self-devoting proposition, urged him forward by every act of friendship and encouragement until, through indescribable suffering of hunger, cold and lassitude, they stood once more on the bank of the Ohio River.

Fortunately they could all swim, and it was only necessary to construct from the limbs of trees and drift-wood on the shore, a raft large enough to bear their disabled friend, and push it before them while swimming across the river. Linn was so much exhausted that his friends feared he would perish in the water, and urged him to get on the raft with Fields; but the gallant boy declined their friendly offer, assuring them that his father had taught him to swim very well, and that he was still strong enough to assist in getting their friend across the river.

At the moment the raft was launched in to the water, the distant yell of the Indians in pursuit was heard. They had struck the trail of the youths and were now almost upon them. Straining every nerve, the gallant boys soon gained the middle of the river, while the frail raft appeared as if it would go to pieces under the slight weight of Fields. As the Indians arrived one after another at the water's edge, they fired at the fugitives, but fortunately the distance was so great they were unable to do them any injury; and the reports of their guns attracted the attention of some settlers working on the Kentucky side of the river, who immediately came to their relief.

Although exhausted and half dead, Linn still retained his hold upon the raft, but entirely insensible, and at first it was thought he had expired. He was carried home, and after remaining for three days wholly unconscious, awoke to a sense of external things in the arms of his mother. His life was spared, and he grew up to a manhood of great energy and exalted worth. Many years afterwards, when the country had become peaceful, Linn met his old enemy the Indian, whom in his boyhood he had deprived of so large a portion of his face, and touched with his horrid appearance, bestowed on him an annuity for life. [16]

The tender heart of Asael endeared him to most everyone he met, especially Nancy. But under circumstances unknown to history, he and Nancy passed away in 1806. Their departures left their two children, Mary Ann and Lewis Fields Linn orphans. Yes, the sentimental Asael named his son after the dear friend whose life he helped save years previous. Parentless, Mary only thirteen and Lewis twelve found their way to St. Genevieve and grew up under the supervision of their half-brother Henry Dodge. Endowed with the indefatigable spirit of his ancestors, Lewis determined the course for his life to be in medicine. By the age of fifteen he was beginning his studies in the profession. This early passion for healing proved beneficial to many an American warrior, as Lewis served under his step-brother Henry in the War of 1812 as a physician.

Lewis would prove to have a very noteworthy career as a physician; one punctuated by his sensitive personality and good looks. His frequent habit of treating patients who had no means of payment bolstered his reputation. No one was turned away from the good doctor. And he made house calls, often many miles away.

This genuine spirit of caring ingratiated him to the public at large. His attractiveness was both physical and emotional, and soon won him a place in politics. At thirty-three years of age he switched careers by popular acclaim to the U.S. Senate; representing the state of Missouri. After ten years of service, and having garnered the approbation of his colleagues on both sides of the aisle for his fairness and sincerity, he became one of those unfortunates who died in office at only forty-seven years of age.

Well, it has been a long and almost exhausting story of Nancy Hunter and her lineage, but believe it or not there is still more. If we return to Moses Henry Dodge's life for a moment, we'll discover one more curious personality in this mix; that of Augustus Caesar Dodge. This descendent of Nancy Hunter had an interaction with Indians of the West as well, serving under his dad, Moses, in the Black Hawk War. Augustus, like so many in his family, became quite popular amongst his fellow citizens and soon found his way into politics. He won election to the U.S. Senate for seven years as representative of the state of Iowa, before which he had served as a delegate from that territory. In later years he became an Ambassador to Spain and then settled into the position of mayor in Burlington, Iowa.

Though she never saw it, at one point in time the progeny of Nancy Ann Hunter Dodge/Linn pulled off a political feat that is yet to be matched. For a period of three years, 1841-1843, all three male descendents of Nancy were warming seats in the Capitol Building in Washington DC. Her first son, Henry Dodge, was there as a delegate from the Territory of Wisconsin. Her grandson, Augustus Dodge was there as a delegate from the Territory of Iowa. And Lewis Linn was there as a Senator from Missouri. As if that wasn't enough of an historical feat, to this day Nancy's children are the only ones to serve simultaneously in the Senate as father and son. Once all these territories had become states, Henry was seated as Senator from Wisconsin, while Augustus was Senator from Iowa.

Except for an Indian arrow having missed its mark by a matter of inches, after being fired against a child fetching cows at Fort Jefferson, none of the heroics noted above would ever have transpired.

Amongst the inhabitants of Fort Jefferson were two other families whose story has only survived because of its being recorded in the memoirs of an early Ohio Valley explorer named Daniel Trabue. The names of the actors in this tale are unknown, but the recounting of it, though sad and tragic, highlights the ways of selfishness and selflessness better than many a sermon.

When it became inevitable that Fort Jefferson should be abandoned, the inhabitants left in all directions. Some went back to

Portraits of descendents of Nancy Ann Hunter who from 1841-1843 simultaneously served in the Congress of the United States. Left to right: (Moses) Henry Dodge, her son; Lewis Fields Linn, her grandson; and Augustus Caesar Dodge, also her son.

Louisville, where most had come from, while others went north to Kaskaskia in Illinois country or south to Natchez, a settlement further down the Mississippi River. This story recounts what happened as two of these families left Fort Jefferson and travelled to Natchez.

As Mr. Daniel Trabue explains it, "A very Remarkable accurance happened to two men that landed at the falls of Ohia now Lewisville." [17] The men had left their homes in what was known as the Monongahela country, probably in the region of today's Pittsburgh. They headed west for a fresh start after feeling that they were somehow being taken advantage of in their current jobs. Having sold most of their goods and bundling their families up for the long ride, they were off to the burgeoning settlement at Louisville, Kentucky. It was from this community that George Rogers Clark had recruited them and most of his settlers for Fort Jefferson.

> Some time after [the two men had arrived at Louisville], Col. R.G. [sic] Clark proposed a settlement Down on the Mississippi at or near the Chickasaw bluffs...
>
> ...This place at the Cheekasaw bluffs proved very sickly, and several of this company Died... One of these men Died and left his wife a widow. The other Man's wife Died and left him a Widower. And as they was Obledged to go a way, they got in a flat bottom boat — this man and his children and this widow woman and her children, all in one boat — and

Descended the Massepee [Mississippi] with an intent to go to knatches [Natchez].

They had but a scant allowence of provision, and it intirely give out. And they run their boat on a log and could not get it off. The boat was near the shore so that they could go on shore. They cut hand sticks and tryed to shove off the boat but could not. This man had a Good Gun and Amonition and went several times a hunting for something to eat but all without suckceess. And they weare nearly starved to Death, and in those Days it was seldom any boats passed up and Down.

This man proposed to the widow that they should cast lots with their children and kill one to eat to save the rest of their lives. She objected and said she had rather all Die together and advised him to hunt again. He Did but without suckcees.

This man said he would kill one of his own children and Did cast lots. And the lot fell on a small Girl. And this girl knew of the plan and she walked up and Down on the shore crying, while this widow woman insisted it must not be Done and told this man they must make another attempt to get of[f] their boat. But he refused to help. And this woman encourged all the children to help and Do their very best, and they shoved off the boat. This woman thinks the water raised a little.

And all went along together, but this man had got very fractery and peevish. And the woman and children Managed the boat mostly themselves. And as they was moeving, it appeared their was some hope. And this little girl's life was spared from Day to Day.

And at length they meet a French Man in a Ceel boat a going to the Elenoy [Illinois] at Caskasey [Kaskaskia] and they petetiond him for food. And he said he had scarce but he would give them some. This woman informed the Frenchman that they ware not all one family and to Give her and her children's portion to themselves. And he Did so. And she give her children a little at a time and eat but little her self at one time, while this Man eat so much he actuly Died.

And this widow and boath sets of children all did arrive at knatches. And some of her friends some time after that heard of her Destress and went to her and took her and her children around to Baltimore and then to her own people again. [18]

Maybe it was only a few hundred people who spent time within the walls of Fort Jefferson. And maybe it seemed to be for an insignificant length of time. But over that short span, in that place, the few lives we've come to know give evidence to bravery and endurance unimaginable to many of us today. Through their sufferings of disease, malnutrition, and chronic Indian attacks many of the survivors moved on and flourished. Others were lost. Though there is no physical evidence of Fort Jefferson today, its legacy lives on through the descendents of these brave, adventurous souls who inhabited it by choice in an attempt to forge a new life and to protect their newborn country. ♦

ANECDOTE.

A serious Question. — About 1794, an officer presented a western chief with a medal, on one side of which President Washington was represented as armed with a sword, and on the other an Indian was seen in the act of burying the hatchet. The chief at once saw the wrong done his countrymen, and very wisely asked, "Why does not the President bury his sword too?"

In Samuel G. Drake's, Biography and History of the Indians of North America, 1848 [19]

XIII.
RESERVED FOR CONNECTICUT.

While they were still under the rule of the King of England, many of the colonies had legal holdings of lands that were laying beyond the Appalachians. Claims to these lands were still in place as the colonies transitioned into states at the end of the Revolution. The tracts were varied in their shapes and sizes by state. Geographically, Connecticut's stake was an extension of their state's northern and southern borders all the way across the continent to the Mississippi River; interrupted only in part by portions of New York and Pennsylvania.

As the country was getting on its feet in 1787, the federal government was on the verge of turning a large chunk of the West into the Northwest Territory so that they could gain revenue through the sale of parcels of land to settlers. Before that could happen, however, the states with claims in the region had to cede them to the federal government. All did, except for Connecticut, who managed to hold a portion of its western lands in reserve. Hence, it became known as the Western Reserve of Connecticut.

The Reserve stretched over one hundred and twenty miles from what would become the eastern boundary of the state of Ohio to a few miles west of the current city of Sandusky. It extended northward a few miles into Lake Erie and southward to approximately the 41st parallel latitude where Akron is found. In 1792, 500,000 acres of the most western portion of this reserve were designated as "The Sufferers' Lands" or "The Fire Lands." The sufferers referred to were citizens of Connecticut towns who incurred extreme losses to their persons and property at the hands of British attackers during the Revolution.

Nine Connecticut towns, most of them seaport villages, were ransacked, plundered, and extensively burned to the ground by English troops. These harbors had warehoused massive stores of goods that would have been used by the revolutionaries in their war effort had the British not destroyed or stolen them. As the British became aware of these depots, they planned and executed quick overnight forays into the towns. Fires were set to foodstuffs, ammunition, and all sorts of supplies that the Americans were in dire need of in the war effort. They also targeted buildings, residences, and almost everything else in the business districts along the waterfronts. In some of these raids the death toll was light, but a few towns suffered hundreds of fatalities. These were not the traditional fights of the Revolution in which battle lines had been drawn; these were precision strikes employing the element of surprise. Once the enemy had arrived on the scene and wreaked their havoc they retreated as fast as they had appeared, usually under the cover of night. Such assaults had an after-effect on the inhabitants of the towns that was personally, physically, and financially staggering.

A few accounts from early historians give us an idea of what had transpired. One example was the major assault on New London and Groton, two ports situated across from each other at the mouth of the Thames River in Connecticut (not to be confused with the Thames River in Canada). It was carried out in September of 1781 near the end of the war. The tale begs for attention because of its many surprising and disturbing details.

For one thing, the attack upon these sister ports was conducted by the notorious traitor, Benedict Arnold, who at this time was in control of a British fleet. Having already turned his back on his American heritage, this day he would turn his back specifically on former friends and neighbors. He had grown up in Norwich, Connecticut, just ten miles up the Thames River, and had often frequented both New London and Groton as a young man.

In the evening before the day of the attack, warnings were circulated throughout the two towns that British ships were witnessed accumulating near Long Island, just a few miles across the sound. However, because such alerts were so prolific, like the boy who cried wolf too many times, few of the townspeople gave this one any serious concern. Most carried on as usual and then retired for the night. By dawn they would discover that this was no false alarm.

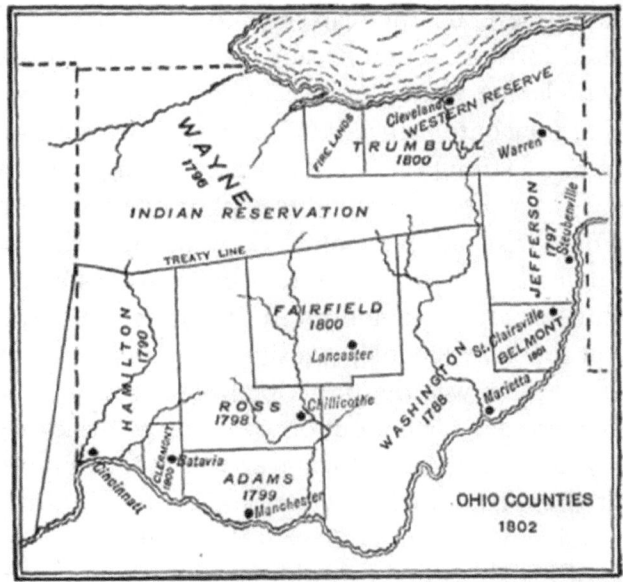

Map showing the counties of Ohio, including the Connecticut Reserve and the Firelands just before Ohio became a state in 1803. Found in book: *The Evolution of Ohio Counties*, by J.F. Laning, 1896.

As had happened on so many other occasions during the American Revolution, it seemed that the Almighty had a hand in the events of this day in favor of the Americans. Here's why. The British had planned to sail their ships directly into the mouth of the Thames River in the middle of the night. Their troops were to disembark to the shores of the harbor and quickly infiltrate the towns. After destroying the stores at hand, primarily by setting them ablaze, they would evacuate before daybreak. Ideally, all this would be carried out in such haste that no retaliatory forces could be mustered against them. However, when the time to set sail had arrived, the winds suddenly strengthened and shifted. They began blowing directly against Arnold's fleet. This forced a delay. Arnold decided to have his troops board small boats which they rowed against the wind into the ports. It took until mid-morning for them to land. They had lost the cover of darkness and the Americans became aware of their presence.

Just after the British made landfall, coincidentally or Providentially, the winds would shift again. They turned one hundred and eighty degrees, enabling several American ships to escape upriver. These were vessels targeted for destruction because they were laden with all sorts of material goods, foodstuffs, and weaponry. Thanks to the change in wind direction they outdistanced the range of British cannons.

Each town had a stronghold for its defense, though they were not as formidable as most. Fort Trumbull was positioned above New London while Fort Griswold overlooked Groton across the river. As the British troops had approached, cannon blasts were heard from Fort Griswold. But the firings were not directed at the enemy, rather they were aimed at the townspeople, as a signal. At a specific interval, two shots were fired. This was the prescribed message to the militia and other able-bodied men farther out of town that an attack was at hand, and that they needed to make their way to the fort. However, it was at this point that Arnold made a very quick and shrewd move. His American training clued him as to what that cannon fire was all about. He had one of his ships fire a third shot at the proper time interval which changed the meaning of the signal. The three blasts meant that there had been a general triumph of some sort, just the opposite of the true situation. The backup of men in the distance were confused by the firings and so were delayed in getting to the forts.

As the British troops made their way through the streets of both towns, residents began to flee to the outskirts.

> No sooner were the terrible alarm guns heard, than the startled citizens, leaping from their beds, made haste to send away their families and their portable and most valuable goods. Throngs of women and children were dismissed into the fields and woods, some without food, and others with a piece of bread or a biscuit in their hands. Women laden with bags and pillow-cases, or driving a cow before them, with an infant in their arms, or perhaps on horseback with a bed under them, and various utensils dangling at the side; boys with stockings slung like wallets over their shoulders, containing the money, the papers, and other small valuables of the family; carts laden with furniture; dogs and other household animals, looking strange and panic-struck; pallid faces and trembling limbs — such were the scenes presented on all the roads leading into the country. [1]

While the women and children scrambled to get out of town, little by little, the men from the outlying areas found their way in. Though severely outnumbered, they assembled in the forts with determination to protect their families and businesses. The redcoats, nearly a thousand on each side of the river, began their destruction near midday. Units marched up and down the streets so familiar to Arnold with torches in hand. Many of the establishments of his former friends and neighbors were not spared.

> It is said that Arnold himself with extended sword, pointed out the way to the troops with this emphatic command — "Soldiers! Do your duty."
>
> Of course vengeance and destruction had no check: shops, stores, dwellings, piles of lumber, wharves, boats, rigging, and vessels, were soon enveloped in smoke and flame. Hogsheads [barrels] were knocked in; sugar and coffee lay in heaps, and rum and Irish butter, melted in the fire, trickled along the street, and filled the gutters. [2]

Reports varied, but most of them seem to show that Arnold did not order the torching of family homes. However, many were burnt down. He later claimed that unknown stores of powder inadvertently exploded and spread the damage to personal dwellings. This was true in some cases, but not all. One account details that,

> the market wharf, the old magazine and battery, the court-house, jail and jail-house, the Episcopal church, and several contiguous shops and dwelling-houses, were soon a heap of ashes. [3]

Renegade soldiers seemed to take matters into their own hands as well, making on-the-spot decisions over the fate of any residents they happened to encounter. For instance, there was an elderly fisherman who begged a soldier that his small boat be spared from the torch. He was denied. While in another part of town as a unit of Redcoats approached, a woman's plea to have her home spared had touched a soft spot in the heart of its British commander.

> ...gathering her little children around her, [she] went out to meet them. Dropping to her knees before the captain, she told him that her husband had been gone several long years, and she knew not what had become of him; she had nothing left but a group of helpless children and yonder house with its simple furniture, which she entreated him not to destroy. The officer raised her from the ground, and brushing a tear from his eye, said, "Go in, good woman! you and your property are safe; none of my men shall disturb you." [4]

A footnote provided by an early historian, brings the tale to a satisfying conclusion.

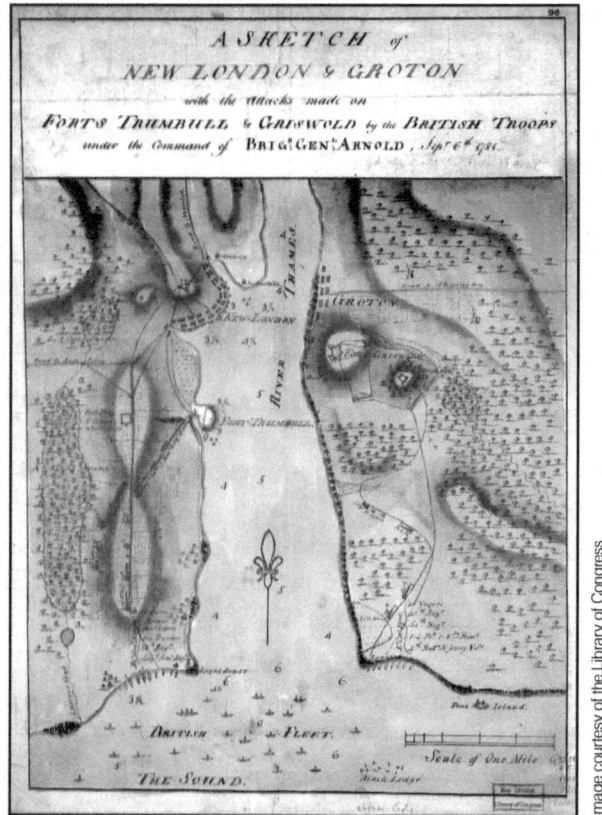

Map of the attacks on New London and Groton Heights, 1781. This military sketch shows the movement of British troops and the American garrisons of Fort Trumbull and Fort Griswold.

Her husband was a sea-captain and trader, who being in Europe when the war broke out and meeting with reverses and difficulties, had continued there, trading and waiting for an opportunity to return home. The very day Arnold was burning New London, he arrived with his vessel in the Sound, and discovering the hostile fleet in season, put back and lay close, till the next day. When the enemy had departed, he slipped into the harbor in the dusk of evening, and landing made his way through the smoldering streets to his own threshold; where lifting the latch, he paused, and before speaking to wife or children, fixed his eyes on two ancient portraits of his ancestors, hanging upon the wall, and with a humor peculiar to his character, saluted them and expressed his satisfaction at finding them still on duty, at their post. [5]

As the market streets of New London went up in smoke, the other half of Arnold's forces moved upon the fortress in Groton. It was hoped by the British that the fort's cannon, once taken, could be used to reach the ships escaping upriver. To the relief of the Americans, the winds had taken the vessels just far enough out of the reach of their own artillery in the fortress as well as that on the British ships. Such good fortune, however, was not to befall the Americans who were still defending the town from within the garrison.

Approximately one hundred and fifty men had run to Fort Griswold to defend their harbor-town. Nearly all were common citizens, untrained in military affairs. But that did not diminish their bravery. Twice through the fight they refused a flag of surrender. When a substantial British force finally stormed the fortress, the few American military officers in charge led the determined residents in its defense. Inevitably, their resistance failed; but not before they had taken out several British officers whose popularity was such that their death fueled the fury of the remaining troops. Once inside, the commanding British officer

> cried out, as he entered, "Who commands this fort?" "I did, sir, but you do now," replied Col. Ledyard, raising and lowering his sword, in token of submission, and advancing to present it to him. The ferocious officer received the sword, and plunged it up to the hilt in the owner's bosom; while his attendants rushing upon the falling hero, dispatched him with their bayonets. [6]

The fortress fell into a frenzy. The Americans nearby immediately rushed to avenge the blatant murder of their colonel. Many of them were later found dead with twenty to thirty piercings each. Horrendous as this sounds, it was just the beginning of the British savagery. Consider that the Americans had just surrendered; yet

> as the British marched in, company after company, they shot or bayoneted every American they saw standing. Three platoons, each of ten or twelve men, fired in succession, into the magazine [ammunition stores], amid the confused mass of living men that had fled thither for shelter, the dying and the dead. This fiend-like sport was terminated by the British commander, as soon as he observed it, not on the plea of humanity, but from fear for their own safety, lest the powder deposited in the magazine, or scattered near, might be fired, and they should all be blown up together. An explosion, it was thought, might have taken

place even earlier than this, had not the scattered powder and every thing around been saturated with human blood. [7]

The assault did not end until eighty-five Americans lay dead in Fort Griswold; their bodies piled up within the fort walls stripped of any clothing or other plunder worth taking. The wounded were left to fend for themselves and about thirty men who had survived in reasonable condition were escorted to the British ships as prisoners.

Fire had dominated the street scenes on both shores of the Thames River, and so it seems fitting that the lighting of the fortress itself would be the perfectly scripted denouement to end this real life tragedy. As it played out, before the last of the British troops departed for their ships, they torched the barracks near to the fort. But previous to the fire being set, a trail of powder was strategically laid from those barracks to the large magazine within the fort. As Arnold and his fleet sailed out of Long Island Sound they watched with the anticipation of seeing the fortress evaporate into the night sky with a tumultuous explosion. They were disappointed. Unbeknownst to them, a few daring American citizens had run to Fort Griswold just as the last of the British troops were departing. They quelled the fires at the barracks, discovered the fuse of powder, and disturbed its path to the magazine; thus sparing the bodies of the dead Americans left within the fortress from a final desecration.

The heroism shown by the ordinary citizens of these towns was extraordinary. Unfortunately, their loss of property and lives was multiplied across several Connecticut sites during the Revolution. Though only few of the original victims would be able to directly benefit from the gesture, eleven years later the government of their state tried to compensate them for their losses. Over the Appalachians, Connecticut still owned their Western Reserve. The farthest west acreage of that block was given to those who suffered through these British attacks. It became known as the Firelands. This was a generous allotment by the government, but there was still a sizable Indian population in that part of the reserve who saw the land as their own, so settling there was a very risky proposition. It would take a few more years, when in 1795 through the Treaty of Greenville, the Indians would legally sign over the eastern two-thirds of the reserve to the U.S. However, heading westward from the Pennsylvania border this agreement only opened land up to the Cuyahoga River which is the area of Cleveland today. The Firelands were the portion even further west which was still officially Indian territory.

It was at about this time in 1795 that the Connecticut legislators started to realize that their western reserve property was becoming more trouble to maintain than it was worth. Therefore they sold the entire portion which had been secured by the Treaty of Greenville to a private investing firm known as the Connecticut Land Company. This group would take on the expense of surveying the land and then selling it in parcels to would-be settlers. The superintendent of the surveying team was General Moses Cleaveland, who founded the city that was bestowed with his name.

By 1800, Connecticut turned over the rest of its western reserve lands, the Firelands, to the federal government. And just three years later, in 1803, it all would become part of the new state of Ohio. But even as state property, the Firelands were not conducive to settlement because they were situated too far to the West where the population of Native Americans remained high. Not until 1805, when the Treaty of Fort Industry was signed along the Maumee River in present-day Toledo, would the Indian nations of the region finally cede the Firelands over to the Americans. It's not clear how many of the Connecticut families who were directly affected by the British attacks during the Revolution actually settled in the area because the signing of this last treaty came some twenty-five years after the fact. But whether they or their children did, they should have at least received monetary compensation from the sale of the Fireland parcels to others.

For all these reasons, the Firelands were the last of the Reserve to attract settlers; most not arriving until after the War of 1812. Pioneers had trickled into the eastern areas of the reserve much earlier. The trip in from the coastal states required a great deal of perseverance and endurance as one early historian notes:

> Of the first settlers, some men walked the entire way from Connecticut; some rode horseback part way, sharing the horse with others; some rode in ox carts; some drove oxen; some came part way by land and the rest by water; some came on sleds in mid-winter; some plowed through

Illustration of family emigrating to New Connecticut, 1817-1818.
From an engraving in Peter Parky's Recollections and reprinted in book:
History of Youngstown and the Mahoning Valley, Ohio, 1921.

the mud of spring, or endured the heat of summer; some had bleeding feet, and some serious illnesses. Sometimes it was a bride and a groom who started alone; sometimes it was a husband, wife and children; sometimes it was a group of neighbors who made the party. Children were born on the way, and people of all ages died and were buried where they died. But after they came, their experiences were almost identical. [8]

They were identical in their challenges. For these earliest settlers life was quite difficult on many levels. Most had to cope with being isolated by many miles from a friendly smile or a helping hand. All manner of situations required assistance beyond what a single family might be able to manage alone. Structures needed to be built, crops planted, grains ground to flour, and livestock nurtured, just to name a few.

When injuries and disease struck, it was rare to find a physician who could arrive in a reasonable amount of time. Then too, there were still some antagonistic Indians about the region and wild animals roamed at will. Long trips were required to find a town where one could stock up on supplies. Ultimately, many people couldn't handle these types of stresses and strains and eventually returned to their original homes in the East.

One of the first residents to succumb to the rigors of the wilderness was named Mary, the wife of John Young. In 1797, John was surveying lands in the reserve when he discovered a charming spot along the Mahoning River which he thought would be perfect for his family to settle upon. Married just a few years before John left to survey the western reserve, Mary had been enjoying a simple life with her young son in a New York community recently established by her father, Hugh White. When approached by her husband about the prospect of moving west, she agreed to the adventure. Over the next six years in the wilderness, the Young family would grow as Mary bore two more children. It was a custom on the frontier to open your home to any traveller, offering them food and even a bed if needed. This practice, when added to the daily challenges and strains of raising a family in such an environment, finally overwhelmed Mary. Her eldest son states:

> In 1803 our mother, finding the trials of her country life there, with the latch-string always out and a table free to all, too great with her young family for her powers of endurance; our father, in deference to her earnest entreaties, closed up his business as best he could and returned with his family to Whitestown and to the home and farm which her father had provided and kept for them. [9]

After only a few years, for the sake of his wife and family, John Young left the settlement that bore his name, Youngstown, for the settlement that bore his father-in-laws name, Whitestown.

John Young was not the only city founder who left the reserve early. Moses Cleaveland, after heading up a team of surveyors from the Connecticut Land Company in 1796, returned to his hometown of Canterbury, Connecticut just months after laying out the town that would bear his name. He would never return to the Ohio region, let alone to his city at the mouth of the Cuyahoga River.

A surprising number of the travelers and settlers in the Western Reserve kept journals or diaries of their experiences. Even more remarkable is that most of these documents have survived to this day. They shine an uncensored light on all aspects of life in the wilderness of Ohio as it blossomed into statehood.

Take, for example, the account of a young investor from Connecticut who came to the reserve to assess first-hand the 41,000 acres that was left to him by his father, former Chief Justice of the United States, Oliver Ellsworth. The daily journal kept by Henry Ellsworth spells out the simple reasons why he chose not to settle on the Ohio lands, but instead return to the comforts of Connecticut. His decision was not unlike others who were among the first to consider such a move.

It was the summer of 1811 when Ellsworth and his brother-in-law, Ezechial Williams, travelled across the lands of the Reserve. Their trip lasted a few weeks. As was the custom on the frontier in the course of such a journey, they found food and a night's rest at the homes of generous families they met along the way. Most of these people, for good or not, proved to be quite intriguing.

It was just a few days into their journey when the two men found themselves somewhere between Warren and Aurora, Ohio. They stopped for the night at the home of a man who gave them a testimony of how a friendly Indian in the area saved his son's life. The story was that for some nineteen weeks his boy had suffered with a severely swollen leg and other distresses as a result of a rattlesnake bite. He had been seen by physicians from the area periodically, but none of them had provided a cure. The man then said that

> perceiving that his leg was much swollen and would soon be destroyed, he sent for an Indian Doctor who collected some indigo weed and placed the root on the place of the bite and wound up the leg with the leaves of the same plant. The consequence of the application was a removal of the swelling in 24 hours, and in a few days the young man was able to pursue his usual occupation. [10]

Today, while certain varieties of indigo provide the dye to color our jeans blue, wild strains of this plant are still sometimes used medicinally because they are known to stimulate the immune system to fight off infections.

Sketch of John Young - by Barnum Hitchcock prior to 1825 and found in book: *History of Youngstown and the Mahoning Valley, Ohio*, 1921.

Ellsworth and Williams soon moved on until they found rest at the dwelling of another stranger. The homeowner's name was Oliver Snow and they were in a small village called Mantua, Ohio. This stop would prove to be the most discomforting one of their entire trip. Ellsworth noted that the abode was quite small and then, with a bit of sarcasm, described their uncomfortable situation.

> It was well nigh 10 o'clock before we could get anything to eat, and when it was provided no mortal could taste of it who saw the sluttish [unclean] manner in which it was cooked. In all my life I never see [saw] so much dirt and filth in any human habitation as in this man's hut. The landlady said "she was out of eatables of present but would knock up a custard." And so she did and then hung up her bake pan to make something which she called cake merely because it had sweetning in it. Finally the banquet was ready and we set down and performed the usual exercises of eating and drinking, without any pleasure and with little refreshment. [11]

Things grew much worse as the two men planned to turn in for the evening. Ellsworth gives an almost whimsical account of their long night.

> Being a good deal fatigued we told the lady of the house we would retire as soon as our bed was prepared. She was not able to furnish us but one bed and that very narrow. It was of no use to complain since we could not better our condition. We retired and no sooner got into bed

Portrait of Henry Leavitt Ellsworth
found in the United States Department of Agriculture yearbook, 1902.

and rendered it seemingly impossible to lie another moment. Nor were the bedbugs far behind in the chace. I have heard travelers complain of fleas and bedbugs and I thought I knew full well the disagreeable sensation they produced, but before this I have had an inadequate conception. I had lain only 30 minutes before my whole body was covered with blotches. My uneasiness, I may add pain, forced me to get up and putt on my clothes, hoping that these would prevent their torture and afford me a few minutes respit. The experiment was useless. The vermin grew worse and worse every minute, and I jumped out bed determined not to lie there any longer. I went to the fire, and, after sitting by the dim light reflected from a few coals an hour or more, I put on my great coat and lay down on the hearth in the same small room where the whole family lodged, consisting of man and wife, a hired man, and 4 daughters. As for Mr. Williams, who had the foresight to sleep with his clothes on, he thought my torments the effect of imagination. I concluded the best way to convince him of the reality was to let him lie a few minutes longer.

I had not lain by the fire more than 20 minutes before I heard him groaning, one symptom (thought I) of at least imaginary distress. Wishing to give him a fair trial of his invulnerability I let him lie some time without my disturbance. At last I went in to hold consultation upon the subject. By this time he was full convinced that some carnivorous creature infested the bed, and he wished me to light a candle and discover the enemy.

It was 1/2 past 12. I stumbled across the room (and they [the people] lay so thick on the floor that I could scarcely take a single step without running against somebody) and lighted a candle by which the vermin were discovered. Mr. W. started up and we resolved to go out into the barn and "turn in" upon the straw.[12]

In the morning the pair were again on their way westward, praying that their next accommodations would be better than what this night had been at Oliver Snow's house. As it happened, just five years later, the Snow family built a larger home across the street from the one these gentlemen had visited that night. That new home, after many upgrades over the past two hundred years, is still in private use as of this writing. Further, Mr. Snow would have another prominent visitor some twenty years after Ellsworth and Williams had come by. It was Joseph Smith, who was beginning to establish his Church of Latter Day Saints in nearby Kirtland, Ohio. Apparently Smith made a great impression on Mr. Snow, as he was soon converted and many years later two of his children would go on to hold prestigious positions within the new church.

Another gentleman who travelled through the western reserve region and documented his findings was John Melish. He not only toured the south shores of Lake Erie, but also much of the new United States west of the Appalachians. As a geographer and entrepreneur, he recorded his physical observations as well as his personal insights and forecasts for the lands. His findings and opinions would be published in books which were designed to entice families in England to immigrate and settle in the wilderness of the new country.

In the course of Melish's tour in 1811, he visited several villages along and about the Cuyahoga River Valley (the vicinity of Cleveland). He found some to be healthy, like Hudson, Ohio, which he noted was

> an old and thriving settlement; the people have fine dairies, and make a great quantity of excellent cheese and butter for the supply of other parts of the country, and for the New Orleans market.[13]

On his way to Hudson, he discovered a few other charming towns with populations that appeared both happy, healthy, and flourishing in the midst of breathtaking scenery. But interspersed and just a few miles away from the river, circumstances were often very different. Settlers on a creek called Tinker's were not fairing as well. Melish spent the night with a family here and explained:

> The landlord was [away] from home, and the family were ill provided. They had no bread, nor wherewithal to make it; they had no beef, and no sugar; but they had some bad tea, bad potatoes, and pork such as I have seen in North Carolina. They made a sort of non-descript dish, by stewing a few slices of potatoes with the pork, and served it up, swimming in butter. [14]

Melish also expounded on the general travel conditions he encountered from the town of Canton until he arrived at Cleveland.

> Traveling had been far from agreeable; the roads were muddy, and often deep; and the country was one dull plain, without a single object to exhilarate the imagination, or cheer the spirits; and latterly the people looked pale and sickly. But I was buoyed up with the anticipation of the beauties of Lake Erie, to which I posted with all the alacrity of impatience. I noticed, as I went along, that the country on the banks of the Cayahoga river were improved; the road led by a high bank, from whence there was a fine view to the westward; the bottoms on the river were extensive and fertile; though I observed the seeds of disease in its slow, sluggish, winding course, choked up with a vast quantity of vegetable matter undergoing decomposition; and at every settlement I passed, the pale, sickly visages of the inhabitants confirmed the remark. At last Lake Erie appeared. with a beautiful, blue, placid surface, checkering through the trees...
>
> ...I pursued my way to the tavern. But, O! what a contrast was there! the people looked pale, sickly, and dejected. I learned that they had been afflicted with a very severe sickness this season. It was periodical, they said, and generally fever and ague; but this season it had been worse than usual, and accompanied with some very severe cases of bilious fever. I found that this had proved a complete check upon the improvement of Cleveland, which, though dignified with the name of a city, remained a paltry village containing a few houses only... [15]

Melish himself envisioned that Cleveland could become a significant harbor and suggested endeavors to make it so. He promoted the idea of cutting a clear channel across the sandbars and the decaying swamp that had clogged the Cuyahoga River and kept it from flowing swiftly into the lake. Such an action would certainly open the harbor to occupation and free the area of disease-breeding stagnation. A few years later Melish's suggestions were implemented, along with the building of the Ohio-Erie Canal. Both ventures sparked a more rapid growth of Cleveland, until it became the city it is today; the largest in the area first known as the Connecticut Reserve.

Yet another traveller through the region was Zerah Hawley. His tour began in the fall of 1820 and lasted about a year. He was considering moving to the reserve area from Connecticut as a few of his brothers already had. But the letters he regularly sent back to one of his siblings in Connecticut made it clear that aside from a few of the places he visited, he was not impressed with the western lands. Although his visit came a decade after the others we've heard about, his impression suggests that little had improved over the years. He noticed many of the same things others had, like the attractiveness of the lakes and rivers, but he also compared and contrasted the lifestyles of the many settlers. A religious man, he couldn't help but sermonize to his brother about the manners and behaviors of the people living on this frontier.

> One custom in particular I shall mention, which can not be denied or excused, which is very indelicate, and has a very demoralizing tendency. It is this. Sleeping promiscuously in one room. In almost every house, parents and children, brothers and sisters, brothers and sisters-in-law, strangers and neighbours, married and unmarried, all ages, sexes and conditions, lodge in the same room, without anything to screen them from the view of each other. This I affirm, is not the case of a solitary instance; but it is a general practice, not in the poorest families only, but among the richest and most respectable, as the inhabitants themselves will tell you. And this is done in some cases which I could particularize, where there is not the least shadow of necessity; even in houses where there are apartments sufficient to accommodate each sex separately, adult brothers and sisters, and young men and women, no ways related, sleep in the same bed chamber...
>
> ...Of the existence of this practice, I do not write from report; but from my own knowledge, and I do not exaggerate in the description.

> This may be considered as one great step towards a state of barbarism, and is a rapid approach to the custom of our savage bretheren of the wilderness, who sleep without ceremony around fires of their cabins. And as example has great influence, the rising generation is likely to have less delicacy on this subject than the present, so that there is a great prospect that the manners and morals of the people in this particular especially, will deteriorate rather than ameliorate. It is also probable that people of better manners, moving from other parts of the country, will partake, (in some degrees at least,) of general evil, and perhaps in time become as bad as others. [16]

Perhaps Hawley was finding reasons to not move away from his Connecticut home, because the picture of immorality he paints of the settlers is drawn with a broad brush. It doesn't seem reasonable to believe that all the people of the region had the numerous flaws of character as he implies. He finds that the citizenry on the whole fails to meet his standards of morality and diligence; rather than considering that these people may have needed deeper relationships because of their isolation and hardships. Here is an example of his further observations.

> People here possess a great share of curiosity, especially in one particular, i.e. a great desire to be acquainted with the business of others; so much so, that anything uttered in a manner supposed to be secret, will, some how or other, be known in a few days time to almost every individual, in a dozen towns, and you are wholly at a loss to determine in what manner the information could have been communicated. Frequently when a person has mounted his horse, and has set out on some business of his own, he is, without ceremony, bluntly asked, "where are you going?" If he inform the inquirer, he will add, "what are you going there for?" If he satisfies him in this particular, he proceeds to inquire, "what are you about to do?" &c. &c. appearing to feel as much or more interest in his affairs that he does himself, or than he does in his own.
>
> If one could be convinced, that this solicitude, concerning his affairs, originated in a desire to promote his interest, or from any motives of friendship, it would be gratifying enough; but when it is known that curiosity is the cause of all this apparent solicitude, it is extremely disgusting and odious, and highly reprehensible. [17]

He went on to criticize the work ethic and pace of life all about.

> All appear at ease, whether their business drives or not, and it is a notorious fact, that people (in many towns) are very deficient of industry. It

is not an uncommon circumstance, but happens to many, I believe, every year, that a part at least, of their pumpkins, corn, and potatoes, remain in the fields until the snow falls, and thus are lost, for want of a little more industry.

Instead of preparing wood for the summer, in winter, as is the custom in the Eastern States, men frequently meet in considerable numbers, and spend half the day in idle chit-chat, or invidious remarks concerning their neighbours, each of whom, if you were to believe the assertions of some one individual, is either a debauchee, a drunkard, a cheat, or a swindler. [18]

One more comment seems to cast criticism on the practice of sharing things with one's neighbor. Although he acknowledges that all the members of a community are willing to share anything they have, the implication is that he would rather live as he apparently had been, much more self-sufficient and making do with what one has.

The people here in general are very fond of borrowing, it is no matter what, is it any thing you have which they fancy they want, so that you must expect to lend all your crockery, should it chance to be wanted, and if broken, they will be very sorry, and in a short time, you will neither have any to lend or use yourself. They are, in their turn, very good to lend also, and are not in the habit of refusing you any thing you need, if they can spare it as well as not. [19]

Quite a different picture of life in New Connecticut is painted by Emily Nash. A surprisingly mature view of the conditions and practices of frontiersmen is seen through the eyes of this young girl. Emily Nash came to Troy Township, about thirty miles east of Cleveland, in the midst of the War of 1812. At a time when some families were leaving the area for fear that the British at Detroit and in Canada might sweep over the region, six-year-old Emily moved in with the rest of her family in the hopes of making a fresh start. In comparison with Zerah Hawley's opinions, Emily seems to capture the essence of how these people lived in community that fulfilled the biblical teachings to love thy neighbor.

It is clear from the childhood years of her journal, that each member of the family played several roles from the earliest of age. The sloth that Hawley had inferred to be rampant across the land, had not taken root in Emily's household. One example comes from the fact that when she was merely eight years old, Emily was found behind the plow, driving the oxen across her family's farm fields because her brother had suffered a disabling injury. Everyone picked up where the other left off and lended a hand. The industry and resolve to help others is evident in Emily's telling of how they first got settled into a cabin that they had built.

> Farther was a carpenter and he brought his chest of tools. He went to work splitting planks and hewed them smothe with his broad ax. So in a few days we had a smothe whitewood floor. Then he made some bedsteads out of poles. Then we had a nice place for our beds and began to take comfort. In a few days he took the sled boar[d]s and made a nice door then he made a table hewed out with his broad ax four feet long and three wide. Then we were so comfortable that Harvey Pratt wished to come and board with us. He had taken up some land near by us. He wanted to work for his board. We wanted his work to help build a chimney for our house before winter came upon us. In a short time we had a chimney and a good stone hearth and a winder. Then farther began to chink [fill in] between the logs. This he did evenings. [20]

Emily's journal also reveals the important role of women on the frontier, especially how their handiwork paid the bills. This excerpt further highlights their day-in and day-out work ethic that resulted in an abundance of product to trade for food. It also casts light on how that, "food" was often threatened by wolves as it grazed.

> Mother found all the work spinning and weaving that we could do. There were two famalies in Burton [a village nearby] Mr John Ford and Mr [Eleazar] Hickock that wanted lots of spinning and weaving. Their familys were boys and wore home made clothes would and pay us in any thing we wanted. Mr Ford let us have a cow and twelve sheep and wanted women work for pay. He let us have meat and lots of provision so we made out to live and not go hungrey. If it had not been for the womens work we could not get along, for provisions is very high it being in the time of the war...
>
> ... we have got the cow and sheep paid for all spinning and weaving. We had considerable provisions besides the cow and sheep. Came to get the count book and foot up the number of yards wove and the runs of yarn spun. It seems that it could be compared in number to the sands on the sea shore. The account filled a long book that I wish every body

could see. Now we have a span of horses, a yoke of oxen cows, and twelve sheep and nothing to feed them. Only what they can get in the woods. The sheep we have to yard nights to keep them from the wolves that are real thick. The cattle can fight their way but the wolves bit off one of the oxes tails, only left a piece about six inches long. He could not keep off the flies with such a short tail. [21]

Anyone ever pestered by flies can sympathize with that poor ox! But there were far worse things afoot in 1812 to be troubled by. A draft of frontier men was called to combat the potential threat of attack by British troops. The immediacy of the muster is seen in Emily's telling of it. Suddenly, the young girl had to face life without that sense of security only her father had provided.

One morning he [Emily's father] was out drawin the brush top over the ground when a man rode up to him with potmantoe [portmanteau] and valease [valise]. He took a paper out of his pocket. he tells farther he had come on urgent business and wished his attention that [General William] Hull had surrendered his armey. There has came a draft for every able bodyed man to go to Cleveland to defend and protect the west frountear from the threatning foe. He told him he had better go with him up to Burton. There was a big number going from there. Colonel [Jedediah] Baird had got a company ready to start. Perhaps he could git a chance to ride from Burton.

So farther comes in to the house and changes his clothes for better ones and starts off with Judge Vene Stone on foot. When he gets to Burton he finds a chance to join with Colonel Beards company. Mother is sick with the ague [fever]. Every man has gone to the defense except old Mr Eldred he was too old for the draft and Darby Lamoin [Lemoine] not old enough for the draft. It was a trying time for us all. Mother not able to leave her bed with ague. There had been some rain that day about sundown. The bullfrogs and a host of other frogs up about half a mile west of us set up such a howling that it fritened us dreadful bad. We thought it was the indians come to kill us with drums and tin pans and horse fiddles and every sort of thing that could make a bad noise... Darbey Lamoin came over to see how Mother was feeling to have farther gone and we left alone. John and I had made up our minds that we would go to Parkman. We hated to leave Mother to be killed so we began to cry. So Darbey says I will go up that way and see what it is. He gets up on a stump and lisyens a short time then comes to the house and says don't cry any more children I think it is not the indians but frogs...

> Farther came home feeling well. We were glad and over joyed. We feared we should never see him again. He only went to Cleveland. When they got there they found things were not so bad as they feared so the folks came home. [22]

Luckily, the family was quickly intact once again. Certainly other families across the reserve experienced the same relief as their fathers, husbands and brothers returned home.

One final circumstance that Emily shines light upon is the intricacies of childbearing during this period of time. Giving birth and caring for the newborn was not without its difficulties and dangers. In time, physicians grew in numbers as the population increased, so each year health care improved incrementally. But in these early years, if available at all, doctors were usually on the move through the expanse of the region tending to emergencies wherever they happened to arise. They would have to be tracked down by word of mouth and then would require a good deal of travel time from town to town to find them.

For want of a physician to assist in the birthing process, and for various other reasons, new mothers on the frontier had to rely on other women in their neighborhoods for help. After giving birth, some of the women had to ask other mothers to act as wet nurses. Because of the many responsibilities already on a woman's plate, the addition of a child required more time than the average mother had available. Just as teenage girls of today are often called upon to babysit, so it was in the pioneer home. Young girls would care for the children while mom worked at weaving, spinning, making clothes, cooking, and all other manner of chores about the household. Emily, when merely eleven years old, was called upon by her mother for a duty we might consider quite odd today. On a day in March of 1814 she explains with understandable embarrassment that

> Mr [Elijah] Ford came to farthers this morning real earley and told me there was a girl babey to his house and wanted me to go over there and see her. So I put on my bonet and went home with him. When I got there the house was full of folks. They showed me the girl babey. I thought it was not a pretty babey and was going home. Mother says I must not go till I had drained Mrs [Ester] Fords breasts. I told her I did not want too before the folks. She told me I must and should. Mrs Ford told me she would give me some callicos [dresses] some time. Then I drained her breasts. I wished I had staid at home with farther and the girls. [23]

No doubt! Young girls across the country, let alone on the reserve, had to be absolutely exuberant when Orwell Needham was awarded a patent for the first mechanical breast pump in 1854.

As one might expect, death during or after childbirth was all too common; and then for either the child or the mother. Emily would have to bear the grief of losing both a brother and a sister just a few years apart. Both were barely toddlers. In 1814, a child who had serious deformities was born. Emily explains:

> The doctor says the cause of its being so feeble is Mothers having the ague so long and her working so hard before it was born. It has fits. We fear it cannot live long. We have to tend it on a pillow for there is no back bone — onley half away down to the hips. We will try to take good care of it while it lives. It is a hansom child. It is distressing to see the little thing have a fit. [24]

The baby passed away after only five weeks. Three years later, Mrs. Nash bore twin girls. They were named Philenia and Philansia. Emily was frequently called upon to care for them and claimed they were a handful. None-the-less they were loved by the entire family until one day when the inexplicable happened. Emily noted that

> Philansia went out of doors this morning to play as usual after breakfast. When she had ben out about half an hour she came in crying with the cold. Mother takes her up in her lap. Her hands were cold, her finger nails purple, she appeared real sick. She began to doctor her for worms. She thought the worms was the trouble. She grew worse and wors. Farther went to Parkman [a nearby town] after Doctor Scott in haste but she grew worse all the time. befor nin oclock she was dead. The doctor did not know what ailed her. She was taken sick at nine in the morning and died at nine in the evening. [25]

On a lighter note, Emily recorded the day that her brother and the neighbor girl, both likely pre-teens at the time, accidentally discovered the devil's brew.

> Now farther and Mr [Elijah] Ford ar thinkin about trying to build each of them a framed house. They are going to try to make their own brick for chimneys. They are making a brick kiln on Fords land. They have got a man to mould the brick and work is going on finely. The[y] have a jug of Whiskey there to drink now and then. Brother Alden and Lovina Ford are there every day to see their farthers work and to play. They see the men go to the jug and drink now and then so they think

they can go there and drink any time. They go and drink as though it was water. They call it good drink and go often and drink. After they had drank several times the[y] found they could not walk without falling down. They tried to walk but they went this way and that way staggering over the brick and made tiptoe tracks till they fell down dead drunk. Their farthers carryed [them] home in their arms. they appeared like dead children. After the brick was burned the children see them tracks in the brick. They thought they were bairs tracks till their farthers told them all about their drunk drinking Whiskey for warter. They had no remember of the thing. I think they will let the jug alone… [26]

As all these men and women from the New England states began settling onto the Connecticut Reserve, the missionaries and ministers of various denominations were not far behind. They were received with mixed reactions by the frontiersmen. Most of the population was indeed already deeply rooted in their Christian faith, no matter the denomination, and looked forward to regular Sunday sermons of encouragement. But some had fled the states, at least in part, to escape the preacher as well as their past.

Before the Western Reserve had opened up for settlement, there were already ministers traveling across the Northwest Territory to spread the word of God. The Methodists referred to theirs as circuit riders. These preachers would complete a prescribed course, visiting towns and villages along the way. This travel could take a few weeks or even months, when the preacher would regroup and circle back again. This practice of systematically moving about a region was not limited to the Methodists. Baptists, Congregationalists, and Presbyterians were the most predominant denominations to minister in this manner, but many others did so as well. In this way the first pioneers had their spiritual needs addressed. Only when a town grew to a substantial size was it able to support a resident preacher of its own.

The determination of these mobile men of God was not to be questioned. Their dedication is validated by a common expression of the day. Whenever ominous weather was making its approach, one would usually note that, "There's no one out today, but crows and Methodist preachers."[27] Though the comment speaks to a particular denomination, it exemplifies the dedication of all touring ministers of that day.

One of the first men to serve the spiritual needs of the settlers in the Western Reserve was Joseph Badger. As a member of the Missionary Society of Connecticut, Badger accepted an appointment to this region late in 1800. He was a Congregationalist and spent thirteen months of his first tour preaching in numerous locations. Some visits were to individuals who were isolated from any human contact, while other trips were made to communities that had grown to a dozen families or more. In 1801, Badger began his second loop of his circuit, but this time he found many of the residents were having second thoughts about making a life in the wilderness.

> I now revisited all the settlements in this part of the Reserve and endeavored to encourage the people with hopes of a brighter day. Their hard beginning would soon pass away. The soil was good, and industry would soon produce plenty. Found here and there professing Christians mourning the loss of their former privileges, and wondering why they had come to this wilderness, where there was no house of worship nor gospel ordinances. I observed to them that they had been moved here by the hand of God, to plant the church in this wilderness. It is a land capable of an extensive and dense population; and in a few years churches will be erected and ministers breaking the bread of life in them. [28]

The schedule Badger followed was brisk and dangerous. An edited version of just a few weeks from his diary gives one an idea of the pace of his travels and the size of the communities he visited.

> In the month of June I visited Mesopotamia and Windsor; found seven families in the former and three in the latter place... I returned to Warren, and thence pursued a course through Nelson (planted with one family,) and reached Mantua about dark. Here were two or three families and several young men, opening for themselves places for habitation. I made an appointment to preach here on the Sabbath, and went onto Aurora. Returned on Sabbath morning with Esquire Sheldon's family, and preached to a small assembly in Mantua.
>
> Invitation had been given to the few scattering inhabitants to assemble at the cabin of Esquire Hudson in the town of Hudson, and celebrate the fourth of July... Preached here the next Sabbath; visited all the families and preached again the Sabbath following.
>
> On Monday I returned to Aurora, from which I took the only road from south to the lake; got very wet in a thunder shower. Arrived in Newburg before dark. In this place were five families. Preached here on the Sabbath:

on Monday visited Cleveland, in which were only two families. Here I fell in company with Judge Kirtland. We rode from here to Painesville; found on the way, in Euclid, one family; in Chagrin one; in Mentor four, and in Painesville two families. Next day rode to Burton, preached on the Sabbath, and visited the families in this place. From this I found my way to Austinburg. In this place were ten families, and about the same number in Harpersfield. Visited all the families in these settlements, and preached to them three Sabbaths. Thus were visited and the gospel preached to all the families on the Reserve.[29]

In mid-August, 1801, Badger began his trip home to his wife and six children living in Massachusetts. Among other things, his journal dated September 6 points out that good relationships had existed between the Americans and the Indians living in the eastern end of the reserve.

Swam our horses by a canoe across the Cuyahoga, and took the Indian path up the lake; came to Rocky river, the banks of which were very high, being almost perpendicular rock on the west side, for some distance. At the north termination of the high rock we found a passage up the bank, but very steep. While cutting the brush to open a way for our horses, we were saluted with the song of a large yellow rattlesnake: removed it out of our way, ascended the bank, and pursued our course along a range of high rock, supposed to be about fifty feet. The wind blowing fresh nearly on shore, would often throw the spray over us. Arrived at Black River and encamped.

7th, — In the morning we found a bark canoe, with which we passed the river, and swam our horses. We pursued our Indian path to Huron river, where we arrived about three o'clock in the afternoon. Proposed to tarry with Delawares and talk with them on the Sabbath. We were led by a young man across the Huron, where the water was midside to our horses, and into a large corn-field to an Indian cabin: here we tied up our horses and fed them corn fodder. The woman of the cabin presented us with a knot bowl of string beans boiled in fresh water, and buttered with bear's oil. I told the woman we should want some of her corn bread when we went on our journey.

Sabbath, we recrossed the Huron, rode up to the village, held our talk with the Indians, who heard us attentively, and got back before dark. They treated us kindly, and with the best they had.

9th, Monday, — We started as early as we could see to follow our path, our hostess having furnished us with a bread cake baked in the embers, and well filled with beans, like plum cake. Soon after we started it began

Engraving of Reverend Joseph Badger by W.T. Norman in the book: *A Memoir of Rev. Joseph Badger*, 1851.

to rain moderately. When we came to the great openings, we saw some miles before us a smoke; we concluded to ride to that before we took our breakfast. There we found an Indian man and his wife, sitting by their fire. We took out our scanty supply; and after asking a blessing began to eat. The man, noticing our small store, stepped to a basket, and handed me part of a loaf of good Indian bread; the woman, almost the same instant, took out of another basket a piece of honeycomb well filled. We made a good breakfast, returned most of the bread, thanked our friends, and went on our way. [30]

Badger continued on his journey home, finally arriving there on New Year's Day, 1802. After just a few days of recuperation, he reported to his religious superiors in a nearby town. They were very pleased with efforts and proposed that he permanently move to the reserve with his entire family. He agreed to the proposition and would receive a modest salary for doing so. Its not clear how his wife and children felt about the situation, but Badger's journal seems to infer that they all had nervous concerns.

The subject of removal to a distance of six hundred miles, began now to fill our minds with very serious reflections. We could carry no furniture excepting a few light articles such as brass utensils for cooking, clothes and bedding, with a small supply of table furniture. Our family of six children must now be taken from school, to grow up in the woods without any advantage of even a common school, for years; and in circumstances extremely difficult to make them or ourselves comfortable with clothing. But we concluded to submit our cause to Him who feeds the ravens and clothes the lilies of the field.[31]

Obviously, Badger's faith was authentic and he like others of his calling spent most of his life traveling and preaching to the people of the reserve. He would need a deep reliance on the Lord more often than not. One instance of such dependence came on a day when he was traveling alone through the woods with darkness falling fast.

[I] rode up the stream some distance, to find a tree fallen across, on which I might pass with safety. Having found one reaching from bank to bank, I stripped my horse, looked out the most favorable spot for his getting through, tied up his bridle, and drove him in. As he leaped from the bank he plunged all over in the water; but driving down with the current, he soon found a place to get out. I then took my portmanteau and crossed over; returned an took my saddle. Having caught my horse, I proceeded on amid showers of rain. Had by this time become drenched with water, but continued my course, until nearly dark I came to the only ford on Grand River within ten miles; passed over, intending to encamp on the upland bank where some trees were broken down. Rode up to the place and started some animal on the opposite side. I rode a little around to see what company I had fallen into, and was met by a large bear.

Supposing the brute would run, as several had done with which I had met before, I slapped my hands and halloed at him. But instead of running, he raised his hair on end, and snapped his teeth violently. As I had no weapon for defense, I thought best to leave the ground, turned to the left, and walked my horse partly by him, when the brute stepped directly on behind and within a few paces. By this time it had become so dark I could see nothing around, not even my hand holding the bridle, and the bear was snapping and approaching nearer. I had in my hand a large heavy horse-shoe, took aim by his noise, and threw the shoe, but effected no alarm of the enemy. To ride away was impossible, in a pathless wood, thick with brush and old fallen timber. I concluded to resort to a tree, if I could find one.

I reined my horse first to the right, and then to the left, at which instant some sloping limbs brushed my hat. On feeling them, I found them to be long, pliable, beech limbs. I reined my horse again, and he came with his shoulder close to the tree. I tied the bridle to the limbs, raised myself on the saddle, and by aid of the small limbs began to climb. I soon got hold of a limb large enough to bear me, and at this instant the evil beast came to the tree with a violent snuffing and snapping. I thought, by the action, he had begun to climb. I fixed my standing on the limb, took out a sharp knife, the only weapon I had, and prepared for battle. But I soon heard him snuffing near the horse's nose as he was chanking the boughs and leaves within his reach. I then ascended about forty feet, as near the top of the tree as I thought was safe; found a convenient place to sit on a limb, and tied myself with a large bandanna to the tree, so as not to fall if I fell into a drowse.

The bear continued smelling at the horse until he passed round him to the opposite side of the tree, and all was still but the chanking of the horse. By the roaring of the thunder it appeared a heavy gust was approaching. It soon began to rain powerfully, with heavy peals of thunder with wind. At this time the horse shook himself, which started the bear to a quick rush a few rods, at which point he stopped and snapped his teeth violently, and there continued, until a few minutes before light he went off. My horse standing at the tree without moving a foot from the place I left him, and in no way frightened by the approach and management of the bear, seemed peculiarly Providential [32]

And so we get a glimpse of the life of an itinerant preacher as he spread the truths of the bible to any of the earliest pioneers and Indians of the reserve who would listen. Badger lived a full life of eighty-nine years ministering all his days. In a letter to his family dated 1843, just a couple years before he passed away, he penned these words of advice that are perhaps more poignant at the time of this writing than they may have been in his day.

Let me say a few words to my dear grandchildren. If you intend to be respectable, and useful in the circle of society in which you may spend your future years, if God should prolong your days, avoid wasting your time, in unprofitable scenes of amusement. Carnal pleasures can not be innocent, they lead to death. Make no use of novels in your reading, they generally contain moral poison. Truth in books, as they relate to historical facts, or religious instruction, are infinately preferable to novel trash, or chaff in the whirlwind. Make yourselves well versed in geography, and the history of your country, and of the world, so far as you can. Cultivate a benevolent spirit, do a little to aid in sending the gospel, and school instruction to the heathen, at home and in foreign lands... but above all, read your Bibles every day with prayer; and remember, and keep the Sabbath day holy to the Lord. [33]

Whether it was a traveling missionary, a son evaluating his inheritance, a young girl growing through adolescence, or a man surveying a wilderness; the handful of accounts these souls have left to posterity present us with a glimpse of what life was like in New Connecticut. It seems all of them had a deep appreciation for the natural beauty of the countryside with its great lake and flowing rivers. But it was obviously a very arduous territory in which to begin a new life. Many understandably couldn't withstand it. The fortitude of these earliest inhabitants deserves to be recognized and appreciated. In a short time, the region was absorbed into the state of Ohio and life became a little less burdensome. However, those original names, the Western Reserve and the Firelands, echo to this day in institutions like Case Western Reserve University and the Firelands campus of Bowling Green State University, as reminders of those first pioneers. ♦

ANECDOTE.

A beggar in England was picking a few of his old acquaintances off his clothes when a nobleman passing by accosted him. You dirty rascal what are you about? "nothing sir" replied the beggar but guillotining a few aristocrats. "Aristocrats! you seditious scoundral how dare you call such vermin aristocrats?" "I cannot find a better name for them, may it please your honour, they always live on the poor."

In the Centinel of the North-Western Territory, July 12, 1794 [34]

XIV.
THE MUD DUCK.

What a Coot! It looks like a duck as it forages in the marshlands of today's northwest corner of Ohio; however the American Coot is actually a bird. It can fly, but usually stays low to the ground for short distances. When it swims it most resembles a duck, but below the surface its long, lobed toes instead of webbed feet, paddle it along. The lobes act as flaps of sorts that help the bird to propel itself through the water as well as giving it extra support as it walks on muddy grounds. The coot often prances through mucky waters hunting for insects and edible plants.

This particular bird was known to the Indians of the Northwest Territory as the "Little Rail" or the French title "Poule D'eau" which translates literally to "hen of the water." They were found in large numbers in the Great Black Swamp of the early 1800s and are still populating the southern shores of Lake Erie today. In her book, *Wau-Bun*, Juliette Kinzie relates the lore of Native Americans surrounding this interesting creature.

> The Indians have the genius of Aesop for depicting animal life and character, and there is among them a fable or legend illustrative of every peculiarity in the personal appearance, habits, or dispositions of each variety of the animal creation.
>
> The back of the little rail is very concave, or hollow. The Indians tell us that it became so in the following manner:
>
> There is supposed, by most of the Northwestern tribes, to exist an invisible being, corresponding to the "Genie" of Oriental story. Without being exactly the father of evil, Nan-nee-bo-zho is a spirit whose office it is to punish what is amiss. He is represented, too, as constantly occupied in

entrapping and making examples of all the animals that come in his way.

One pleasant evening, as he walked along the banks of a lake, he saw a flock of ducks, sailing and enjoying themselves on the blue waters. He called to them: "Ho! come with me into my lodge, and I will teach you to dance!" Some of the ducks said among themselves, "It is Nan-nee-bo-zho; let us not go." Others were of a contrary opinion, and, his words being fair, and his voice insinuating, a few turned their faces towards the land – all the rest soon followed, and, with many pleasant quackings, trooped after him, and entered his lodge.

When there, he first took an Indian sack, with a wide mouth, which he tied by the strings around his neck, so that it would hang over his shoulders, leaving the mouth unclosed. Then, placing himself in the centre of the lodge, he ranged the ducks in a circle around him.

"Now," said he, "you must all shut your eyes tight; whoever opens his eyes at all, something dreadful will happen to him. I will take my Indian flute and play upon it, and you will, at the word I shall give, open your eyes, and commence dancing, as you see me do."

The ducks obeyed, shutting their eyes tight, and keeping time to the music by stepping from one foot to the other, all impatient for the dancing to begin.

Presently a sound was heard like a smothered "quack," but the ducks did not dare to open their eyes.

Again, and again, the sound of the flute would be interrupted, and a gurgling cry of "qu-a-a-ck" be heard. There was one little duck, much smaller than the rest, who, at this juncture, could not resist the temptation to open one eye, cautiously. She saw Nan-nee-bo-zho, as he played his flute, holding it with one hand, stoop a little at intervals and seize the duck nearest him, which he throttled and stuffed into the bag on his shoulders. So, edging a little out of the circle, and getting nearer the door, which had been left partly open, to admit the light, she cried out,–

"Open your eyes–Nan-nee-bo-zho is choking you all and putting you into his bag!"

With that she flew, but Nan-nee-bo-zho pounced upon her. His hand grasped her back, yet, with desperate force, she released herself and gained the open air. Her companions flew, quacking and screaming, after her. Some escaped, and some fell victims to the sprite.

The little duck had saved her life, but she had lost her beauty. She ever after retained the attitude she had been forced into in her moment of danger – her back pressed down in the centre, and her head and neck unnaturally stretched forward into the air.[1]

THE MUD DUCK

The American Coot – also known as the Mud Hen.

The tale is a sad one that attempts to explain the somewhat awkward appearance of a special bird that today goes by many names. Depending on which subtle differences it holds, it can be considered a member of the coot, rail, or gallinules families. But, because it lingers in the muddy bogs along bodies of water, and is often spotted covered in the mud that it wades through, it is commonly referred to as a "mud hen." That nickname has ended up being applied to several pieces of Americana.

One of these iconic "Mud Hens" is the F-15E Strike Eagle fighter jet used by the United States Air Force since 1988. Similar to the F-15 of a decade earlier, the difference in the "E" model is that it flies lower and has air-to-ground superiority as well as air-to-air striking prowess. Its two large fuel tanks give it a bulge on its underside that somewhat inhibits high altitude flights. This large underbelly, painted a dark gray, matches the characteristics of the real mud hen who also flies low and has a dark, bottom-heavy under-carriage usually covered in mud.

There is also a special train locomotive that debuted in America at the turn of the twentieth century. It was run by the Denver & Rio Grande Line and after a few decades of upgrades became known as the K-27 class engine. Built in 1903, this workhorse was an imposing black machine designed to pull heavier loads than previously possible through mountain inclines and sharp curves. The tales of how this locomotive came to be nicknamed the "mud hen" vary a bit. One story is based on the fact that this bold, black engine tended to wobble as it moved along. This was said to resemble the waddle of a duck, which they mistakenly thought the mud hen was at the time. Another explanation says that the name came about because the locomotive frequently became covered in mud, much like the hen, especially if it derailed; which was far too frequent.

Perhaps the most recognized attribution of the mud hen name is to the Triple A, minor league baseball team from Toledo, Ohio. Baseball was being played as early as 1883 in the region, but in 1896, the Toledo "Swamp Angels" team began playing on a field just offshore from the bay at the mouth of the Maumee River. This was just down river from the site of the historic 1794 Battle of Fallen Timbers and the sieges on Fort Meigs in 1813. The field itself was less than ideal. With poor drainage it would often remain muddy for long periods after rains. That was only natural as it was within sight of the marshland along the bay where the American Coot flourished. As the fans watched the players get covered in mud like the nearby hens, they warm-heartedly started calling the boys the "mud hens." The name stuck and when the second half of the '96 season began the name was made official.

Should you spot an old coot, the feathered variety, wandering through the muck along a waterway, remember that it is not an oddity by design, it may be the result of an awful experience with an ornery spirit of ancient Indian legend. ♦

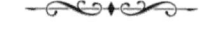

ANECDOTE.

A few days ago high words happening between two lawyers of some eminence, concerning superiority of abilities in the profession, one of them on account of the diminutive size of his antagonist, jeeringly told him, if he did not cease his prating [babbling] he would put him in his pocket; upon which the little gentleman smartly replied, that if he did, he would have more law in his pocket, than he ever had in his head.

In the Centinel of the North-Western Territory, December 19, 1795 [2]

XV.
MY HUSBAND WENT TO WAR.

A collective sigh of relief could be heard across North America and Great Britain the day the American Revolution ended in 1783. The bloodshed had stopped. The men were coming home. This meant life was going back to normal. Husbands were reunited with their wives and fathers were once again providing for their children. But it was not to last. Those rebellious colonists were now Americans and the new lands they had just gained in the West seemed to be imploring them to venture over the mountains and resettle upon them. And that's just what they did. It was this course of action that in just a few short years would disrupt the family unit once again.

As it happened, the arrival of Americans into what became the Northwest Territory drew the attention and animosity of the Native Americans. After all, this land had been the Indians' for centuries, and now without any negotiations, these strangers were staking claims to it. Conflicts were inevitable. At first the Indians tried to dissuade the intruders by having a handful of warriors assault individual family homesteads. The frequency of these attacks increased in proportion to the number of settlers who put down roots. Soon, bolder attacks in greater numbers were organized. Eventually, Indians stormed American fortresses.

In just seven short years, the aggressions escalated to all out military battles once again. It was 1790 when Washington's Indian Wars began in the territories of Indiana and Ohio. This meant that men from all parties involved were being called to defend their respective peoples. Though it may have appeared to be a fight between the Americans and the Indians, the British were very much involved as well.

England had just ceded the frontier lands to the Americans and as a result were supposed to have vacated the region, but they were still hanging around. Why? They had a vested financial interest in trading with the Indians. This business had been in place for decades and they were nowhere near ready to have it taken over by the Americans, even if the Treaty of Paris said they were supposed to abandon all such posts. One means to securing this lucrative market for the British was for them to lend aid to their customers. This took the form of arms and ammunition to be used against the American influx. On many levels, this was one of those win/win situations. The Indians and the British had a common enemy, the Americans. The Indians wanted the Americans off of their lands and the British wanted them away from their business dealings. What better way to build trust between the two traders than for the British to ally themselves with their customers and provide them with arms and ammunition to stave off their common foe?

To the Americans of the 1790s, the British tried to present an illusion of non-involvement by keeping their own soldiers from partaking directly in the fighting; however it was a shallow disguise. Many of the guns and bullets fired by the Indians at the Americans in these conflicts were made in England. Not too many years later, in 1812, the British abandoned their "hands-off" charade and made a formal alliance with a confederation of Indian tribes which was led by Tecumseh. This second Revolution, as some refer to it, finally ended in 1815 and its conclusion marked the end of the heaviest fighting in the Northwest Territory. However, through those early decades of fighting, few note the status of the women who had to cope with husbands being absent, returning with serious injuries, or perhaps not coming home at all.

Women from all three of the battling parties faced the same emotional turmoil. Love doesn't change from culture to culture. The situation of the Indian woman was slightly different from that of a British or American wife, but only from a geographical standpoint. The conflict had come to the Indians. They were living on the land in question when the outsiders intruded. That fact played into the style of battle the male warriors would employ and the effect the fighting would have on the rest of the family. Especially early on, they did not have to travel far to engage their enemy. Often, they could launch a small raid, or even a more substantive attack, and be back at their home villages in a matter of a few days or even the very same night.

While the warriors were off fighting in this manner, the women remained in the village and took care of the routine family matters, albeit never escaping worry for their loved ones. Only if the battles were expected to be a protracted affair, and at a great distance from their villages, would some Indian women pack up their children and goods and follow their men into such a dangerous situation. This scenario played out during the War of 1812.

At this time select warriors from numerous tribes had joined together in an alliance led by Tecumseh. In turn this coalition allied with the British military. None of the combatants in the War of 1812 ever really knew where the next engagement would occur. Never-the-less, base camps of operation were established. A major post of the British who were dealing with the conflicts in the Northwest Territory was setup along the northern shores of Lake Erie in Canada. Known as Fort Malden, and located just south of Sandwich (Windsor, Ontario), it was the site from which the British General Henry Proctor and Tecumseh would set out to do battle wherever it became necessary. Because this new war was expected to be a long-term endeavor, the wives of many of the warriors involved had packed up and re-established makeshift villages in outlying areas around the fortress. The numbers of Indians and their families encamped here would vary over time, as new warriors would arrive and others return to their original villages; but at the beginning of the war well over a thousand warriors along with their wives and children came to Canada.

Through 1812 and 1813 several battles would be fought within one hundred miles of Fort Malden. The Indian women and children would remain in the villages near the fort while the men went off to fight. However, several setbacks were suffered by the British and Indians over the course of the first year. Oliver Perry's Lake Erie victory over the British fleet in September of 1813 turned out to be the most decisive blow. Because of it, a full retreat from Fort Malden was called for by Proctor. It had become obvious that U.S.

General Harrison was coming after them with a superior number of American troops. The fort was torched and everyone; the British troops, the Indian warriors, and their respective wives and families, went into a full retreat along the Thames River in Upper Canada. They were heading eastward to Lake Ontario in hope of reinforcements. At a distance of a mile or two, the Indian wives trailed the troops. On October 5, Harrison caught up with the fleeing army and the Battle of the Thames ensued. Tecumseh was killed that day and the Indian confederation dissipated. The Indian wives and children returned with the survivors to their home villages.

The options of involvement were a little different for the wives of British and American soldiers. One thing to note is that some women were living close to the action on the frontier while others were quite distant. American soldiers came from homes in the states and in the Northwest Territory. British troops were recruited from the former colonies, Canada, and England itself. Wives of men serving in both forces had a choice of remaining at their homes or joining the troops as camp followers.

Surprisingly, many of the British wives living in England did come to North America. If they hadn't they may not have seen their husbands for three or more years. The adjustment such a move required varied from person to person. Officer's wives had the best of it, usually settling into a home near a fortress with their husbands. Many of the trappings of their English homes were available in such accommodations, making their transition comfortable. The wive's of the enlisted men had to make a more difficult adjustment, usually taking up a space in the men's barracks or the fort itself.

Wives and family members of officers were known to be present in the British camp at the Battle of the Thames. In fact, General Proctor was heavily criticized for abandoning his troops for a period of time during their retreat from Fort Malden. He left to make proper arrangements for his wife and others to be safely positioned away from any potential fighting.

In an account from the northern regions of Ohio, we can gain some insights of what it was like for a wife to cope with life while her husband was off to war in 1812. Little is known about her life before and after, but for more than two months in 1812, while living in the

Women depicted doing the laundry on the frontier.
Painting titled: *La Lavandaja*, by Nicolo Cavalli 1760-70.

newly settled township of Deerfield, Sarah Day kept a diary of her daily activities and emotions. Her husband, Alva, had volunteered for the Ohio militia just as soon as he learned that the war was officially declared. This left Sarah home alone to take care of their four children and to wonder daily if Alva would ever return. The wording and grammar she used in her journaling is a bit disjointed at times, but one can readily feel her emotions and understand how the community was heavily involved in her life.

It was on July 1 that Sarah saw her husband off.

> The day of the departure of my companion, designing to march with his volunteers to Sandusky, I parted with him at the center, returned with a heart laden with sorrow... [1]

Several friends and neighbors had accompanied her to say farewell to Alva. They came,

> they said, to cheer my spirits, but in vain, for I neither enjoyed their company with any degree of satisfaction, nor they mine. Mrs. [Ruth] Tibbals wished me to assist her in altering a straw bonnet; my assistance being but small to her I so regretted; thronged with company I retired to bed with a heavy heart. I slept but little. [2]

Who hasn't suffered through tough situations that were muddled by well-meaning friends or relatives? Each day the neighbor ladies engaged Sarah in activities that were both necessary and therapeutic. They mended garments, washed clothes, spun wool, and performed any number of household chores together, hoping to lessen Sarah's loneliness; but some days she just wanted to be alone. She noted that she found some additional comfort from religious services held on the Sabbaths.

Five days after he had left, the first word arrived from Alva:

> [I] received a letter from my absent companion by Mun [Day]; states that he is in good spirits; marched this day from Ravenna for Sandusky. When I opened the letter my heart ached for him; I thought to myself, wo be to you; I am in great doubts whether you will ever return, but said nothing; at night with a mind agitated with grief and in meditation did I raise my heart to my God for his safety. [3]

Only a week later, she confides how she is struggling through her despondency over Alva's absence and how it was compounded by the hearsay that her neighbors were sharing.

> This day's labor is washing and sewing on straw bonnet; my house is thronged with company and my spirits so sad that I cannot make myself sociable with them with using my best endeavors. My ear has just now been saluted with the rumor that is passing — our volunteers had sailed from Cleveland and that their stores of provisions had been taken by the Indians, — a very unlikely story and an old woman's whim at the story is; the provision part I did not credit. [4]

That evening several of the men of the town came to her home with more rumors suggesting that even more men were being drafted into service and that many American ships had been lost to the British on Lake Erie. She dismissed the stories as foolishness until real verification was at hand. In the morning another letter arrived from Alva reporting some details of his continued march. Sarah read the letter aloud to a group of her neighbors who had gathered at her house to hear the words of her husband.

The rumors of additional enlistments into the military proved to be true. On the night of July 17, Sarah relays that she

> was visited by the young people, Joseph Hartzel with his flute. Joseph Hartzel and Merrick Ely told me that they came to see me for the last

time as they were drafted to go into the army. What a pity thought I, as they were under age, but apparently both in good spirits while sorrow lay on their brow.[5]

More and more of the community was now coping with loved ones being sent away to fight. The women left behind continued to try to comfort each other by sharing meals and working together on spinning, sewing and weaving projects, all of which were needed to be bartered for food and other family necessities. One more week would go by before another note arrived from Alva.

> I received a letter from my companion dated July 17th; with joy unspeakable I read the acceptable letter. By this letter I have a faint hope he will return at August court. The idea I harbor of such a thing to take place is so faint that I guess I may faint away upon it or not, which I please, for I shall not see him; oh, the distance and length of time which separates us, but be patient old head, when the wars are over I may see him again.[6]

Sarah traveled to her father's house to read him these latest two letters from Alva, as well as a copy of General Hull's proclamation given to her by a relative. This decree was Hull's proud opening statement as he entered into Upper Canada on the opposite side of Lake Erie. "The army under my command has invaded your country and the standard of the United States waves on the territory of Canada," Hull wrote. He continued to reassure the neutral residents of that region, "I come to find enemies not to make them, I come to protect not to injure you." Unfortunately in just a matter of weeks Hull would fall from this self-made perch of benevolence when he surrendered Fort Detroit to the British.

Things remained quiet and routine with Sarah for a couple weeks, but then rumors stirred again. This time word came that Fort Malden was taken from the British by General Hull. It would only take until the next day's mail to have this notion proven wrong. On August 12, Sarah writes:

> This day to my great disappointment received no letter [from Alva], the mail brings fresh news from the army; states that Malden is not taken and the Detroit mail is stopped by the British, and the Detroit mail was guarded with two hundred men; before they reached Sandusky they were molested by the British; one man's horse was shot

from under him; he took his heels and ran without hurt or injury and told the news; what would be the consequence he did not know, and that five hundred British had come in on American ground; [they] lay between Detroit and Sandusky, all which I did not credit but very little. Peter Mason came at evening; I asked him what he thought of the news; his answer was he did not believe that there were so many British landed, no more than he believed there were so many Hells, neither did he believe the mail was guarded with so many men, so it remains for a further hearing.[7]

The historic truth is that Fort Malden most likely could have been taken by General Hull, but he backed away from the attempt at the last minute. The mail from Detroit was stopped and controlled by the British, but it was likely done by far less than the two hundred troops rumored. And the British would make landfall on American soil in the Lake Erie region noted, but not until May of the next year when they attacked Fort Meigs in today's Perrysburg, Ohio.

Another week would go by before Sarah would face more distress. Word of mouth news came from the mail carrier that Alva was quite ill and recuperating somewhere along the Maumee River. No letter arrived from Alva himself to verify the postman's report, and so Sarah could do nothing but wait and pray for good news. As it happened, Alva soon returned intact to Sarah. He would go on in later years to become an associate judge in the state of Ohio.

The journal of Sarah Day is short and somewhat unspectacular, but it chronicles the mental turmoil suffered by a wife who was left alone to tend to her family while her husband was away and in persistent danger. It's striking honesty shows how little human nature has changed over two hundred years. Neighbors and friends still rally, as they did for Sarah, to console each other in stressful times, rumors still fuel many of our discussions, and an anxious soul still needs stretches of solitude to function properly.

While Sarah Day's story spotlights the life of a wife and mother who chose to remain in her home, another account from the War of 1812 details the circumstances of an American wife, who in union with other wives, followed alongside the troops.

Lydia had been married only four years to her longtime friend, Josiah Bacon, when he was commissioned as a lieutenant in the army. It was 1811, and rumors of another all out war with the British and Indians were flying about. Josiah was ordered to report with his company to Pittsburgh. Eventually, he would be ordered farther west to Vincennes in the Indiana Territory where trouble was brewing between the Americans and an ever-growing village of Indians along the Tippecanoe River. Lydia Bacon was not willing to remain at their Boston harbor home alone. She decided that she would travel with her husband into a dangerous and uncertain situation.

Through her journal, Lydia reveals what life was like among the camp followers. Her journey began at Fort Independence in Boston where her husband had been previously stationed. The troops and civilians, including Lydia's teenage sister boarded a ship which would take them to the first stop in their travels, Philadelphia. Arriving in mid-May, the Bacons soon visited relatives with whom the younger sister would remain. Additional companies of Josiah's regiment arrived at the encampment just outside of Philadelphia over the next few weeks. Lydia befriended the wife of one of the newly arrived officers. With other wives, they would proceed by land to Pittsburgh riding behind the troops in stage coaches.

There were plenty of occasions to wonder at the beauty of the countryside along the way. As they approached the foothills of the Allegheny Mountains, Lydia noted the landscape, the farms, and cultural nuances of what today is known as Pennsylvania Dutch country.

> The land… is rich and highly cultivated. Large farms with barns of spacious dimensions, built of stone, meet the eye in every direction. But our attention was particularly attracted by the sight of Dutch girls performing the labor of men in the fields, and we were greatly amused by seeing large numbers of swine feeding in rich clover up to their backs. I had often heard of "pigs in clover" but never saw it realized before. [8]

In contrast to the repeated delightful scenes of nature in the countryside, the next leg of the trip over the mountains turned out to be quite unpleasant.

> The stages over the mountains were very bad, the roads equally so; and we are obliged to walk the horses in the ascent for several miles

together. Sometimes for a change we would all get out and walk, and during the roughest of the way the seats were taken out from our vehicle, straw spread upon the bottom of it, and the passengers stowed in like baggage. But to those who desired to view the landscape as we passed along, the last arrangement was most unsatisfactory, and we resolved that we would rather endure the jolting upon our seats than be deprived of this pleasure. So the seats were restored, and you may just imagine to yourself Lydia seated at the coach window, to which she was obliged to hold on with both hands, straining every nerve and muscle to maintain her equilibrium.

On one side my neighbor's elbow was constantly pounding me, on the other the stage, which was neither lined or stuffed, was bruising me, while my head was often thrown against the top till I feared my brains would be dashed out. But all this I bravely endured for the sake of beholding the scenery.

At a distance the mountains towered to the clouds, and in some instances the tops were lost in them. On one side, and within a foot or two of the carriage wheels fell an awful precipice, at whose base a beautiful river quietly glided along, unmindful alike of the danger or the admiration of the travelers. After a little turning we would ride through this stream and then again cross it upon a rude bridge, and often afterward it would be seen in the distance. We were obliged to lock the wheels upon descending the mountains, and when we came to a narrow place in the road the driver would blow his tin horn vociferously to warn any teams which might be approaching to avoid danger by stopping where we could safely pass them. The distance across the mountains by the road which we traveled was one hundred and sixty miles, and this it took us several days to accomplish. [9]

At last they arrived at Pittsburgh in mid-June. Lydia explains the living conditions.

The military quarters are small and will not accommodate all our regiment. The Colonel resides with his staff at the quarters, with the exception of my husband who prefers to live with his wife, the rest board or live in hired houses. Lieut. G. and wife, Josiah and myself, with some of our brother officers, have hired a new brick house on Market street, and all live at one table. For this my husband provides, and sees that our fare is cooked and served in good order. [10]

Lydia benefited from the fact that her husband was an officer and the quartermaster of the regiment. This gave him the ability to rent a house in which he and fellow officers could temporarily reside with their wives instead of in the tents of the regulars. As well he could readily access any foodstuffs they might desire, because of his title. However, their stay in Pittsburgh was short-lived. In late July, orders came down that they were to move down the Ohio River to Newport, Kentucky.

Lydia boarded one of the fleet of keel boats the regiment commanded and spent the next two weeks observing the scenery of the Ohio Valley as she drifted down the river. Aside from some bad weather and delays due to low water, most of the excursion was comfortable. On August 9, they arrived at Newport. Here Lydia describes the region and expresses some of her more intimate emotions.

> This is a military depot. Cincinnati lies directly opposite, and it is said to be a flourishing town. I intend to see it to-day. The view, as seen from this side of the river reminds me more of Boston than any place that I have yet seen. Thirty years ago it was almost a wilderness. I can only account for its rapid growth by the fact that the settlers are principally Yankees. I long much to see my dear mother and sisters, and New England friends, but as my beloved husband was obliged to come here, I have never for a moment regretted that I accompanied him. It is great comfort that we can be together, and I have the satisfaction of feeling that I am performing my duty. This place is healthy, we are both well, the season is delightful, and we have an abundance of fruit, which is here both plenty and cheap. How long we shall be allowed to remain here is altogether uncertain. We are now awaiting farther orders. I hope they may be to stay here or to return to Pittsburgh, but fear we shall be destined still farther west. [11]

Her boding over their next move was borne out within a few weeks when they learned that they were going on to Vincennes in the Indiana Territory. They arrived on October 1 and found the town preparing for a military move against the Indians who had a burgeoning village further along the Wabash River to the North.

A few days before arriving at Vincennes, Josiah suffered a freak accident while duck hunting on the shores of the Ohio. As he refilled the pan of his gun with powder, it flashed, and in turn ignited his entire horn and its contents of a half pound of powder. The result scorched his face and burnt off his eyebrows. He was unable to see

The Battle of Tippecanoe - fought November 7, 1811.
Painting copyright by Kurtz & Allison, 1889.

for most of two weeks. Lydia explains that

> a simple curd made of new milk and vinegar cured his eyes, and an application of oil and brandy alternately applied to his face healed it rapidly.
>
> Just after he was burnt, I took a violent cold by being out to view a comet, which had just made its appearance, and was quite sick in consequence. We were two pitiable objects, neither able to help the other and yet both needing assistance. [12]

Because of his injury, when the troops under Governor Harrison took their leave on October 5, Josiah was ordered to stay behind until healed. He was put in command of Fort Knox, a small stockade a few miles upriver from Vincennes. (This Fort Knox is not to be confused with the Army post and bullion depository still occupied in Kentucky.) There he and Lydia convalesced together for a few days. Her journal entries over this period explain their situation:

> Oct. 8th. So here we are at Fort Knox, a stockade or military depot on the banks of the Wabash. I have not a single female associate, but I

have my husband and so all is well. I venture alone sometimes outside the pickets, but although a soldier's wife, I lay no claim to heroism. And, as I do not relish the idea of being scalped by our red bretheren, I never venture far, but strive to content myself with those sources of enjoyment which are within my reach. I read, write, sew, converse, and think of absent friends whom it seems to me I never loved better than now. Josiah's eyes are getting strong fast, and he is impatient to rejoin his regiment. Indeed, he has besought the physician to pronounce him well enough, and has besides written to his colonel, requesting that he will order him to join him.

Oct. 9th. My husband has received the order to rejoin his regiment. This is very much to his satisfaction, though not exactly to mine. Inglorious ease suits me better than it does him. Although he has been here only a week, we must pack up and be off to Vincennes again.

Oct. 10th. My dear husband is gone to the army, and I am boarding at Vincennes, with a Mrs. Jones. I have a very pleasant companion in Mrs. Witlock, the wife of an officer commanding another regiment. They are Virginians. I have had a return of the fever and ague, and Mrs. W. has nursed me like a sister. The troops are eighty miles from this place, building a fort [Fort Harrison]. The Indians in that neighborhood have as yet manifested no decided hostility towards them, but they are so deceitful and treacherous that no reliance can be placed upon their good will. The British furnish them with arms, ammunition, and rations. I hear that Colonel Miller has been very ill, and was obliged while sick to lie down upon the ground in a tent. He is now better. I should like to ask him and the rest (who were so impatient to go) how they like their new situation. We have had no cold weather here yet, though it is now November. Indeed, I have not once sat by a fire during the past six months. We expect to stay here all winter, which is a disagreeable prospect to me, for I do not much fancy the place or the people. Dear New England, I love thee better than ever. Oh, shall I be so happy as to visit the blest scenes once more, for blest indeed they are to me. [13]

On their way up the Wabash River, the American troops had stopped to build Fort Harrison just outside of the present-day city of Terre Haute, Indiana. From this new base, constructed as a fall back for safety and for supplies, they continued on to the village known as Prophetstown near today's Lafayette, Indiana. Here The Prophet, the brother of Tecumseh and spiritual leader of the village, had assembled well over a thousand followers and the population was continuing to grow. In Governor Harrison's view this had become an immediate threat to the settlers of the Indiana Territory. For this reason, he led a body of troops that now included Josiah up to the site in an act of intimidation. Harrison was supposed to negotiate with The Prophet the day after they had encamped outside of the village, but just before the dawn of November 7 the warriors attacked. The Prophet, while his wiser brother Tecumseh was away, had convinced his followers that they were impervious to the Americans' bullets and would surely win the day. The Great Spirit had told him so. And so the battle ensued. The Americans overpowered the warriors and destroyed most of their village. It would forever become known as the Battle of Tippecanoe, having been fought along the river of that name. It would also become a huge feather in the political hat of Harrison; so much so that, "Tippecanoe and Tyler Too," became his campaign slogan when he ran for president with John Tyler in 1840.

Though some vague information about a battle along the Wabash had come to Vincennes earlier, it took more than three weeks for definitive word about the status of Harrison's troops to arrive. On November 30, Lydia recorded:

> Oh, what a day was that when we at Vincennes heard of this battle of Tippecanoe. Receiving at first a mere report of the attack and victory without any official communication, and of course without any details, each of us expected to hear sad news from our dear ones, and for hours our souls were harrowed to the quick, and agonized with suspense and dread. At length the express arrived with letters, yet his feelings were so excited, that he could not select and deliver them, but poured them out indiscriminately into my lap. I was so overcome with apprehensions for my husband that I could neither see nor read, and passed them into the hands of a lady who stood by me. Her husband not being in the war, she was more calm and composed, and soon was enabled to find me my letter. When told that the address was in Josiah's own handwriting, I could hardly believe it. My bodily weakness was great, being just recovering from the ague and fever, and this, aggravated by my intense anxiety respecting my dear husband, caused me to sink fainting upon the nearest chair. Recovering soon, however, with Mrs. G kneeling on one side of me, Mrs. W on the other, and Mrs. J in front of me.

I opened the letter and began to read it aloud. I had proceeded only to the third or fourth line, which contained assurance of his safety, when we all burst into tears and thus relieved our aching hearts. Then I was able to finish the precious document, and found that my beloved husband (now more dear than ever) and those whom we most valued had escaped without serious injury. There were but two married men killed from our regiment, and they were soldiers. Only one married officer from the 4th was wounded. How often have I heard or read of Indian fights until my blood chilled in my veins, without thinking that I should ever be so personally interested in one.

Our situation at Vincennes was very much exposed while troops were absent, for every body left that could handle a sword or carry a musket, and we women remained without even a guard. Mrs. W. and myself had loaded pistols at our bedside, but I very much doubt whether we should have had presence of mind enough to use them, had we found it necessary. If the Indians had been aware of our situation, a few of them could have burnt the village, and massacred the inhabitants. But a kind Providence watched over us, and kept us from so dreadful a fate. [14]

Soon, Josiah was back in Vincennes with the victorious troops. The wounded were attended to, but several did not survive. Lydia and Josiah would carry on in this community through the winter. The comforts of her New England home and family tugged at Lydia's heart, but she often adamantly defended her decision to join her husband. She explained to her mother:

> Never, no, never for a single instant, have I been sorry that I accompanied my husband. On the contrary, I feel grateful to the Author of all our blessings that I was permitted to come, to be with him when sick, and to encourage and comfort him under various ills which flesh is heir to. [15]

Lydia would experience several unique events during the remainder of this adventure. One night she was awoken by the uncanny shaking of her entire house. At first her neighbors and Lydia thought it was the stampede of attacking Indians, but soon learned that what they had felt that night and several times since were the widespread New Madrid earthquakes. On another occasion, she was able to get a sneak peek of an Indian Council held in town. The color of the event was not lost on her. She cowered in the background noting the markings, ornamentation, and powerful oration skills of the Indians.

Later, she had a more pleasant visit to a sugar-camp where maple trees were being tapped for their sweet nectar.

On March 31, 1812, orders arrived to leave Vincennes and head to Detroit, a mere six hundred miles away. It took nearly six weeks of packing before the whole body finally moved out on May 14. Lydia had been learning to ride horseback and came to enjoy it, but now was a little wary of being about it over such a distance. None-the-less, she counted herself lucky to be the wife of an officer, which gave her the privilege of riding. She often empathized with the wives of the enlisted men who were utterly exhausted at having to walk the entire distance over treacherous terrain. There were just not enough wagons to carry both them and the supplies.

As unpredictable as the weather always is, Lydia spoke of a particular day that highlights the discomforts a prolonged rain could bring. Soaked through and through, the ladies sought to dry themselves for the night at a large fire the men had cleverly built against a green tree. Its high branches provided an expansive canopy to deflect the rain and the flames provided warmth enough to dry their clothes, albeit slowly while they were still being worn.

At the end of May, Louisville was reached. Here, and again at Newport, Cincinnati, and Urbana, the troops were greeted with an outpouring of gratitude from the citizens. Dinners were often prepared by the townspeople for the enlisted and officers alike. Arched banners appeared reading, "To the Heroes of Tippecanoe." After such a long stretch of adventure in the wilderness, this show of appreciation had to warm their hearts.

At Urbana, a little north of Dayton in the Ohio country, the troops joined with those of General Hull. Tensions were rising in the area of Fort Detroit and much of Upper Canada, so Hull was ordered to move troops to the region. Rumors abounded that war with the British Canadians was imminent. Therefore the regiments united and progressed north together. A team of men went ahead of the main body, clearing a path through much of this untraveled wilderness. The trail they blazed became known as Hull's Trace and extended from today's Dayton, Ohio to Detroit, Michigan. Some of this route has been absorbed into our modern highway system, the rest has been reclaimed by nature.

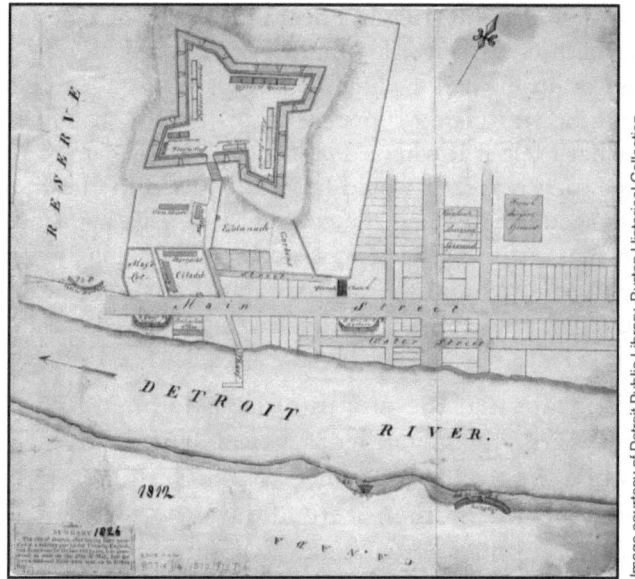

Map from 1812 showing the structure of Fort Detroit
and its proximity to the Detroit River.

When they arrived in the northern regions of the Ohio country, they found themselves in what became known as the Great Black Swamp. Just south of today's Findlay, Ohio, Hull found the travel nearly impossible. Out of necessity, he ordered his men to build a fortress where they could regroup for a few days. Following in the footsteps of General Anthony Wayne twenty years earlier, Hull would build Fort Necessity as the first link in a chain of forts where goods could be stored and where troops could fall back for protection if necessary. So difficult was travel through the mud of this swampland that some of the horses were lost, dropping dead in the so-called road from the fatigue. In some of the muddiest stretches, trees had to be cut and laid next to each other. The corduroy roads thus created allowed for somewhat easier passage, albeit a bumpy one.

Amidst all the dangers of her journey, one day Lydia was nearly taken out by friendly fire of sorts in her own tent. While they were camped near the old British Fort Miamis, in today's Maumee, Ohio, she explains that:

> As I was sitting at the door of our tent, enjoying the beautiful twilight

and musing upon absent friends, I heard the report of a gun and felt the wind of something passing close to my ear. Presently an officer came up with a ramrod in his hand, which he said had just fallen upon his tea-table, where he was taking supper with his family outside of his tent. This was what I felt as it whizzed past my ear. But what an escape! Had it gone one inch nearer, it would have penetrated my head, and inevitable death would have been the consequence. This happened through the carelessness of a militia man, who in discharging his gun, forgot to elevate it, or to remove the ramrod. Thus I am constantly preserved through dangers seen and unseen, and have a renewed call to adore the God of Providence. [16]

From this location at the mouth of the Maumee River, Lydia and the other officers' wives boarded a vessel sent down to them from Detroit. While the troops continued to march the remaining seventy miles to Detroit, the women were allowed by General Hull to sail with the army's supplies across Lake Erie to the post. They gloriously anticipated that in a few hours they would be within the comfortable confines of Fort Detroit. No more mud, mosquitoes, illness, sleeping on the hard ground, or precarious long rides on the back of a horse. However, fate had other plans for Lydia.

When they were within a mere twenty miles of their destination, a ship approached them. It was British; sent from Fort Malden, which was situated across the Detroit River from Fort Detroit. They seized the U.S. vessel and took Lydia and the other wives into custody as they announced that war between the two countries had been officially declared. Suddenly, the ladies were prisoners of war.

Luckily, the British treated their female captives with the same dignity they would bestow on English officer's wives. Lydia was even allowed to negotiate that they be transported to Fort Detroit. Though all the supplies on the U.S. ship were a bit of prized booty for the British, Lydia managed to get possession of Josiah's and her own baggage and take it with her to the American fortress. A few days after settling into Fort Detroit, the main body of US troops safely arrived. The reality of war was starting to settle in. Josiah was ordered to join a company that went to Brownstown, a settlement north of Detroit, where they were to engage the enemy Indians led by Tecumseh. Though many regulars were killed in the skirmish that ensued, no officers were lost and Josiah returned unharmed.

A few days later, the British were suspected of erecting a battery to attack Fort Detroit from across the river. They covered their actions by first erecting a large building, behind which they went about putting their guns in place. On August 15 the building came down in rapid order by the British troops and the grand battery was exposed. General Brock, in command of the British forces, sent a messenger with an order for General Hull to surrender. It was rejected and so the cannon fuses were lit. The bombardment went on for some time, but having little effect on the fortress it was ceased for the day. Lydia and others had been ordered to a more secure area of the fort, but they were feeling safe enough to make a dinner and tea in the evening. Perhaps it made them feel normal in the midst of a surreal situation. In a letter to her mother, dated August 19, Lydia gives an eyewitness account of the horrid effect the British artillery had on the Americans when the assault was renewed the following day.

> Soon as the morning of the 16th arose the cannon commenced to roar with apparently tenfold fury; and alas! it did not continue long without doing execution. The enemy's bombs and shot began to enter the fort. Some of the ladies were employed in making cylinders, viz: bags to hold powder for the cannon. Others were scraping lint, that it might be ready in case of necessity, to dress the wounds of the injured soldiers. While thus engaged, a twenty-four pound shot entered the room next to where we were sitting. Two officers who were standing in the room were cut entirely in two, their bowels gushing out as they fell. The same ball, after doing such horrid execution, passed through the wall into another room where a number of persons were standing. Here it took off both legs of one man, and sliced the flesh off the thigh of another. The man who lost both his legs died very soon. Thus one of these angry messengers killed three men and wounded a fourth in a moment in time...
>
> ... Soon after this another ball of equal size entered the hospital room. A poor fellow who lay sick upon his bed, and was asleep, had his head instantly severed from his body; and his attendant was killed by the same blow, the shot striking him in his breast. The enemy had got the range of the fort so completely that it was now judged unsafe for the women and children to remain any longer in it, So we were all hurried to the root-house, which was on the opposite side of the fort,

and was bomb proof. Never shall I forget my sensations as I crossed the parade ground to gain this place of safety. You must recollect, dear mother, that my feelings had been under constant excitement for many weeks, and now were wrought up to the highest pitch. Complain I would not, weep I could not; but it seemed as if my heart would burst. My hair stood erect upon my head, (which in the hurry of the escape was uncovered), as I raised my eyes and caught a glimpse of the bombs, shells and balls which were flying in all directions…

… On looking from the door of the root-house to the quarters opposite I saw a ball knock down one of the chimneys, and was afterwards told that the same shot killed a man who was on duty upon the parapet the other side of the building. About this time the enemy effected a landing on our side, under cover of their armed vessels. Of these they had a sufficiency to demolish Detroit if they chose, while we had not a boat in order to carry a single gun. General Brock's effective force was also double ours, and the Indians were now let loose on the inhabitants. In addition to this our supply of provisions and ammunition was extremely small, and a part of General H ——'s most efficient troops were at this juncture at some distance from Detroit, having been sent away on duty a short time previous to the summons to surrender. Under these circumstances General H., after consultation with Colonel Miller, thought it best to capitulate, and obtained the best terms he could. A white flag was accordingly displayed upon the parapet as a signal for the cessation of hostilities. Immediately the cannon ceased to roar, and all was still. [17]

The British flag was raised in place of the stars and stripes. Lydia and Josiah, were shuffled along in the company of General Hull and other military personnel onto the British ship *Queen Charlotte*. Once again, Lydia was a prisoner of war. They all disembarked at the British Fort Erie. While here, Lydia herself says that Providence looked down on them once again. While they were with General Hull, they happened to catch the attention of General Brock as he was on his way out of the fortress for Montreal. Hull took the opportunity to request that Josiah be released from custody, seeing that he had his wife with him. Brock agreed, and suddenly the couple was free to leave for their New England home. It would be several weeks of travel from the great falls of Niagara to Boston, but this excursion was made with lighter hearts than the one made months previous. Now they were eager to reunite with family and friends. The rest of their lives, Lydia and Josiah dedicated their themselves to service for the Lord through the Presbyterian church. Josiah became an elder and Lydia a religious teacher in the church school.

The life of many a man was taken in the course of wars in the Northwest Territory. Their sacrifices are told and retold throughout history books. However, little is said about the effect their absence, temporary or final, had on the rest of their families. From the sneak peeks into the lives of these two women and others, it is clear to see that the frontier wars had an effect that cascaded over the entire family, be it Indian, British, or American. ♦

ANECDOTE.

How to Cook a Husband. — As Mrs. Glass said of the hare, you must first catch him. Having done so, the mode of cooking him so as to make a good dish of him is as follows: Many good husbands are spoiled in the cooking; some women go about it as if their husbands were bladders, and blow them up; others keep them constantly in hot water, while others freeze them by conjugal coldness; some smother them in hatred, contention, and variance; and some keep them in pickle all their lives.

These women always serve them up with tongue sauce.

Now it can not be supposed that husbands will be tender and good if managed in this way; but they are, on the contrary, very delicious, managed as follows: Get a large jar, called the jar of carefulness (which all good wives have on hand), place your husband in it, and set him near the fire of conjugal love; let the fire be pretty hot, but especially let it be clear; above all, let the heat be constant; cover him over with affection, kindness, and subjection; garnish with modest, becoming familiarity, and the spice of pleasantry; and if you add kisses and other confectionaries, let them be accompanied with a sufficient portion of secrecy, mixed with prudence and moderation.

We should advise all good wives to try this receipt, and realize how admirable a dish a husband is when properly cooked.

In Harper Magazine's Book: American Wit and Humor, 1859 [18]

XVI.
A LYTLE INDIAN INFLUENCE.

The relationship between the early frontiersmen and the Indians in the Northwest Territory was a complex one. It is often assumed that the two parties never got along; probably because so many history books have implied that such was the case. There certainly was plenty of blood shed to support that perspective; but that is not the whole story. Friendships and business relationships were common. Each individual circumstance was different. The reality is that positive relationships are just not as exciting to read about as a good fight. Look at the news reports of today, only a tertiary mention of good deeds is ever heard. As they say, "If it bleeds it leads" on the evening news. History has often taken the same approach, but it doesn't mean that all was nastiness on the frontier.

War is going to put a damper on anything, and an atmosphere of war did loom over the Northwest Territory for most of its existence. It was just a part of daily life for the Indians and the Americans to be on guard against a surprise attack. Each horrid assault would draw a revenge attack, and so it went. Therefore it was easy for generalizations to be made against a differing culture if the only exposure a person had to it was a violent one. But, for those individuals who took the time to develop a one-on-one relationship with each other, the discovery of the good traits of their societies often became evident and even admired.

One example of this can be seen in the "civilizing" campaign that the Americans implemented. While this attempt to persuade Indians to integrate into the American way of life was considered abhorrent to leaders like Tecumseh, other Native Americans saw value in the transition. Likewise, numerous Americans found the simpler village life of the Indians to be a very warm and loving environment. Diaries and journals of white people who were kidnapped by tribes and raised as Indians often tell a similar, endearing story. Numerous accounts report that when exchanges of captives occurred, it was often the case that white children did not want to leave their adoptive Indian homes and return to their biological parents. There was something about the Indian culture that they loved.

The Native Americans have had a profound influence on many aspects of American life, symbolically, legally, and practically. Take the appreciation of the Bald Eagle. It had been revered by many Indian tribes for centuries. When the Americans decided upon a national symbol for their country; the power, courage, and majesty of this bird, so admired in the Indian culture, seemed most fitting for theirs as well. Thankfully, Benjamin Franklin's suggestion of the wild turkey, so prolific in the land at the time, was overridden. When the Constitution of the United States was drawn up, the Iroquois nation's structure of government was at least loosely used as a template. And, everyone knows how harmonious the Native Americans are with Mother Earth. Many of their beliefs and skills still serve us well as incredible guides to survival in the wilderness. Who can argue with their wisdom of holding a profound respect for all of nature. Hundreds of millions of boys and girls have learned and implemented these Native American approaches to life over the past century through the Scouting program.

One pioneer who was heavily influenced by her numerous encounters with the Native Americans throughout her life was Eleanor Lytle. Her name would lengthen over time; first to Eleanor Lytle McKillup and then to Eleanor Lytle McKillup Kinzie through her successive marriages. The professions of her two husbands repeatedly exposed her to the Indians of the West, both for good and evil. None-the-less, these experiences would not only shape her personality, but would eventually influence her children's' lives, and in due time indirectly impact the lives of children worldwide.

When Eleanor was only nine years old, she was living in a precarious area of Pennsylvania, just a few miles from Fort Pitt. The Indian situation in this part of the country was a mix of friendly and enemy tribes. It was 1779. The Revolution was in full gear and tribes had allied themselves either with or against the Americans. The Lytle family was living where the Iroquois, who had joined with the British, crossed paths with the Delawares and other tribes who had sworn allegiance to the Americans.

One morning, Eleanor, affectionately called Nelly by her parents, went out to play as usual with her brother in the clearing at the back of their cabin. He was seven years old and she nine at the time. As it happened, while sitting on a log some distance from their house, the two children were suddenly swept up from behind into the arms of two Seneca Indians. The warriors ran off into the woods with their captives. Unknown to Eleanor, other Seneca warriors of the Iroquois nation stormed her house and took her mother and baby brother captive as well. Her father was away at the time.

As evening approached, the Indians decided to cease their running and make camp for the night.

> ... the poor children could no longer restrain their grief, but gave vent to sobs and lamentations.
>
> Their distress appeared to excite the compassion of one of the party, a man of mild aspect, who approached and endeavored to soothe them. He spread them a couch of long grass which grew near the encamping-place, offered them a portion of his own stock of dried meat and parched corn, and gave them to understand by signs that no further evil was intended them.
>
> These kindly demonstrations were interrupted by the arrival of another party of the enemy, bringing with them the mother of the little prisoners, with her youngest child, an infant of three months old. [1]

In the meantime, Eleanor's father had returned and discovered an empty household. After frantic searches and inquiries with neighbors, he eventually headed to Fort Pitt with some friends for help. As he approached, he was relieved to find another of his sons and a daughter, two of his five children, intact and resting on a ridge. They, at the ages of merely six and four, had escaped the attack by hiding and running through the fields and woods. Mr. Lytle was given a contingent of troops from the fort to help him find the rest of his family. They set out in all directions until word came that it was likely the Seneca who had made the attack. This led the soldiers to the village of an Indian chief presumed to be Cornplanter. Here, Mr. Lytle found his wife and the rest of his children, well most of his children. Days previous, as the captives were being led to the Seneca camp

> one of the older Indians offering [offered] to relieve the mother from the burden of her infant, which she had hitherto carried in her arms. Pleased with the unexpected kindness, she resigned to him her tender charge.
>
> Thus they pursued their way, the savage who carried the infant lingering somewhat behind the rest of the party, until, finding a spot convenient for his purpose, he grasped his innocent victim by the feet, and, with one whirl, to add strength to the blow, dashed out its brains against a tree. Leaving the body upon the spot, he rejoined the party.
>
> The mother, unsuspicious of what had passed, regarded him earnestly as he reappeared without the child — then gazed wildly around on the rest of the group. Her beloved little one was not there. Its absence spoke its fate; but, suppressing the shriek of agony, for she knew that the lives of the remaining ones depended upon her firmness in that trying hour, she drew them yet closer to her and pursued her melancholy way without a word spoken or a question asked.
>
> From the depths of her heart she cried unto Him who is able to save, and He comforted her with hopes of deliverance for the surviving ones, for she saw that if blood had been their sole object the scalps of herself and her children would have been taken upon the spot where they were made prisoners. [2]

Mr. Lytle began negotiations with Cornplanter for what was left of his family.

> A treaty was immediately entered into for the ransom of the captives, which was easily accomplished in regard to Mrs. Lytle and the younger child. But no offers, no entreaties, no promises, could procure the release of the little Eleanor, the adopted child of the tribe. "No," the chief said, "she was his sister; he had taken her to supply the place of his brother who was killed by the enemy — she was dear to him, and he would not part with her."
>
> Finding every effort unavailing to shake this resolution, the father was compelled to take his sorrowful departure with such of his beloved ones as he had had the good fortune to recover...
>
> ...Commending her [Eleanor] to the care of their heavenly Father, and, cheered by the manifest tenderness with which she had thus far been treated, they set out on their melancholy journey homeward, trusting that some future effort would be more effectual for the recovery of their little girl. [3]

Mr. Lytle managed to get the Indian agent of the territory, Colonel Johnson, to try to negotiate Nelly's release, but to no avail. In fact, each year for four years the attempt was made, always without results. Over those years, the Seneca on the whole treated Eleanor to a lot of special attention. After all, she was the new sister of the chief. Cornplanter himself, as well as his mother, tended to her every need. She was special. However, all the fuss over Nelly took its toll on Cornplanter's marriage. Cornplanter had to have at least been in his mid thirties at this time, so Eleanor had to be more of a daughter than a sister to him. Either way, his wife had soon had her fill of young Eleanor and attempted to poison her. Luckily, the plot was foiled, but the wife was made an outcast of the village as a result.

Many of Eleanor's memories of her home were fading as time went by, but not those of her mother. She would never lose the feelings of her mother's unconditional love and tenderness. With the end of the Revolution in 1783, the relations between the whites and Indians had softened, at least temporarily. This boded well for that year's negotiations for Eleanor's release from Cornplanter. The Lytle family had even moved from Pennsylvania to the Fort Niagara area to be closer to the Seneca village where their daughter was being held.

Again it would be Colonel Johnson, the Indian agent who had a long-standing friendship with the Seneca, who was called upon to visit Cornplanter. This year he chose to go at the time of one of the Seneca's more exuberant celebrations: the Festival of the Green Corn. The atmosphere was relaxed and cordial.

> Observing that the hilarity of the festival had warmed and opened all hearts, he [Johnson] took occasion in an interview with the chief to expatriate upon the parental affection which had led the father and mother of his little sister to give up their friends and home, and come hundreds of miles away, in the single hope of sometimes looking upon and embracing her. The heart of the chief softened as he listened to this representation, and he was induced to promise that at the Grand Council soon to be held at Fort Niagara, on the British side of the river, he would attend, bringing his little sister with him.
>
> He exacted a promise, however, from Colonel Johnson, that not only no effort should be made to reclaim the child, but that even no proposition to part with her should be offered him. [4]

Soon the chief was off to the Great Council with his Nelly astride a horse and riding at his side. It is assumed, though not clearly stated, that Eleanor knew that her parents might be at the council. Regardless she had promised Cornplanter that she would never leave him unless he granted her that indulgence. Her parents were certainly aware of her coming as they waited and watched the stream of boats arrive near the fortress. As they peered into the distance for Cornplanter and their daughter,

> at length they were discerned, emerging from the forest on the opposite or American side. Boats were sent across by the commanding officer, to bring the chief and his party. The father and mother, attended by all the officers and ladies, stood upon the grassy bank awaiting their approach. They had seen at a glance that the little captive was with them.
>
> When about to enter the boat, the chief said to some of his young men, "Stand here with the horses, and wait until I return."
>
> He was told that the horses should be ferried across and taken care of.
>
> "No," said he; "let them wait."
>
> He held his darling by the hand until the river was passed — until the boat touched the bank — until the child sprang forward into the arms of the mother from whom she had been so long separated.
>
> When the chief witnessed that outburst of affection, he could withstand no longer.
>
> "She shall go," said he. "The mother must have her child again. I will go back alone."
>
> With one silent gesture of farewell he turned and stepped on board the boat. No arguments or entreaties could induce him to remain at the council, but, having gained the other side of the Niagara, he mounted his horse, and with his young men was soon lost in the depths of the forest. [5]

The family was reunited. Fearing that Cornplanter could have a change of heart, Mr. Lytle decided to put some distance between them. Yet again he moved his family to a new home, this time at Detroit. Eleanor never saw her Indian big brother again, but never forgot him well into her later life.

Just a year later, at the tender age of fourteen, Nelly got married. Her husband was Daniel McKillup, a member of the Detroit militia who rose to the rank of captain over the next ten years. In 1778, when Eleanor was a happy eight year old playing games in Pennsylvania,

Daniel was serving as a corporal in a Butler's Ranger unit somewhere near the Niagara region. A few years later in 1782, while Eleanor was tending to chores and frolicking with Indian children in the Seneca camp, her soon-to-be husband was fighting under the famed British leader Lt. Colonel William Caldwell at the Kentucky Battle of Blue Licks. Years later, now married to Eleanor and leaving her alone to tend to a newborn baby, Daniel would serve once again under Caldwell. This time the year was 1794 and he was called into service at the British Fort Miamis along the Maumee River, near present-day Toledo, Ohio. The British there, had anticipated a clash between the Indians and the Americans who were approaching under the command of General Anthony Wayne. The confrontation occurred as expected and was later known as the Battle of Fallen Timbers. Eleanor would become a widow as a result, Daniel was killed in action.

The circumstances of Daniel's death are somewhat controversial in the annals of history. Most sources say that he was a captain leading one of several companies of Canadian militia into the conflict. [6] However, in her book titled, *Wau-Bun*, Eleanor's daughter states:

> This gentleman [McKillup] was killed near Fort Defiance, as it was afterwards called, at the Miami Rapids, in 1794. A detachment of British troops had been sent down from Detroit, to take possession of this post. General Wayne was then on a campaign against the Indians, and the British Government thought proper to make a few demonstrations in behalf of their allies. Having gone out with a party to reconnoitre, Colonel McKillup was returning to his post after dark, when he was fired upon and killed by one of his own sentinels. [7]

A few other sources also cite this scenario of McKillup's demise, but they are probably based on this account which was first published in 1856.

The fact that Eleanor was told that her British/Canadian husband was killed by friendly fire on a scouting exercise some forty miles to the south of the action, has garnered the attention of some of today's truth seekers. The fact is that in 1794, the British were not ready to officially start another war with the Americans. The last one had just been settled eleven years earlier. They wanted to keep their illegal posts in place in the Northwest Territory so that they could continue their very profitable trade with the Indians. It was no secret that they were supplying the Indians with arms and other goods to do battle with the Americans, but direct intervention of Englishmen into the fight was not supposed to be discovered.

A diary kept by a couple of volunteers from Kentucky who were in the battle as part of the militia, reinforces the fact that some British, albeit Canadian, men did fight at Fallen Timbers when it states that towards the end of the battle, "the Indians and their white allies part British and some French retired in a very precipitate manner leaving their dead and some of their wounded on the Field." [8]

It seems that there was a good deal of subversive activity. The British were likely trying to keep the involvement of the Canadian militia, which included Daniel McKillup, under wraps. Several accounts say that this militia of forty to sixty men were dressed as Indians. It is true that the Canadians were known to dress in Indian-style attire at times, but it seems that in this circumstance they were likely deliberately disguised. Though it is tough to prove definitively, the account that states Daniel McKillup was killed at Fort Defiance, which is provided by the British of that day, was likely given to cover up their direct participation in a fight against the Americans.

None-the-less, Eleanor Lytle McKillup was left to raise her newborn child alone at the age of twenty-four. She moved in with her parents outside of Detroit for a few years until 1800 when she married her second husband, John Kinzie.

John was a dynamic spirit trained as a silversmith in his youth and was operating several trading posts in the Northwest by the time he was in his mid-thirties. John lived in Detroit much of his early life and from there coordinated his business affairs, which were extensive. He had established a major trading center in Kekionga, the large Indian settlement near Fort Wayne. Other posts were built in villages that would soon become the cities of Upper Sandusky and Defiance in Ohio. Another went up in St. Joseph of the Michigan territory.

Before he married Eleanor in 1800, John had a long term cohabitation with Margaret McKenzie; a woman who years earlier had been a captive of an Indian chief in the Detroit region. Margaret and her sister Elizabeth had gained their freedom as a result of John's negotiations with the chief. Both girls had been kidnapped by Indians in an ironically similar fashion to Eleanor's capture. Margaret would bear

John three children while they lived together. However, after a surprise visit from their biological father sometime in the 1790s, Margaret and her sister had a change of heart about their futures. They decided to return to their father's home in Virginia. Margaret took John's children with her, leaving him alone with only his business affairs to tend to in Detroit.

It is suspected that John and Eleanor had probably known each other throughout their years of living in Detroit. Sometime after Margaret's departure, they married. In 1803, their first son was born and given the name John; at which point they moved to John senior's trading post on the St. Joseph River. In 1804, news of Fort Dearborn being built just a hundred miles away along the south shores of Lake Michigan enticed John to move again. He would settle in what would soon become Chicago. Many history books name John as the city's father. He bought the only home in the area from Jean Baptiste Point du Sable, whom historians note as the city's first non-indigenous person to permanently settle in the area. Therefore du Sable is referred to as the city's founder.

How it is that the region came to be known as "Chicago" is in itself interesting. One of the earliest references to the area comes in the 1670s by the French explorer LaSalle who referred to it as "Checaguo." This was how the Indians of that day spoke of the region and the river. The French missionary, Marquette, of that same period mentioned meeting a highly regarded Indian of the Illinois tribe named "Chachagoussiou." The English translation of these words in various spellings is often believed to mean some form of, "wild onion." Accounts say that the region was abundant with wild onions, probably garlic, which lends credence to why this name was applied to it. Eleanor's daughter gives another twist to the story.

> The origin of the name Chicago is a subject of discussion, some of the Indians deriving it from the fitch or polecat [skunk], others from the wild onion with which the woods formerly abounded; but all agree that the place received its name from an old chief who was drowned in the stream in former times. That this event, although so carefully preserved by tradition, must have occurred in a very remote period, is evident from an old French manuscript brought by General Cass from France. [9]

Uncertainty creeps in because no one can agree whether an Indian

The Kinzie Mansion and Fort Dearborn.
Illustrated by Benson J. Lossing and shown here
as it appeared in his *Pictorial Fieldbook of the War of 1812*, 1868.

from the past was named after the region that he lived in, or whether the region was named after him. But whether it was an abundance of onions, garlic, or even skunks; and in spite of how the spellings have changed, Chicago has apparently always had a special "air" about it.

By 1804, when John had moved into this area, he already had long-established contacts with numerous tribes and was considered a staunch friend to the Indians. Despite diverse loyalties of the tribes to the Americans or the British, he and his family were considered to be "hands-off" in the midst of any conflicts. John and Eleanor were loyalists to Great Britain at this point in time, but it was perhaps a loose affiliation. Business seemed to take precedence over patriotism.

In the decade following John's move to Chicago the civilian population grew rapidly. Homes and businesses sprang up all around Fort Dearborn and John would become a leader of the community. He maintained his score of trading posts, adding several more throughout the Illinois and Wisconsin territories and most of the sales with the inhabitants of the fort were coordinated through John. Life was good for a while, but tensions began to rise by 1811. Threats of large scale conflicts between the Indians and the Americans had become a reality when the Shawnee Prophet and his followers clashed with William Harrison's troops at the Tippecanoe River. That was just a hundred miles to the south of Chicago. It became evident that all-out war was on its way and Fort Dearborn was put on high alert.

In early April 1812, just five months after the fight at Tippecanoe, trouble did come to Chicago. A raid of Potawatomi Indians was made upon a few of the homesteads surrounding the fort. Several residents were murdered. Most of the others escaped to safety within the walls of the fort. Only a lone cannon, fired as a warning, scared off the attackers. A few more random attacks were withstood over the next few months. Then on August 7 a Potawatomi chief named Catfish came to the fort. He brought with him papers from General Hull.

> These announced the declaration of war between the United States and Great Britain, and that General Hull, at the head of the Northwestern army, had arrived at Detroit; also, that the island of Mackinac had fallen into the hands of the British.
>
> The orders to Captain Heald were, "to evacuate the fort, if practicable, and, in that event, to distribute all the United States' property contained in the fort, and in the United States' factory or agency, among the Indians in the neighborhood." [10]

When all this news was read to the officers in command, Catfish requested a private talk with John Kinzie. A trust and friendship had been long established between the Potawatomi Indians and John's family. But, when the war was declared, the Indian loyalties to the British were sealed. The Americans in and around the fort were in serious peril. Catfish, unbeknownst to his fellow Indians, made an effort to protect as many Americans as he could. Though John was in the British camp, he knew all the Americans and seemed to likewise not want to see a massacre take place. Catfish begged John to convince Captain Heald, commander of Fort Dearborn, to stay put. Catfish reasoned that there was enough food to last the inhabitants many months. Within that time reinforcements could arrive to help their situation. He further explained how the American families would be an easy target of the Potawatomi as they moved east to Fort Wayne because the women, children, and wagons full of supplies were not conducive to a fast escape.

Despite John's entreaties, Captain Heald felt his force was inadequate to defend the fortress and that food would not last as long as others projected. He ordered that most of the ammunition as well as barrels and barrels of alcohol be disposed of in the river and wells. The other supplies of blankets and foodstuffs were dispersed to the Potawatomi. William Wells and a small band of the Miami Indians from the Fort Wayne area arrived to assist the Americans, still expecting them to remain at Fort Dearborn. Their arrival was a day late, as all the supplies had been given away and the only recourse was to move out.

On the morning of August 15, the Americans left the fortress with only a token amount of powder and balls in hand for their defense. Though a contingent of the Potawatomi felt as Catfish had, that their long friendship with the residents meant that they should help them gain safe passage to Fort Wayne, most of the younger warriors tasted blood. Before they departed, John received word from a band of Potawatomi living along the St. Joseph River, Indians who were his true friends, that the Potawatomi at Fort Dearborn who said they were planning to safely escort the families to Fort Wayne, actually had other plans in mind. There was a foreboding in the air that no one could deny.

John made arrangements for Eleanor, his four younger children, and several others to board a small boat with a couple of his Indian friends who had pledged to guide them safely to the St. Joseph River while John and his eldest son marched with the Americans. John hoped that his presence on the journey might deter an assault. He was mistaken.

Eleanor's vessel had coasted no more than a half mile from the fortress when a messenger came to them with a warning to stop where they were, near the mouth of the river. From here Nelly saw the musket smoke rising in the distance. She knew it meant the assault had begun and feared the worst for her husband and son as she cuddled her other children. One Chicago historian explains the movements of the Americans:

> Their course lay south along the shore of the lake. A range of low sand hills extended south between the lake shore and the prairie to the westward. The advance under Captain Wells had reached a point about a mile and a half distant from the fort (at present intersection of Eighteenth Street and Calumet Avenue), when Wells "was seen to turn and ride back, swinging his hat around his head in a circle, which meant in the sign language of the frontier, 'we are surrounded by Indians.'" As he came nearer he shouted to Captain Heald, "They are about to attack us;

form instantly and charge upon them." The escort of Pottawattomies which had been promised to Captain Heald by that tribe had left the fort in their company, but instead of remaining with the column had diverged in their course and were now on the prairie west of the sand hills. It was this "escort" which had suddenly become the attacking party. The heads of the Indians could now be seen bobbing up and down beyond the sand hills "like turtles out of the water."[11]

The five hundred Potawatomi proceeded to overpower the caravan. The Miami Indians who had come with William Wells fled. While engaged in the fighting Wells himself witnessed an horrific action that he could not bear. A single warrior had jumped into a wagon filled with children of the white families. While huddled together the warrior tomahawked each one of the twelve to death. Wells was heard to exclaim, "Is that their game, butchering the women and children? Then I will kill too!" He galloped back to take his revenge on the families in the Indian camp near the fort, but he would meet his demise on the way. Less than thirty of the eighty-plus Americans survived the event; John and his son luckily included.

Mrs. Kinzie and the others, still under the protection of their Indian allies, came back to her home across from the fort where she was reunited with her husband and son. Soon the dwelling was infiltrated by some enemy Indians from the Wabash River region who held little allegiance to the Kinzies. They were plotting to kill all the residents in the home, but were temporarily delayed by the friendly Indians on guard. As it happened:

> They entered the parlor in which the family were assembled with their faithful protectors, and seated themselves upon the floor in silence.
>
> Black Partridge [a friend of John's] perceived from their moody and revengeful looks what was passing in their minds, but he dared not remonstrate with them. He only observed in a low tone to Wau-bau-see, —
>
> "We have endeavored to save our friends, but it is in vain — nothing will save them now."
>
> At this moment a friendly whoop was heard from a party of newcomers on the opposite bank of the river. Black Partridge sprang to meet their leader, as the canoes in which they had hastily embarked touched the bank near the house.
>
> "Who are you?" demanded he.
>
> "A man. Who are you?"

"A man like yourself. But tell me who you are,?" — meaning, tell me your disposition, and which side you are for.

"I am a Sau-ga-nash! [English-speaking man]"

"Then make all speed to the house — your friend is in danger, and you alone can save him."

Billy Caldwell, for it was he, entered the parlor with a calm step, and without a trace of agitation in his manner. He deliberately took off his accoutrements and placed them with his rifle behind the door, then saluted the hostile savages.

"How now my friends!" A good-day to you. I was told there were enemies here, but I am glad to find only friends. Why have you blackened your faces? Is it that you are mourning for the friends you have lost in battle?" (purposely misunderstanding this token of evil designs.) "Or is it that you are fasting?" If so, ask our friend, here, and he will give you to eat. He is the Indian's friend, and never yet refused them what they had need of."

Thus taken by surprise, the savages were ashamed to acknowledge their bloody purpose. They, therefore, said modestly that they came to beg of their friends some white cotton in which to wrap their dead before interring them. This was given to them, with some other presents, and they took their departure peaceably from the premises. [12]

Thus the timely arrival of Billy Caldwell, who was also known as Sauganash, probably saved the lives of the Kinzie family. Caldwell was the son of a union between British Colonel William Caldwell and a Mohawk woman. Billy gained renown as both a British/Canadian and Potawatomi leader.

Though rescued for the moment, the Kinzies were still in the midst of a lot of angry Indians. They watched the Potawatomi burn Fort Dearborn to the ground the following day. Two days later all of the Kinzies were being escorted to safety in the St. Joseph area where they would remain with the more peaceful band of Potawatomi who had been helping them through the dangerous maneuvers of the past few days. In November, Eleanor and the children were led to Detroit where the British had retaken control of the fort. John stayed behind to take care of some business with the Indians and then made the trip eastward in January 1813. They were living peacefully in a house near the fort where one of their larger rooms was being used as a hospital. Wounded Americans from the Raisin River affair were nursed by Eleanor and John.

Illustration of Indian ambush of Americans fleeing Fort Dearborn. Shown here as it appeared in book: *Cassell's History of the United States*, 1880.

However, not long after this living situation had been established, the British commander, General Proctor, grew heavily skeptical of John's loyalty to the crown. William Harrison, in command of the U.S. Northwest Army had been building Fort Meigs just across the lake throughout January and February. Proctor suspected Harrison may invade Canada soon, and further suspected John of having had traitorous communication with him. Proctor would not rest until he had John Kinzie restrained.

One of Proctor's officer's called on John under the guise of Proctor's wanting to talk business with him. John accepted, but was abruptly surprised when he was put under arrest in a home near Fort Malden. When Eleanor learned what had happened, she contacted several Indian chiefs who were her friends and they road to Proctor's quarters demanding John's release. Considering that the Indians were allied with the British, Proctor did not want to create an internal problem. Besides, he was always wary that a false move could turn their allegiance against him. John was therefore released and reunited with Eleanor; momentarily. A short time later Proctor sent officers to arrest him again. They were successful, but a few hours later John's Indian friends arrived at his house and upon learning what transpired, they again crossed the river and acquired John's release from Fort Malden. Then

> a third time this officer made the attempt, and succeeded in arresting Mr. Kinzie and conveying him heavily ironed to Fort Malden, in Canada, at the mouth of the Detroit River. Here he was at first treated with great severity, but after a time the rigor of his confinement was somewhat relaxed, and he was permitted to walk on the bank of the river for air and exercise.
>
> On the 10th of September, as he was taking his promenade under the close supervision of a guard of soldiers, the whole party were startled by the sound of guns upon Lake Erie, at no great distance below. What could it mean? It must be Commodore Barclay firing into some of the Yankees. The firing continued. The time allotted the prisoner for his daily walk expired, but neither he nor his guard observed the lapse of time, so anxiously were they listening to what they now felt sure was an engagement between ships of war. At length Mr. Kinzie was reminded that the hour for his return to confinement had arrived. He petitioned for another half-hour.
>
> "Let me stay," said he, "till we can learn how the battle has gone."
>
> Very soon a sloop appeared under press of sail, rounding the point, and presently two gun-boats in chase of her.
>
> "She is running — she bears the British colors," cried he — "yes, yes, they are lowering — she is striking her flag! Now," turning to the soldiers, "I will go back to prison contented — I know how the battle has gone."[13]

Eleanor's daughter continues her documentation of what transpired after the defeat of the British fleet by Oliver Perry.

> Matters were growing critical, and it was necessary to transfer all prisoners to a place of greater security than the frontier was now likely to be. It was resolved therefore to send Mr. Kinzie to the mother-country. Nothing has ever appeared which would explain the course of General Proctor in regard to this gentleman. He had been taken from the bosom of his family, where he was living quietly under the parole which he had received and protected by the stipulations of the surrender. He was kept four months in confinement. Now he was placed on horseback under a strong guard, who announced that they had orders to shoot him through the head if he offered to speak to a person upon the road. He was tied upon the saddle to prevent his escape, and thus they set out for Quebec. A little incident occurred, which will help to illustrate the course

invariably pursued towards our citizens, at this period, by the British army on the Northwestern frontier.

The saddle on which Mr. Kinzie rode had not been properly fastened, and, owing to the rough motion of the animal on which it was, it turned, so as to bring the rider into a most awkward and painful position. His limbs being fastened, he could not disengage himself, and in this manner he was compelled by those who had charge of him to ride until he was nearly exhausted, before they had the humanity to release him.

Arrived at Quebec, he was put on board a small vessel to be sent to England. The vessel when a few days out at sea was chased by an American frigate and driven into Halifax. A second time she set sail, when she sprung a leak and was compelled to put back.

The attempt to send him across the ocean was now abandoned, and he was returned to Quebec. Another step, equally inexplicable with his arrest, was soon after taken. This was, his release and that of Mr. Macomb, of Detroit, who was also in confinement in Quebec, and the permission given them to return to their friends and families, although the war was not yet ended. It may possibly be imagined that in the treatment these gentlemen received, the British commander-in-chief sheltered himself under the plea of their being "native-born British subjects," and perhaps when it was ascertained that Mr. Kinzie was indeed a citizen of the United States it was thought safest to release him. [14]

As a result of this uncanny series of events, John found himself a free man. Until he got back home, Eleanor had to worry and wonder what would become of her husband who she assumed was somewhere in the Atlantic heading for England. Things were in quite a stir about Detroit and Fort Malden after the naval victory of the Americans on the lake. General Harrison, as expected, arrived at Detroit on September 29. The relieved Americans assembled to cheer him on. Eleanor, with all of her children, went to meet him. The Kinzies were known to Harrison and obviously prominent residents of the town as they provided accommodations for him to spend the night at their Detroit home.

John's return marked the end of his and Eleanor's death-defying adventures. The War of 1812 ceased in 1815 and two years afterwards with the re-building of Fort Dearborn they would return to their home in Chicago. Life went on quietly and profitably for years to come. Their progeny would prove that the influence of the Native Americans on Eleanor's life and her husbands' was deep-seated as it would be passed

Portrait of Juliette Gordon Low – founder of the Girl Scout program. Shown here at age 27 in painting by Edward Hughes, 1887.

down through the generations.

On October 31, 1860, the great-granddaughter of Eleanor was born in Savannah, Georgia. Her birth name was nearly as lengthy as Eleanor's, Juliette Magill Kinzie Gordon, but it would change to Juliette Gordon Low with her marriage to Mackey Low. The couple established homes in both England and America and were able to rub elbows with the aristocracy of the former because Mackey's father was a prominent land owner of the day. That connection proved fortuitous to Juliette. Though her husband passed away in 1905, Juliette was still involved in British society when one day in 1912 she met Sir Robert Baden-Powell. Just a couple years previous, he had established the Boy Scouts Association. Juliette had an epiphany. She is said to have called a family member exclaiming, "I've got something for the girls of Savannah, and all of America, and all the world, and we're going to start it tonight!"

Epitomizing the traits of Eleanor from a century previous, Juliette always felt inclined to guide young girls to become women of character, self-confidence, and self-sufficiency. That instinct, combined with her lifelong interest in the arts, nature, and animal life, led her to create what would blossom into the largest educational organization for girls in the world. Today the alumni of the Girl Scouts can extend their thanks for all that they learned about being a strong, upstanding, and prepared woman all the way back to Eleanor Lytle McKillup Kinzie.

A close look at the intricacies of the Girl Scout programs will reveal many roots with the Native Americans. Living conditions are significantly different from what they were a century ago when Juliette began her organization; and certainly very different from two centuries previous when Eleanor lived. There are few occasions when tracking an animal, starting a fire without matches, or reading signs from nature of changing weather conditions are critically needed skills. Yet, it is the Indians' deeper sentiments: respect for Nature, esteem for themselves, and reverence for the Great Spirit, that lies as an undergirding to both the Boy and Girl Scout organizations. The Native Americans were prepared for anything, hence the motto, "Be prepared." Through the experiences she had with the Indians of her day, whether they had been good or bad, Eleanor not only learned a respect for the earth, but even more importantly learned respect for herself and others. Three generations later, Juliette would encourage young girls to be steadfast in facing any challenge, to set fear aside, and to engage whole-heartedly with others. ♦

ANECDOTE.

In a late naval engagement a brave, economical seaman
on board the Royal Charlotte, had his leg separated from his thigh
by a cannon-ball, just at the knee, some of his shipmates had taken
up Jack's leg, and were going to throw it overboard, when he called out,
"D_ _ n my eyes, you may do what you please with the leg,
but give me the silver buckle out of the shoe."

In the Centinel of the North-Western Territory, November 21, 1795 [15]

XVII.
KEEN INDIAN INSIGHT.

As the "West" continued to be settled into the 1790s, it became obvious that conflicts would continue to escalate. Then president, George Washington, came up with a program that he felt was a wise solution to the settlement situation. He proposed a "civilizing" movement which enticed the Indians to assimilate into the American lifestyle. On the surface the proposal was good for both parties; but the brunt of the effort fell to the Indians who would have to shift cultural gears. The women had to give up their farming duties to their husbands and turn to spinning, weaving, and household chores. The men needed to give up hunting and take on the farming of crops and livestock. It was rationalized that since the Indians no longer needed to hunt if they followed this scenario, they didn't need access to unlimited land. The government would give them a tract of land as they became citizens of the United States. In turn, all the left over Indian land could be sold for profit by the government to Americans.

The program met many obstacles. While the older Indians generally agreed to the plan, the younger members of the tribes strongly resisted. The federal authorities had designated certain regions as exclusive Indian lands, but some of the state governments undermined these designations. Settlers either ignored laws and took possession of lands earmarked for the Indians, or the state politicians sold the federal Indian lands to gain their own profit. The entirety of this situation frustrated Washington who seemed to truly want the best for all parties.

A man who lived through this transitional period of the late 1700s in frontier America was John Heckewelder; a Moravian missionary who worked among the Delaware (Lenape) Indians as an assistant to the renowned David Zeisberger. Reverend Heckewelder became very intimate with the Delaware who were repeatedly forced to move to new locations in the territory because their professed neutrality in the Revolution was questioned by everyone involved. Though they truly were seeking peaceful non-involvement, over a hundred of them were brutally murdered at their village of Gnadenhutten in Ohio by American militia who didn't trust them. In later life, Heckewelder chronicled his experiences with the Delaware tribe.

An often overlooked sketch in his documents comes from an anonymous Delaware man. It gives us an intriguing story of how he came to believe that assimilation into the American way of life was right for him. In a time when the white men generally considered the Indians to be intellectually inferior, Heckewelder explains that the episode he shared with this man

> is strongly characteristic of the good sense of the Indians and shews how much their minds are capable of thought and reflection.
> Seating myself upon a log, by the side of an Indian, who was resting himself there, being at that time actively employed in fencing in his cornfield, I observed to him that he must be very fond of working, as I never saw him idling away his time, as is so common with the Indians. The answer which he returned made considerable impression on my mind; I have remembered it ever since, and I shall try to relate it as nearly in his own words as possible.
> "My friend!" said he, "the fishes in the water and the birds in the air and on the earth have taught me to work; by their examples I have been convinced of the necessity of labour and industry. When I was a young man I loitered a great deal about, doing nothing, just like the other Indians, who say that working is only for the whites and the negroes, and that the Indians have been ordained for other purposes, to hunt the deer, and catch the beaver, otter, racoon and such other animals. But it one day so happened, that while a hunting, I came to the bank of the Susquehannah [River], where I sat down near the water's edge to rest a little, and casting my eye on the water, I was forcibly struck when I observed with what industry the Meechgalingus [Sun-fish] heaped small stones together, to make secure places for their spawn, and all this labour they did with their mouths and bodies without hands! Astonished as well as diverted, I lighted my pipe, sat a while smoking and looking on, when presently a little bird not far from me raised a song which enticed me to look that way; while I was trying to distinguish who the songster was, and catch it with my eyes, its

mate, with as much grass as with its bill it could hold, passed close by me and flew into a bush, where I perceived them together busy building their nest and singing as they went along. I entirely forgot that I was a hunting, in order to contemplate the objects I had before me. I saw the birds of the air and the fishes in the water working diligently and cheerfully, and all this without hands! I thought it was strange, and became lost in contemplation! I looked at myself, I saw two long arms, provided with hands and fingers besides, with joints that might be opened and shut at pleasure. I could, when I pleased, take up anything with these hands, hold it fast or let it loose, and carry it along with me as I walked. I observed moreover that I had a strong body capable of bearing fatigue, and supported by two stout legs, with which I could climb to the top of the highest mountains and descend at pleasure into the valleys. And is it possible, said I, that a being so formed as I am, was created to live in idleness, while the birds who have no hands, and nothing but their little bills to help them, work with cheerfulness and without being told to do so? Has the Creator of man and of all living creatures given me all these limbs for no purpose? It cannot be: I will try to go to work. I did so, and went away from the village to a spot of good land, built a cabin, enclosed ground, planted corn, and raised cattle. Ever since that time I have enjoyed a good appetite and sound sleep; while the others spend their nights in dancing and are suffering with hunger, I live in plenty; I keep horses, cows, hogs and fowls; I am happy. See! my friend; the birds and fishes have brought me to reflection and taught me to work!" [1] ◆

ANECDOTE.

Toleration. — In the year 1791, two Creek chiefs accompanied an American to England, where, as usual, they attracted great attention, and many flocked around them, as well to learn their ideas of certain things as to behold "the savages." Being asked their opinion of religion, or of what religion they were, one made answer, that they had no priests in their country, or established religion, for they thought, that, upon a subject where there was no possibility of people's agreeing in opinion, and as it was altogether matter of mere opinion, " it was best that every one should paddle his canoe his own way." Here is a volume of instruction in a short answer of a savage!

In Samuel G. Drake's, Biography and History of the Indians of North America, 1848 [2]

NOTES TO THE SKETCHES.

INTRODUCTION.
1. *Centinel of the North-Western Territory*, (Cincinnati, W. Maxwell, August 1, 1795), Col. 1, p. 4.

SKETCH I. An American in Canada.
1. E.A. Cruikshank, *The correspondence of Lieut. Governor John Graves Simcoe, with allied documents relating to his administration of the government of Upper Canada*, (Toronto, The Society, 1923-31), p. 108.
2. An editorial/news story in an unidentified Philadelphia newspaper, July 10, 1800, and reprinted in *The Salem Impartial Register*, July 31, 1800.
3. J. Russell, Jr., *History of the War between the United States and Great Britain*, (Hartford, B. & J. Russell, 1815), p. 112.
4. through 17.
   Rev. A. Wright, *A Pioneer Gone, Obituary of Isaac Hamblin*, in *The Western Christian Advocate*, September 14, 1859.
18. *American Wit and Humor*, (Franklin Square, NY, Harper & Brothers, 1859), p. 10.

SKETCH II. The Melmore Man.
1. William Lang, *History of Seneca County*, (Springfield, OH, Transcript Printing Co., 1880), p. 151-2.
2. Ibid. p. 152.
3. Laura Everett, in notes collected by Joyce Tuckerman Zeigler, *Tuckerman Family History*, Vol. II.
4. Consul W. Butterfield, *History of Seneca County*, (Sandusky, OH, D. Campbell & Sons, 1848), p. 102-3.
5. Laura Everett, in notes collected by Joyce Tuckerman Zeigler, *Tuckerman Family History*, Vol. II.
6. Ibid.
7. Ibid.
8. Samuel G. Drake, *Biography and History of the Indians of North America, from Its First Discovery*, (Boston, Benjamin B. Mussey, & Co., 1848), Tenth Ed., p. 23.

SKETCH III. This Little Piggy Went to War.
1. Robert B. McAfee, *Book and Journal of Robert B. McAfee's Mounted Company*, August 15, 1813, in *Register of the Kentucky Historical Society*, Vol. 26, May 1928, No. 77, pgs. 107-9.
2. Lewis Collins, *History of Kentucky*, (Covington, KY, Collins and Co., 1882) Vol. II, p. 622.

3. Robert B. McAfee, *History of the Late War in the Western Country*, (Originally published in 1816), (Bowling Green, Ohio, Historical Publications Co., C.S. Van Tassel, 1919), p. 415.
4. Collins, *History of Kentucky*, p. 623.
5. *Centinel of the North-Western Territory*, (Cincinnati, W. Maxwell, January 9, 1796), Col. 1, p. 4.

SKETCH IV. The Jersey Boys.

1. Draper notes from Phoebe Miranda and Rachel Kibbey (Daughters of Ben Stites) Draper 3S252-60.
2. *Papers of the Continental Congress, Memorials Addressed to Congress*, (1775-1788, National Archives, Microfilm Pub M247, Roll 49, Item 41, Vol 2), pgs. 537-9; in Harry G. Enoch, *Historical Records of the Enoch Family in Virginia and Pennsylvania*, (lulu.com, 2014), pgs 170-1.
3. Henry A. Ford, A.M. and Mrs. Kate B. Ford, *History of Hamilton County*, (L.A. Williams and Co., 1881), p. 349.
4. Ibid., p. 350.
5. Emilius O. Randall, *Highlights in Ohio Literature*, in *Ohio Archaeological and Historical Quarterly*, (Columbus, OH, Fred I. Heer Printing Co., 1919, Volume XXVIII), p. 260.
6. Bro. Henry Baer, *Three Pioneer Masons of the Early West*, in *The Builder Magazine*, (Joseph Fort Newton, The National Masonic Research Society, December 1928, Vol. XIV, No. 12).
7. W. Maxwell, *The Centinel of the North-western Territory*, (Cincinnati, April 26, 1794), Col.1, p. 3.
8. Henry Howe, *Historical Collections of Ohio*, (Cincinnati, Bradley & Anthony, 1850), p. 323.
9. Letter — Col. John McDonald to Draper, June 30, 1845, Draper 11E28.
10. William Clark, *Notes and Documents, William Clark's Journal of General Wayne's Campaign*, in R. C. McGrane, *The Mississippi Valley Historical Review*, (Oxford, UK, Oxford University Press, Vol. 1, No. 3, Dec. 1914), p. 436.
11. Ibid. p. 442.
12. Bro. Henry Baer, *Three Pioneer Masons of the Early West*, in *The Builder Magazine*, (Joseph Fort Newton, The National Masonic Research Society, November 1928, Vol. XIV, No. 11).
13. Western Spy, *Early Indiana Trails*, July 23, 1799, in Ellen Sieber and Cheryl Ann Munson, *Looking at History, Indiana's Hoosier National Forest Region, 1600 - 1950*, (U.S. Dept. of Agriculture, Forest Service, 1991), pgs 43-4.
14. Judy Adams, *Captain Robert Benham: His Life and Survival on Kentucky's Early Shores*, in *Kenton County Historical Society Bulletin*, (Covington, KY, January 1999), pgs. 2-3.
15. Narrative — Basil Brown to Lyman Draper, Draper 9ZZ121.
16. Louis Phelps Kellogg, *Frontier Retreat on the Upper Ohio 1779-1781*, (Madison, WI, Wisconsin Historical Society, 1917), p. 83.

17. Ibid. p. 84.
18. Mann Butler, *History of the Commonwealth of Kentucky*, (Louisville, KY, Wilcox, Dickerman, and Co. 1834), p. 103.
19. Louis Phelps Kellogg, *Frontier Retreat on the Upper Ohio 1779-1781*, (Madison, WI, Wisconsin Historical Society, 1917), p. 88.
20. Ibid. pgs. 85-6.
21. Ibid. p. 87.
22. Narrative — Basil Brown to Lyman Draper, Draper 9ZZ122-4.
23. John McClung, *Sketches of Western Adventure*, (Dayton, OH, L.F. Clafin & Co., 1852), pgs. 148-9.
24. Narrative — Basil Brown to Lyman Draper, Draper 9ZZ124-5.
25. McClung, *Sketches of Western Adventure*, pgs. 149-50.
26. Ibid., pgs. 150-1.
27. Narrative — Basil Brown to Lyman Draper, Draper 9ZZ126-7.
28 Letter — James Bowman to Draper, July 31, 1845, Draper 11E10.
29. J. Thomas Scharf, A.M., *History of Western Maryland*, (Clearfield Company & Willow Bend Books, 1995), Vol. 1, p. 77.
30. Letter — James Bowman to Draper, July 31, 1845, Draper 11E12.
31. Kellogg, *Frontier Retreat on the Upper Ohio 1779-1781*, p. 90.
32. Elizabeth M. Cooley and Marie Dickore, *The Benham Brothers - Robert, Peter, and Richard: Early Settlers of Southwestern Ohio and Northern Kentucky*, in *Bulletin of the Historical and Philosophical Society of Ohio*, January 1952, Volume 10, No.1, p. 71.
32. *Centinel of the North-Western Territory*, (Cincinnati, W. Maxwell, April 9, 1796), Col. 4, p. 3.

SKETCH V. Jane the Pious.

1. Joseph M. Trimble, *Memoir of Mrs. Jane Trimble, A Tribute of Affection from Her Grandson*, (Cincinnati, R. P. Thompson, 1861), p. 9.
2. Ibid., pgs. 5-6.
3. Ibid., pgs. 35-8.
4. Ibid., pgs. 41-2.
5. Ibid., p. 42.
6. Rev. J. M'D. Mathews, Mrs. Jane Trimble, in *The Ladies Repository and Gatherings of the West*, (Cincinnati, L. Swormstedt and J. T. Mitchell, R.P. Thompson, 1845), p. 345.
7. Ibid., pgs. 345-6.
8. Ibid., p. 347.
9. Trimble, *Memoir of Mrs. Jane Trimble, A Tribute of Affection from Her Grandson*, pgs. 99-100.
10. Ibid., pgs. 183-4.
11. Trimble, Memoir of Mrs. Jane Trimble, A Tribute of Affection from Her Grandson, p. 70.
12. Ibid., pgs. 73-75.

13. Ibid., p. 84.
14. Ibid., p. 85.
15. Ibid.
16. Ibid., p. 88.
17. Ibid., p. 118.
18. Ibid., p. 121.
19. Ibid., pgs. 123-4.
20. Ibid., p. 134.
21. *Centinel of the North-Western Territory*, (Cincinnati, W. Maxwell, August 1, 1795), Col. 1, p. 4.

SKETCH VI.   O Lard! O Lard!.

1. Isaac Lippincott, *The Early Salt Trade of the Ohio Valley*, in *Journal of Political Economy*, (Chicago, The University of Chicago Press, Dec. 1912), Vol. 20, No. 10, pgs. 1029-1052; originally in *General Public Acts of Congress respecting the Sale of Public Lands*, II, p. 286.
2. Chester Raymond Young, *Westward into Kentucky, The Narrative of Daniel Trabue*, (Lexington, KY, The University Press of Kentucky, 1981), pgs. 70-3.
3. *Col. William Fleming's Journal in Kentucky from Nov. 10, 1779 to May 27th, 1780*, in Newton D. Mereness, *Travels in the American Colonies*, (New York, NY, The Macmillan Co., 1916), p. 620.
4. William M. Darlington, *Christopher Gist's Journals*, (Pittsburgh, J.R. Weldin & Co., 1893), p. 43.
5. Elizabeth E. Lea, *Domestic Cookery, Useful Receipts, and Hints to Young Housekeepers*, (Baltimore, Cushings and Bailey, 1859), 10th Edition, pgs. 172-3.
6. Young, *Westward into Kentucky, The Narrative of Daniel Trabue*, p. 73.
7. *Centinel of the North-Western Territory*, (Cincinnati, W. Maxwell, November 9, 1793), Col. 3, p. 3.

SKETCH VII.   Camels That Got Over the Hump.

1. W.W. Dobbins, John E. Reed, *The Battle of Lake Erie, and Reminiscences of the Flaghsips "Lawrence" and "Niagara,"* (Erie, PA, Ashby Printing Company, 1929) 3rd Edition, p. 60.
2. Ibid. pgs. 60-1.
3. Ibid. pgs. 61-2.
4. Ibid. pgs. 62-3.
5. Ibid. p. 63.
6. Alex Slidell Mackenzie, U.S.N., *The Life of Commodore Oliver Hazard Perry*, (New York, Harper & Brothers, 1843), Vol. I, p. 172.
7. Ibid. p. 171.
8. Dobbins, Reed, *The Battle of Lake Erie, and Reminiscences of the Flaghsips "Lawrence" and "Niagara,"* pgs. 80-1.
9. Mackenzie, *The Life of Commodore Oliver Hazard Perry*, p. 176.
10. Ibid. pgs. 174-5.

11. Dobbins, Reed, *The Battle of Lake Erie, and Reminiscences of the Flaghsips "Lawrence" and "Niagara,"* pgs. 84-5.
12. William Besant, *Elementary Hydrostatics*, (London, George Bell & Sons, 1889), p. 52.
13. Dobbins, Reed, *The Battle of Lake Erie, and Reminiscences of the Flaghsips "Lawrence" and "Niagara,"* p. 86.
14. Mackenzie, *The Life of Commodore Oliver Hazard Perry*, pgs. 176-7.
15. Dobbins, Reed, *The Battle of Lake Erie, and Reminiscences of the Flaghsips "Lawrence" and "Niagara,"* pgs. 86-7.
16. Ibid. p.89.
17. Samuel G. Drake, *Biography and History of the Indians of North America, from Its First Discovery*, (Boston, Benjamin B. Mussey, & Co., 1848), Tenth Ed., p. 21.

SKETCH VIII. Wildcat McKinney.

1. James McBride, *Pioneer Biography - Sketches of the Lives of Some of the Early Settlers of Butler County, Ohio*, (Cincinnati, Robert Clarke & Co., 1869) Vol. I, pgs. 211-2.
2. Ibid. p.211.
3. Ibid. pgs. 213-4.
4. *Centinel of the North-Western Territory*, (Cincinnati, W. Maxwell, January 30, 1796), Col. 1, p. 4.

SKETCH IX. Oliver Swift.

1. Draper 7U2-3.
2. Draper 7U3.
3. Draper 7U4.
4. Ibid.
5. Benjamin Drake, Life of Tecumseh and of His Brother the Prophet, (Cincinnati, Anderson, Gates & Wright, 1858), p. 53.
6. Ibid.
7. Ibid., pgs. 53-4.
8. Letter of Lt. Curtis to Jacob Kingsbury, September 21, 1812, Jacob Kingsbury Papers, Chicago History Museum.
9. Letter of Lt. Curtis, Draper, 7U67-8.
10. A Soldier of 1812 (Anonymous), *Recollections of Major William Oliver, Toledo Lucas County Public Library Digital Collections*, 1851, pgs. 7-8.
11. Robert B. McAfee, *History of the Late War in the Western Country*, (Originally published in 1816), (Bowling Green, Ohio Historical Publications Co. C.C. Van Tassel, 1919), p. 280.
12. H.S. Knapp, *History of the Maumee Valley Commencing with the Occupation by the French in 1680*, (Toledo, Blade Mammoth Printing and Publishing House, 1872), p. 159.
13. Journal of Ensign William Schillinger, A Soldier of the War of 1812, in Eastern Shawnee Tribe of Oklahoma Digital Collection, p. 70, (Originally in *Ohio Archaeological and Historical Quarterly*, Vol. 41, No. 1, January 1932, pgs. 52-85).

14. Willard V. Way, *The Facts and Historical Events of the Toledo War of 1835*, (Toledo, Daily Commercial Steam Book and Job Printing House, 1869), p. 43.
15. Ibid.
16. Ibid. pgs. 44-45.
17. Kathryn Miller Keller, The Oliver House, in *Northwest Ohio Quarterly*, Vol. 19, Issue 3, July 1947, pgs. 121-4.
18. *American Wit and Humor*, (Franklin Square, NY, Harper & Brothers., 1859), p. 203.

SKETCH X. The Brothers Clairvoyant.

1. Philip Thomas, *Civilization of Indian Natives*, in *The Massachusetts Missionary Magazine*, (Boston, E. Lincoln, 1807), Vol. 5, p. 268.
2. Ibid. p. 270.
3. Benjamin Drake, *Life of Tecumseh and of his brother The Prophet with a Historical Sketch of the Shawanoe Indians*, (Cincinnati, Anderson, Gates and Wright, 1858), p. 86.
4. Thomas McKenney, *History of the Indian Tribes of North America*, (Philadelphia, Anderson, Rice, Rutter & Co., 1870), pgs. 55-6.
5. Drake, *Life of Tecumseh and of his brother The Prophet with a Historical Sketch of the Shawanoe Indians*, p. 86.
6. Abraham Luckenbach autobiography, diary, and letters in Robert S. Grumet, *Voices from the Delaware Big House Ceremony*, (Norman, OK, University of Oklahoma Press, 2001), pgs. 39-41.
7. *Diary of the Little Indian Congregation on the White River for the Year 1805* in Lawrence Henry Gipson, *The Moravian Indian Mission on White River*, (Indianapolis, IN, Indiana Historical Bureau, 1938), p. 333.
8. Ibid. p. 339.
9. Ibid., pgs. 354-5.
10. Logan Esarey, *Messages and Letters of William Henry Harrison*, (New York, Arno Press, 1975), p. 182.
11. Ibid, pgs. 183-4.
12. Elmore Barce, *The Land of Potawatomi*, (Fowler, IN, The Benton review Shop, 1919), pgs. 26-7.
13. An Inhabitant of Boston (Andrew Newell), *Darkness at Noon or, the Great Solar Eclipse of the 16th of June 1806, Described and Represented in Every Particular*, (Boston, MA, D. Carlisle & A. Newell, May 1806), p. 7.
14. Fred Espenak, *Total Solar Eclipse of 1806 Jun 16*, (EclipseWise.com, Last Updated: Mar 21, 2018), www.eclipsewise.com/solar/SEgmapx/1801-1900/S1806Jun16Tgmapx.html.
15. Letter from Timothy Barnard, Creek Nation, 14th May 1812, in *The Georgia Journal*, May 27, 1812, p. 3, Cols. 1-2.
16. Ibid.
17. McKenney, *History of the Indian Tribes of North America*, pgs. 64-5.

18. Extracted of a letter to a gentleman in Lexington from his friend at New Madrid, (U.L.) dated 16th, Dec. 1811, in the *Kentucky Reporter*, reprinted in *The Georgia Journal*, March 25, 1812, Page 2, Col. 4.
19. Drake, *Life of Tecumseh and of his brother The Prophet with a Historical Sketch of the Shawanoe Indians*, p. 158.
20. William Caldwell to Lyman Draper, Draper 17S221.
21. Ibid. 17S220.
21. Letter of James Galloway to Lyman Draper, January 29, 1841, Draper, 7U66.

SKETCH XI. The Race to Paris — Harmar's Victory.

1. Article I of the Treaty of Paris, 1783.
2. Letter — John Adams to Congress from Paris, September 5, 1783, in Francis Wharton, *The Revolutionary Diplomatic Correspondence of the United States*, (Washington, Government Printing Office, 1889), Vol. 6, p. 674.
3. Edmund Burnett, *Letters of Members of the Continental Congress*, (Washington, DC: The Carnegie Institution of Washington, 1921-1936), Vol. 7, Citation 423, p. 357.
4. Burnett, *Letters of Members of the Continental Congress*, Citation 434, p. 364.
5. Thomas Jefferson, *Autobiography Draft Fragment*, Written February 11, 1821, in *The Thomas Jefferson Papers*, Library of Congress. Series 1, p. 30.
6. Ibid., p. 33.
7. Letter — Thomas Mifflin to William Livingston, January 4, 1784, in Paul H. Smith / Ronald M. Gephart, *Letters of Delegates to Congress*, (Washington, Library of Congress, 1994), Vol. 21, p. 258.
8. Letter — Thomas Mifflin to Franklin, Adams and Jay, in Francis Wharton, *The Revolutionary Diplomatic Correspondence of the United States*, (Washington, Government Printing Office, 1889), Vol. 6, pgs. 754-5.
9. James A. Marusek, *A Chronological Listing of Early Weather Events*, 7th Ed., p. 843, originally in Ben Gelber, *The Pennsylvania Weather Book*, Rutgers University Press, 2002.
10. Jefferson, *Autobiography Draft Fragment*, p. 38.
11. Letter — Thomas Mifflin to Josiah Harmar, January 14, 1784, in Paul H. Smith/ Ronald M. Gephart, *Letters of Delegates to Congress*, (Washington, Library of Congress, 1994), Vol. 21, pgs. 274-5.
12. Letter — Thomas Mifflin to the Chevalier de La Luzerne, January 14, 1784, in Paul H. Smith / Ronald M. Gephart, *Letters of Delegates to Congress*, (Washington, Library of Congress, 1994), Vol. 21, p. 275.
13. Letter — Charles Thomson to Benjamin Franklin, January 15, 1784, in Paul H. Smith / Ronald M. Gephart, *Letters of Delegates to Congress*, (Washington, Library of Congress, 1994), Vol. 21, p. 284.
14. Letter — Morris to the President of Congress, February 2, 1784, in *The Revolutionary Diplomatic Correspondence of the United States*, (Washington, Government Printing Office, 1889), Vol. 6, p. 762.

15. Letter — Franks to Mifflin, in Herbert Friedenwald, *Jews Mentioned in the Journal of the Continental Congress*, in *Publications of the American Jewish Historical Society*, (New York, American Jewish Historical Society, 1893), No. 1. p. 83. Original in *Papers of the Continental Congress*, No. 78, Vol. IX, p. 511.
16. Ibid., p. 84.
17. Letter — Cadwalader Morris to Jacob Read, Feb. 13, 1784, in Paul H. Smith / Ronald M. Gephart, *Letters of Delegates to Congress*, (Washington, Library of Congress, 1994), Vol. 21, p. 355.
18. Letter — Jacob Read to Benjamin Guerard, Mar. 1, 1784, in Paul H. Smith / Ronald M. Gephart, *Letters of Delegates to Congress*, (Washington, Library of Congress, 1994), Vol. 21, p. 398.
19. Ibid., Footnote on p. 398.
20. Letter — Franklin and Jay to Hartley, Mar. 31, 1784. *Harmar Papers, 1783-1785*, Box/Vol. 1, William L. Clements Library, Univ. of Mich.
21. Letter — Hartley to Laurens, Mar. 26, 1784, in *The Revolutionary Diplomatic Correspondence of the United States*, (Washington, Government Printing Office, 1889), Vol. 6, pgs. 789-90.
22. Letter — The President to the Secretary of War, November 19, 1790, in John Bloom and Clarence Carter, *The Territorial Papers of the United States*, (Washington, National Archives and Records Service, 1934), Vol. 2, p. 310.
23. Paul H. Smith, Ronald M. Gephart, *Letters of Delegates to Congress, 1774-1789*, (Washington, Library of Congress, 1976), p. 289.

SKETCH XII. The Forgotten Colony of Clark.

1. William Salter, *A Heroine of the Revolution: Nancy Ann Hunter grandmother of the Honorable A.C. Dodge*, in *The Iowa Historical Record*, (Iowa City, IA, Iowa State Historical Society, April 1886), Vol. II, No. 2. p. 259.
2. Letter — Robert George to George Slaughter, from Fort Jefferson, February 15, 1781, in *George Rogers Clark Papers*, 1771-1781, (Springfield, IL, Trustees of the Illinois State Historical Library, 1912), p. 506.
3. Ibid.
4. Letter — John Dodge to Thomas Jefferson, from Fort Jefferson, August 1, 1780, in *George Rogers Clark Papers*, 1771-1781, (Springfield, IL, Trustees of the Illinois State Historical Library, 1912), pgs. 436-7.
5. Mann Butler, *A History of the Commonwealth of Kentucky*, (Louisville, KY, Wilcox, Dickerman, and Co., 1834), p. 119.
6. Ibid.
7. Ibid.
8. William Hayden English, *Conquest of the Country Northwest of the River Ohio 1778-1783; and Life of Gen. George Rogers Clark*, (Indianapolis, IN & Kansas City, MO, The Bowen-Merrill Co., 1896), p. 675.
9. Salter, *A Heroine of the Revolution*, Vol. II, No. 2. p. 260.
10. English, *Conquest of the Country Northwest of the River Ohio 1778-1783; and Life of Gen. George Rogers Clark*, p. 621.

11. Letter — George Slaughter to Thomas Jefferson, from Louisville January 14, 1781, in *George Rogers Clark Papers*, 1771-1781, (Springfield, IL, Trustees of the Illinois State Historical Library, 1912), p. 493.
12. Salter, *A Heroine of the Revolution*, Vol. II, No. 2. pgs. 261-2.
13. Ibid., p. 263.
14. E.A. Linn and N. Sargent, *The Life and Public Services of Dr. Lewis F. Linn*, (New York, NY, D. Appleton and Company, 1857), Vol. 6, pgs. 8-10.
15. Ibid., pgs. 11-2.
16. Ibid., pgs. 13-6.
17. Chester R. Young, *Westward into Kentucky, The Narrative of Daniel Trabue*, (Lexington, KY, University of Kentucky Press, 1981), p. 144.
18. Ibid., pgs. 144-5.
19. Samuel G. Drake, *Biography and History of the Indians of North America, from Its First Discovery*, (Boston, Benjamin B. Mussey, & Co., 1848), Tenth Ed., p. 27.

SKETCH XIII. Reserved for Connecticut.

1. Frances Manwaring Caulkins, *History of New London, Connecticut*, (New London, CT, Frances Manwaring Caulkins, 1860), p. 547.
2. Ibid., p. 553.
3. Ibid.
4. Ibid., p. 554.
5. Ibid., pgs. 554-5.
6. Ibid., p. 562.
7. Ibid.
8. Harriet Taylor Upton, *History of the Western Reserve*, (Chicago/New York, The Lewis Publishing Co., 1910), Vol. I, p. 38.
9. Ibid.
10. Robert A. Wheeler, *Visions of the Western Reserve*, (Columbus, OH, Ohio State University Press, 2000), p. 101.
11. Ibid.
12. Ibid., pgs. 101-2.
13. Ibid., p. 117.
14. Ibid.
15. Ibid., pgs. 118-9.
16. Zerah Hawley, *Journal of a Tour*, (New Haven, CT, S, Converse, 1822), pgs. 58-9.
17. Ibid., pgs.. 60-1.
18. Ibid., p. 61.
19. Ibid., p. 62.
20. Wheeler, *Visions of the Western Reserve*, p. 130.
21. Ibid., pgs. 130-1.
22. Ibid., p. 133.
23. Ibid., p. 131.

24. Ibid., pgs. 133-4.
25. Ibid., p. 137.
26. Ibid., pgs. 136-7.
27. William A. Powell, Jr., *Methodist Circuit-Riders in America, 1766-1844*, (Master's Theses, Paper 813, 1977), p. 34., https://scholarship.richmond.edu/masters-theses/813
28. Joseph Badger, *A Memoir of Rev. Joseph Badger*, (Hudson, OH, Sawyer, Ingersoll and Company, 1851), pgs. 25-6.
29. Ibid., pgs. 26-7.
30. Ibid., pgs. 28-9.
31. Ibid., pgs. 36-7.
32. Ibid., pgs. 54-6.
33. Ibid., p. 185.
34. *Centinel of the North-Western Territory*, (Cincinnati, W. Maxwell, July 12, 1794), Col. 3, p. 3.

SKETCH XIV. The Mud Duck.

1. Juliette A. Kinzie, *Wau-Bun, The Early Day in the Northwest*, (Philadelphia, J.B. Lippincott & Co., 1873), pgs. 244-6.
2. *Centinel of the North-Western Territory*, (Cincinnati, W. Maxwell, December 19, 1795), Col. 1-2, p. 3.

SKETCH XV. My Husband Went to War.

1. Robert A. Wheeler, *Visions of the Western Reserve*, (Columbus, OH, Ohio State University Press, 2000), p. 87.
2. Ibid., p. 87.
3. Ibid., p. 88.
4. Ibid., p. 89.
5. Ibid., p. 90.
6. Ibid., p. 91.
7. Ibid., p. 93.
8. Lydia B. Bacon, *Biography of Lydia B. Bacon*, (Boston, Massachusetts Sabbath School Society, 1856), p. 9.
9. Ibid., pgs. 10-1.
10. Ibid., p. 13.
11. Ibid., pgs. 20-1.
12. Ibid., p. 26.
13. Ibid., pgs. 27-9.
14. Ibid., pgs. 32-4.
15. Ibid., p. 37.
16. Ibid., p. 54.
17. Ibid., pgs. 66-9.
18. *American Wit and Humor*, (Franklin Square, NY, Harper & Brothers., 1859), p. 23.

SKETCH XVI. A Lytle Indian Influence.

1. Juliette A. Kinzie, *Wau-Bun, The Early Day in the Northwest*, (Philadelphia, J.B. Lippincott & Co., 1873), pgs. 211-2.
2. Ibid., p. 213.
3. Ibid., pgs. 218-9.
4. Ibid., p. 224.
5. Ibid., p. 225.
6. McKillup is cited as being killed on the battlefield in: Le Roy Barnett & Roger Rosentreter, *Michigan's Early Military Forces*, (Detroit, Wayne State University Press, 2003) p. 46; Alan D. Gaff, *Bayonets in the Wilderness*, (Norman, University of Oklahoma Press, 2004) p. 308; Wiley Sword, *President Washington's Indian War*, (Norman, University of Oklahoma Press, 1985), p. 304.
7. Kinzie, *Wau-Bun*, p. 226.
8. Richard C. Knopf, *Two Journals of the Kentucky Volunteers*, August 20, 1794; originally in *Filson Club History Quarterly*, Vol. XXVII, No. 3 (July 1953), pgs. 247-81.
9. Kinzie, *Wau-Bun*, p. 150.
10. Ibid., p. 166.
11. J. Seymour Curry, *Chicago: Its History and Its Builders*, (Chicago, The S. J. Clarke Publishing Company, 1912) Vol. 1, p. 82.
12. Kinzie, *Wau-Bun*, pgs. 186-8.
13. Ibid., pgs. 197-8.
14. Ibid., pgs. 198-9.
15. *Centinel of the North-Western Territory*, (Cincinnati, W. Maxwell, November 21, 1795), Col. 1, p. 4.

SKETCH XVII. Keen Indian Insight.

1. Rev. John Heckewelder, *An Account of the History, Manners, and Customs of the Indian Nations, Who Once Inhabited Pennsylvania and the Neighbouring States*, (Philadelphia, Abraham Small, 1819), pgs. 315-7.
2. Samuel G. Drake, *Biography and History of the Indians of North America, from Its First Discovery*, (Boston, Benjamin B. Mussey, & Co., 1848), Tenth Ed., p. 21.

INDEX.

Abingdon, VA, 87
Adair County, KY, 102
Adams, John, 179-81, 189
Adams, John Quincy, 143
Aesop, 253
Akron, OH, 223
Alabama, 168
Alexandria, KY, 80
Allegheny Mountains, 265
Alleghany River, 117
Amelia (ship), 118-119
American Coot, 253, 255-256
American Revolution, 2, 10, 11, 14-15, 17, 35, 52, 69, 83, 102, 126, 150-151, 179, 182, 192, 194, 198, 201-202, 206, 210, 223-225, 230-231, 257, 280, 283, 300
Amherstburg, ON, Canada, 20
Amsterdam, Netherlands, 121
Anbury (author), 44
Anglo-Dutch Wars, 2
Ann Arbor, MI, 143
Annapolis, MD, 183-187, 189-190
Appalachian Mountains, 1, 4, 6-7, 9-10, 151, 195, 223, 230, 237
Ariel (ship), 118
Arkansas Post, 71
Arkansas (Ozark) River, 71, 73
Arnold, Benedict, 190, 203, 224-229
Articles of Confederation, 16
Athens, ON, Canada, 35
Atlantic Ocean (coast), 1, 2, 8, 14, 180, 199, 295
Auglaize River, 156-157
Augusta County, VA, 86, 96
Aurora, OH, 234, 247
Austinburg, OH, 248
Bacon, Lydia, 265-268, 271, 272-277
Bacon, Josiah, 265-267, 271, 274-277
Baden-Powell, Sir Robert, 296
Badger, Joseph, 247-251

Baird, Colonel Jedediah, 243
Baltimore, MD, 187, 220
Baptist, 246
Barcley, Commodore Robert, 189, 294
Bardstown, KY, 211
Barrett, Captain Abner, 177
Bass Island, 48
Battle of Blue Licks, 285
Battle of Fallen Timbers, 129, 152, 256, 285-286
Battle of Lake Erie, 111, 259
Battle of Point Pleasant, 125
Battle of the Thames, 21, 32, 175, 260
Battle of Tippecanoe, 165, 268, 270
Battle of Wisconsin Heights, 213
Battle of Yorktown, 179
Baum Company, 140-141
Bean's Station, TN, 87
Beate, 159-163
Benham, Joseph S., 80
Benham, Peter, 80
Benham, Robert, 51, 68-81
Beresford, Richard, 185-186
Berks County, 19
Big Warrior, Chief, 170
Black Hawk, 213, 218
Black Hoof, Chief, 163, 167
Black Partridge, 291
Black River, 248
Black Rock, NY, 112, 114-115, 118, 120
Bloomington, IN, 34
Blue Jacket, 159, 168
Blue Licks, KY, 101
Boonesboro, KY, 103
Boston, MA, 44, 265, 267, 276
Boswell, Colonel William, 139
Boudinot, Elias, 182-183
Bowling Green State University, 252
Bowman, James, 79
Boy Scouts of America, 69, 296-297
Bradshaw, James, 17

Bright Horn, 132-133
Brock, Major General Isaac, 21, 112, 275-276
Brookfield, CT, 16
Brown, Basil, 52, 70-71, 73-80
Brown, Case, 39
Brown, Daniel, 36
Brown, Elizabeth, 35, 39, 41
Brown, Ezra, 35-43
Brown, Noah, 116, 122
Brown, Sabrina (Ransom) Parks, 41-42
Brown, Thomas, 52, 79
Brownsville, PA, 52, 70, 79
Brownstown, MI, 274
Buckongahelas, Chief, 161
Bucks County, 19
Buck Creek, 177
Buffalo, NY, 39, 112, 117, 141
Bullit's Lick, KY, 101, 105-108, 110
Bullit, Thomas, 103
Bunker's Hill, 44
Burlington, IA, 218
Burlington, ON, 30
Burnet House, 147
Burnet, Jacob, 68
Burton, OH, 242-243, 248
Butler's Rangers, 285
Cahokia, IL, 203
Caldwell, William, 175-176, 285, 292
Caledonia (ship), 118
California, 42-43
Captain Johnny, 132-133
Case Western Reserve University, 252
Catfish, Chief, 289-290
Cambridge University, 122
Campbell, Colonel John, 74-75
Campbell County, KY, 80-81
Canada, 2, 14, 17-20, 24, 35-36, 39, 48, 120, 241, 259-260, 263, 293-294
Cane Ridge, KY, 92, 94-95, 158
Canterbury, CT, 233
Canton, OH, 238
Cape Cod, MA, 4
Cass, Lewis, 112, 287

Centinel of the North-Western Territory, 63, 67
Chachagoussiou, 287
Chagrin, OH, 248
Chapline, Lieutenant Abraham, 74
Chatham-Kent Museum, 32
Chatham, NY, 35
Chatham, ON, 20, 23, 30, 32
Chauncey, Commodore, 112, 114-116
Cherokee, 4
Chesapeake Bay, 2, 187
Chicago, IL, 41, 130, 287-290, 295
Chickasaw, 207-208
Chickasaw Bluffs, 219
Chillicothe, OH, 98, 101, 151, 203
Choctaw, 208
Choir Invisible, the, 126
Church of Latter Day Saints, 237
Cincinnati, OH, 46, 51, 58-59, 62-63, 65-68, 70, 74, 80-81, 130-132, 140-141, 147-148, 196, 267, 272
Cincinnati Municipal Airport, 58
Cincinnati Reds, 80
Civil War, 14
Clark, George Rogers, 70-71, 73-75, 202-205, 207, 209, 213, 219
Clark, Rev. D. W., 83
Clark, William, 65, 202
Clark's Colony, 202
Clay, General Greene, 137-140
Clay, Henry, 94
Cleaveland, General Moses, 231, 233
Cleveland, OH, 112, 231, 237-239, 241, 243-244, 248, 262
Clinch Mountain, 88
Clinch River, 88, 95, 99
Colbert, James, 208
Collins, Joel, 127
Collins, Lewis, 49
Collins, Mrs., 127
Collins, Stephen, 127
Columbia, KY, 102
Columbia, OH, 58-61, 63-65
Columbia Township, 67

INDEX 315

Columbia-Tusculum, 58
Columbian Scouters, 65
Columbus, Christopher, 2, 4, 58
Columbus, OH, 33
Combs, Leslie, 139
Congregationalist, 246-247
Connecticut, 16, 19, 180, 186, 188, 223, 230-231, 234, 239-240
Connecticut Land Company, 231, 233
Connecticut Reserve, 225, 239, 246
Constitution of the United States, 16, 280
Continental Army, 14, 15, 19, 60, 87
Continental Congress, 54, 56, 180, 182, 198-199
Cooper, James Fenimore, 165
Cornplanter, 281-284
Cornwallis, General, 179
Crab Orchard, KY, 91
Creek, 168-171, 174, 301
Cresap, Michael, 79
Crown, The, 7, 8, 17-18, 35
Cumberland Gap, 9, 90
Curtis, Lieutenant, 135-136
Cuyahoga River, 231, 233, 238-239, 248,
Cuyahoga River Valley, 237
Darkness at Noon, 166-167
Day, Alva, 261-264
Day, Sarah, 261-264
Dayton, OH, 272
Dearborn County, IN, 68
Deerfield, OH, 60-61, 68, 261
Defiance, OH, 156, 286
Delaware (Lenape), 8, 125, 159-160, 162, 164, 166, 248, 281, 299-300
Delaware River, 187
Delaware (state), 180, 186-187
Delay, Henry, 54
Denman, Matthias, 58
Denver & Rio Grande Line, 255
Detroit, MI, 4, 22, 25-26, 28, 42, 75, 112, 142-143, 170, 241, 263-264, 272, 274, 284-287, 289, 292, 295
Detroit River, 20, 22, 30, 273-274, 294
Detroit Road, 27

Detroit (ship), 119
Dobbins, Captain Daniel, 111-115, 117, 121-122
Dodge, Augustus Caesar, 218-219
Dodge, Israel, 210-213
Dodge, John, 206, 210-212
Dodge-Leavenworth Expedition, 213
Dodge, (Moses) Henry, 211-214, 217-219
Dooright, Dudley, 30
Dover, DE, 191
Drake, Benjamin, 156, 158
Draper, Lyman, 70, 76, 79, 102, 175-177
Dudley, Colonel William, 139
East Jersey Company, 56
Eckford, Henry, 115
Eldred, Mr., 243
Elliot, Captain Matthew, 175
Elliot, Captain William, 22
Elliott, J. D., 114-115
Ellsquatawa (see Prophet, the)
Ellsworth, Henry, 234-237
Ellsworth, Oliver, 234
Ely, Merrick, 262
England, 1-2, 4, 5, 8, 14, 17-18, 21, 69, 72, 213, 237, 252, 260, 295-296
Enochs, Henry, 54
Erikson, Leif, 2
Erie, PA, 111-114, 116-119
Erie (ship), 32
Erwin, Mrs., 89
Erwin, William, 89
Esarey, Logan, 163
Essex County, 54
Euclid, OH, 248
Europe, 193-194, 228
Everett, Laura, 38
Exploits of Daniel Boone, the, 69, 78
F-15E Strike Eagle, 255
Ferrari, 28
Ferris, Mr., 56
Fields, Lewis, 215-217
Filson, John, 58
Findlay, OH, 273

SKETCHES OF INTRIGUING PEOPLE

Finley, Rev. James, 97
Firelands, 223, 225, 230-231
Five Medals, 134
Fleming, Colonel William, 107
Florida, 1, 170
Ford, Alden, 245
Ford, Lovina, 245
Ford, Mr. Elijah, 244-245
Ford, Mrs. Esther, 244
Ford, Mr. John, 242
Forsythe, Major, 36
Fort Amanda, 139
Fort Dearborn, 130-131, 287-290, 292-293, 295
Fort Defiance, 139, 285-286
Fort Detroit, 7, 21, 46, 112, 131, 137-138, 204, 210, 263, 273-276
Fort Erie, 113, 276
Fort Findlay, 139
Fort George, 113
Fort Greenville, 67, 152
Fort Griswold, 226, 228-230
Fort Harrison, 269
Fort Independence, 265
Fort Jefferson, 201-204, 206-211, 213, 218-219, 221
Fort Kaskaskia, 203, 209, 213
Fort Knox, 268
Fort Logan, 103, 105, 110
Fort Mackinaw, 111-112, 130-131
Fort Malden, 20-22, 28-29, 30, 46, 48, 112, 259-260, 263-264, 274, 293-295
Fort Meigs, 28, 137-142, 256, 264, 293
Fort Miamis, 137, 273, 285
Fort Necessity, 273
Fort Niagara, 283
Fort Pitt, 7, 21, 69, 213, 280-281
Fort Seneca, 140
Fort Stephenson, 28
Fort Trumbull, 226, 228
Fort Vincennes, 203, 211
Fort Washington, 62-63, 80, 196-197
Fort Wayne, 65, 129-133, 135, 137, 139, 155, 196, 286, 289-290

Fort Wayne, IN, 4
Four Seasons, the, 51
France, 5, 6, 9, 15, 188, 192, 194, 287
Franklin, Benjamin, 179, 181, 185, 189, 191-192, 198, 280
Franklin County, 33
Franks, Lt.-Colonel David, 188-191
Fremont, OH, 28
French & Indian War, 5
Galloway, James, 177
Galvez, Bernardo de, 70-71
Garrard, Captain, 138
General Myers (ship), 32
Genesee County, 19, 39
George, Captain Robert, 204-205, 207-208, 211
Georgia, 168, 180
Gibway Point, 38
Girl Scouts, 297
Girty, Simon, 75
Gist, Christopher, 108
Glass, Mrs., 277
Gnadenhutten, 300
God the Father (Abrahamism), 149
Governor's Island, NY, 192
Grand River, 250
Great Barrington, MA, 16
Great Black Swamp, 253, 273
Great Britain, 4, 14, 15, 35, 111, 175, 180, 193, 257, 288-289
Great Crossings, KY, 45
Great Lakes, 1, 9, 10, 141, 210
Great Miami River, 57
Greenville, OH, 156, 163
Groton, CT, 224, 226, 228-229
Grouseland, 68, 168
Halifax, 295
Hamblin, Hannah, 34
Hamblin, (Hamlin), Isaac, 16, 17, 19, 20, 22-35
Hamblin, Isaac Jr., 33-34
Hamilton County, OH, 68, 81
Hamilton, Henry, (Hair-Buyer), 210
Hamilton, Paul, 114-115, 120

INDEX

Hamlin, William Jr., 19
Hamlin, Elisha, 16, 19
Hamlin, Perez, 16, 17
Hamlin, Rachel, 16
Hardin, Colonel, 197
Harmar, General Josiah, 58, 62-63, 80, 179, 184-186, 188-198
Harmar's Defeat, 199
Harpersfield, OH, 248
Harrison County, 54
Harrison, General William Henry, 21-22, 28-33, 45, 68, 119-120, 132-133, 136-140, 148, 162-168, 174, 260, 268, 270, 276, 288, 293, 295
Harrodsburg, KY, 46, 49, 103, 110, 203
Hartford, CT, 187
Hartley, David, 179, 181, 192
Hartzel, Joseph, 262
Hathaway's Mill, 53
Hawley, Zerah, 239-241
Hayden, William, 209
Heald, Captain, 289-291
Heckewelder, Rev. David, 44, 299-300
Henry, Ann, 211
Henry, Moses, 211-212
Henry, Patrick, 69, 70, 73, 202
Hickock, Mr, Eleazer, 242
Hillsboro, Ohio, 94
Historical Collections of Ohio, 69
Holes, John, 54
Holland, 15
Honey Creek, OH, 39-40
Hood's Point, VA, 204
Horseshoe Ford, 88-89
Hotel de York, 180
Howe, Henry, 64, 69
Hudson, Esquire, 247
Hudson, OH, 237-238, 247
Hudson River, 9
Hull, General William, 20-21, 112, 130-132, 138, 243, 263-264, 272-276, 289
Hull's Trace, 272
Hunter, Nancy Ann, 209-213, 217-219

Huron River, 248
Iceland, 2
Illinois, 10, 71, 204, 207, 219-220, 288
Independence Hall, 182
India, 4
Indian Removal Act, 42
Indian Reserve, 7, 9
Indiana, 10, 129, 140, 163, 209
Indiana Magazine of History, 165
Indiana Territory, 68, 132, 153, 166-167, 257, 265, 267, 270
Iowa Territory, 218
Ireland, 4
Iroquois, 8, 125, 168, 281
Island House Hotel, 146
Jackson, Andrew, 42, 143
Jackson's Fort, 52-53
James Fort, 4
Jamestown, 4
Jaqua, Richard, 36-38
Jay, John, 179-181, 189, 191-192
Jefferson, Thomas, 183-185, 188, 202, 206-207, 210-211, 213
Jenkins, Sarah, 194
Jesuit, 4
Joliet, Luois, 4
Johnson, Colonel (Indian Agent), 283
Johnson, Colonel Richard M., 31-32, 45-46
Jones, Mrs., 269
Juliette Magill Kinzie Gordon (see Low, Juliette Gordon)
Kaskaskia, IL, 70, 72, 210-211, 219-220
Kekionga, 286
Kentucky, 8-10, 23, 33, 45-46, 48, 57, 63, 74, 77, 86-87, 91, 94, 96, 102-104, 106-108, 125-126, 128, 132, 137-139, 158, 171, 176, 197, 204, 207, 211-212, 216, 268, 286
Kentucky Gazette, 126
Kenyon College, 34
Kibbey, (Kibbe, Kibby) Ephraim, 51, 57, 60-68, 80-81
Kibbey, Miranda, 53

Kibbey, Phoebe, 53
Kibbey, Rachel, 53, 59
Kibbey's Road, 68
Kickapoo, 164
Kilbourn, Colonel James, 39-40
King George III, 7-8, 179-180
King George III Proclamation, 6-7
King George's War, 5
King James I, 4
King of England, 6-7, 180-181, 185, 193-194, 223
King Williams War, 5
Kinzie, Eleanor Lytle McKillup, (see Lytle, Eleanor)
Kinzie, John Sr., 286-295
Kinzie, Juliette, 253
Kirtland, Judge, 248
Kirtland, OH, 237
Knox, General, 87-88, 90-91
Lafayette, IN, 209, 269
Lafayette, Marquis de, 189
Lake Erie, 14, 20, 22, 28, 30, 47-48, 111-114, 118, 124, 223, 237-238, 259, 262-264, 274, 294
Lake Huron, 21, 24
Lake Michigan, 4, 287
Lake Ontario, 14, 30, 260
Lalawethika, (see Prophet, the)
La Luzerne, Chevalier de, 188-189
Lamoin (Lemoine), Darby, 243
Lang, William, 36
La Salle, de Cavelier, 4, 287
Laurens, Henry, 189, 192
Lawrence (ship), 111, 119-124
Le Courier de l'Amerique, 191-193
Ledyard, Colonel, 229
Lee, Dr. Arthur, 183-184
LeGrand, Mr., 188
Lenni Lenape, 2
Lewis and Clark, 202
Lexington Green, MA, 19
Lexington, KY, 91, 126, 209
Licking River, 58, 74, 76-77, 80
Limestone, KY, 53, 63

Linn, Asael, 213-217
Linn, Colonel William, 213-214
Linn, Lewis Fields, 217-219
Linn, Mary Ann, 217
Linn, Nancy Ann Hunter Dodge (see Hunter, Nancy Ann)
Linn's Station, 214
Little Miami River, 54, 56-57, 59, 61
Little Rail, 253
Little Turtle, 159, 164, 196
Livingston, Governor William, 185
Logan, Colonel Benjamin, 103
Logan, Johnny, 132-133, 136
London, 4, 190-191, 193-194
Long Island, NY, 191, 224
Long Island Sound, 230
L'Orient, 182, 192
Losantville, OH, 58-59, 61-62, 80
Louisiana, 194, 213
Louisiana Purchase, 1
Louisville, KY, 72-75, 79, 101, 203, 209, 211, 213-214, 219, 272
Low, Juliette Gordon, 296
Low, Mackey, 296
Lower Canada, 14
Lucas County, OH, 143, 146
Lucas, Robert, 143-144
Luckenbach, Abraham, 160-161
Ludlow, Cornelius, 54
Lytle, Eleanor (Nelly), 280-288, 290-293, 295-297
Lytle, Mr. (father), 281-284
Lytle, Mrs. (mother), 282
Mackinaw Island, 111, 289
Macomb, Mr., 295
Mad River, 177
Madison, Pres. James, 21, 112, 114
Mahoning River, 233
Maine, 14, 187
Manhatten, 141
Mannahatta, 2
Mantua, OH, 235, 247
Marietta, OH, 51
Marquette, Fr. Jacques, 4, 287

INDEX

Martin County, IN, 68
Maryland, 180, 182, 186
Marysville, OH, 42-43
Mason, Governor, 143-144
Mason, Peter, 264
Massachusetts, 15, 180, 186, 248
Masterson, Mrs., 127
Maumee, OH, 137, 140, 144, 146, 273
Maumee River, 28, 65, 129, 137, 140-141, 231, 256, 264, 274, 285
Mayflower, 4
Maysville, KY, 48, 56, 63, 101
McAfee, Robert, 49, 138
McBride, James, 127
McClung, John, 75, 77
McDonald, John, 64
McDonald, Thomas, 64
McKee, Captain Thomas, 175-176
McKenney, Thomas, 157, 170
McKenzie, Margaret, 286-287
McKillup, Colonel Daniel, 284-286
McKinney, John "Wildcat", 125-128
Mead, General David, 112, 123
Meigs, Return J., 137, 139
Melish, John, 237-238
Melmore, OH. 39-42
Mentor, OH, 248
Mesopotamia, OH, 247
Methodist, 246
Miami, 4, 196, 290-291
Miami-Erie Canal, 141, 146
Miamis (ship), 32
Michigan, 4, 10, 22, 41-42, 141-146
Michigan Territory, 142-143
Mifflin, Thomas, 183-190, 192, 198
Miller, Colonel, 269, 276
Minnesota, 10
Mississinewa River, 156
Mississippi River, 1, 2, 4, 6, 10, 69-74, 97, 141, 151, 159, 168, 170, 173, 201, 203, 206-207, 219-220, 223
Missouri, 128, 174, 218
Moffitt, Colonel James, 84
Mohawk River, 9

Monmouth County, NJ, 69
Monongahela, 219
Monongahela River, 52, 60-61, 69
Monroe, MI, 22
Montgomery, AL, 168
Montreal, QC, Canada, 276
Moravian, 299
Morris, Cadwalader, 191, 199
Morris County, 54
Morris, Robert, 183, 188-190
Morristown, NJ, 187
Morristown, NY, 37
Motshee Monetoo (Evil Spirit), 149
Mud Hen, 255
Nan-nee-bo-zho, 254
Narragansett Pacer, 88
Nash, Emily, 241-245
Nash, Philansia, 245
Nash, Philenia, 245
Nassau Hall, 182
Natchez (Manchac) (Natchitoches), 71-73, 219-220
Nautical Almanac, 167
Navajo, 4
Needham, Orwell, 245
Nell, 30
Neolin, 159
Netherlands, 10, 121, 182
Nevada County, CA, 43
New Connecticut, 232, 241, 252
New England, 44, 187-188, 246, 267, 269, 271, 276
New France, 2, 6
New Hampshire, 180, 186
New Jersey, 2, 51-52, 54, 56, 60, 69, 180, 186-187
New London, CT, 224, 228-229
New Madrid, MO, 170-172, 174, 271
New Netherland, 2
New Orleans, LA, 69-74, 201, 213, 237
Newport, KY, 45-47, 80, 272
Newport, NY, 267
New York, 2, 8, 16, 36, 38-39, 54, 56, 116-117, 180, 183, 188-191, 223, 233

Niagara, 19, 276, 285
Niagara River, 112, 114, 116, 284
Niagara (ship), 111, 119-121, 123-124
Nichols, Colonel, 112
North America, 1-5, 257, 260
Northampton County, 19
North Bend, OH, 59
North Carolina, 180, 186, 238
North San Juan, CA, 43
Northwest Territory, 10, 21, 41, 45, 56, 58, 81, 83, 94-95, 101-102, 125, 129, 131, 150, 158-159, 202, 223, 246, 253, 257-260, 277, 279, 285
Northwest Ordinance, 10, 195
Northwestern Army, 45, 52
Norwich, CT, 224
Nova Caesara Harmony Lodge No. 2, 51
Ogden, Colonel, 182
Ogdensburgh, 36
Ohio, 28-29, 39, 42, 48, 66-68, 96, 108, 129, 131-133, 137-142, 144-146, 148, 152-153, 177, 204, 223, 225, 231, 233-234, 252-253, 257, 260-261, 264, 272-273
Ohio-Erie Canal, 239
Ohio River, 8-10, 46-48, 52-54, 56, 60-62, 69-71, 73, 80, 102, 132, 141, 152, 195, 201-202, 214-216, 267
Ohio River Valley, 4, 8-10, 51-52, 56, 60-61, 101, 103-104, 125, 151, 203, 218, 267
Ohio (ship), 118-119
Ohio State University, 143
Ojibwe, 24
Oklahoma Territory, 213
Old Kettle Furnace (Durant, Ohio), 109
Oliver House, 147
Oliver, Peter, 131
Oliver, William, 129-141, 143, 146-148
Ontario, 14
Opelousas, 73
Open Door, (see Prophet, the)
Ottawa, 7, 24, 158-159
Owen, Captain George, 209

Owen, George, Jr., 209
Owens, Thomas, 209
Painesville, OH, 248
Parkman, OH, 243, 245
Paris, 1, 126, 180, 182-183, 185-190, 193-194, 207
Parks, William Henry, 42
Parliament, 179, 194
Passy, 192
Patterson, 38
Patton, 208
Penagashega (Change of Feathers), 159, 162
Pennsylvania, 9, 52, 54, 117, 180, 186-187, 191, 199, 223, 230, 265, 280, 283-284
Pennsylvania Dutch Country, 265
Perry, Commodore Oliver Hazard, 28, 111, 116-117, 119-120, 122-124, 259, 294
Perrysburg, OH, 264
Phelps, Mr. T., 106, 110
Philadelphia, PA, 60, 117, 182, 185, 187-188, 190, 199, 265
Piankeshaw, 212-213
Piatt Company, 141
Piqua, OH, 131-132, 203
Pittsburgh, PA, 69-70, 72, 74, 117, 201, 219, 265-267
Plaquemine Village, 73
Plains Indians, 213
Point du Sable, Jean Baptiste, 287
Point Place, 141
Pollock, Mr., 71-72
Pontiac, Chief, 7, 159, 168
Pontiac's War, 159
Porcupine (ship), 118
Port Lawrence (Company), 141
Potawatomi, 131, 135, 289-292
Poule D'eau, 253
Pratt, Harvey, 242
Presbyterian, 246
Presque Isle, PA, 114, 116-117, 120, 122

Prince, Captain William, 165
Princeton, NJ, 182
Princeton University, 182
Proctor, General Henry, 21, 22, 24-25, 27-31, 33, 137, 259-260, 293-294
Prophet, the, 149-153, 155-160, 162-168, 171, 174-175, 269-270, 288
Prophetstown, 163, 174, 269
Providence Plantations, 180
Put-in-Bay, 119
Quakers, 154-155
Quebec, 14, 210, 294-295
Queen Anne's War, 5
Queen Charlotte (ship), 119, 276
Raisin River, 22, 24, 42, 292
Raleigh, Sir Walter, 2
Raven Hill, TN, 88
Ravenna, OH, 262
Rawsee, 38
Read, Jacob, 191
Red River, 73
Redstone Fort, 70
Redstone, PA, 52-53, 59-60, 69, 71
Reeder, 59
Renard, Joseph, 163-164
Republic, OH, 42
Rhea, Captain James, 135-136
Rhode Island, 180, 186
Richard, Fr. Gabriel, 142-143
Rinehart, Caleb, 53
Ripley County, IN, 68
Rochambeau, General Comte de, 179
Rochester, NY, 39
Rocky River, 248
Rogers, Colonel David, 69-70, 72
Rogers, Isaiah, 146-147
Roosevelt, Theodore, 69
Royal Charlotte (ship), 297
Ruddell, Captain George, 173
Ruffin, Elizabeth, 147
Ruffin, Major William, 147
Sackett's Harbor, 38, 114
Salem Impartial Register, 19
Salina (ship), 111-112

San Augustin, 2
Sandusky Bay, 30, 48, 120
Sandusky, OH, 223, 261-262, 264
Sandwich, ON (Windsor), 259
Satan (Abrahamism), 149
Sau-ga-nash (Billy Caldwell), 292
Sauk, 213
Sault Sainte Marie, 4
Saunders, Captain, 112
Savannah, Georgia, 296
Schaponque, 161
Scioto Salt Licks, 101
Scorpion (ship), 118
Scotland, 4
Scott County, IN, 68, 209
Second Great Awakening, 95, 158
Seneca, 281-283
Seneca-Cayuga, 8, 125
Shawnee, 4, 8, 28, 44, 125, 132-133, 136, 153, 156-159, 162-164, 166-168, 174, 176, 204
Shays, Daniel / Rebellion, 14-16
Shelburne, Lord, 179
Shelby, Gov. Isaac, 45, 47, 49
Sheldon, Esquire, 247
Simcoe, Sir John Graves, 17-19
Sioux, 168
Slaughter, Lt.-Colonel George, 204
Smith, Joseph, 237
Snow, Oliver, 235-236
Somers (ship), 118
South Carolina, 180, 185-186, 188, 191
South Lebanon, OH, 60
Spain, 1, 2, 9, 15, 72, 218
Staunton, VA, 87
St. Anne's Parish, 142
St. Clair, General Arthur, 58, 63, 80-81, 147
St. Genevieve, MO, 211-212, 217
St. Joseph, Indiana, 148
St. Joseph, MI, 286, 292
St. Joseph River, 65, 129, 287, 289
St. Lawrence River, 14, 35-37, 39

St. Louis, MO, 2, 4, 42, 70-72, 74, 201, 203
St. Mary's, OH, 132-133, 139
St. Mary's River, 65, 129
Steuben, Baron von, 195
Stewart, Rev. John, 97
Stickney, B. F., 141, 143
Stites, Benjamin, 51-54, 56-61, 68
Stockbridge, MA, 16
Stone, Judge Vene, 243
Suffers' Lands, 223
Susquehanna River, 187
Sylvania Church, 34
Symmes, Anna, 68
Symmes, Judge John, 56-57, 59, 68
Symmes Purchase (Miami Purchase), 56, 61
Tallapoosa River, 170
Tecumseh, 28, 30-33, 137, 149-153, 155-157, 159, 163, 166, 168-171, 174-177, 258, 259-260, 269-270, 274, 279
Temperance Movement, 99
Tenmile, PA, 52, 60-61, 69
Tennessee, 207
Tenskwautawaw, (see Prophet, the)
Terre Haute, IN, 269
Teteboxti, Chief, 164
Thames River (Canada), 14, 20, 24-25, 27-28, 30, 33, 46, 48-49, 260
Thames River (Connecticut), 224-225, 230
Thaxter, Mr., 182
Thompson, Eliza Jane Trimble, 98-99
Thompson, Miss, 127
Thomson, Charles, 189
Thousand Isles, 38
Tibbals, Mrs. Ruth, 261
Tiffin, OH, 39, 140
Tigress (ship), 118
Timbuctoo, CA, 43
Timbuctu, Mali, Africa, 43
Tinker's Creek, 238
Tippecanoe River, 163, 265, 272, 288-289

Toledo Blade Newspaper, 146
Toledo Mud Hens, 256
Toledo, OH, 140-146, 148, 231, 256, 285
Toledo Strip, 142, 145-146
Toledo Swamp Angels, 256
Toledo War, 142-143, 145-146
Trabue, Daniel, 102-104, 107, 109-110, 218-219
Treaty of Paris, 1, 3, 6-7, 9, 151, 179, 181, 191, 199, 258
Treaty of Greenville, 59, 62, 140, 163, 230-231
Treaty of Fort Industry, 231
Treaty of Fort Stanwix, 8, 125
Treaty of Fort Wayne, 167
Trenton, NJ, 185
Trimble, Allen, 89, 93, 95-97, 99
Trimble, Captain James, 86-89, 91, 94-95
Trimble, Cary, 97
Trimble, Dr. Cyrus, 98
Trimble, Jane Allen, 83-91, 93-97, 99
Trimble, John, 95
Trimble, Joseph M., 85, 96
Trimble, Major David, 140
Trimble, Margaret, 96
Trimble, Victoria, 99
Trimble, William, 97-98
Trippe (ship), 118
Troy Township, OH, 241
Tuckabatchee, AL, 168, 170, 174
Tuckerman, Elizabeth "Betsy" (Brown), 41
Tyler, John, 270
Union Railroad Depot, 146
United States, 1-2, 4, 9-11, 13-15, 17, 19, 20-21, 25, 45-46, 54, 102, 111, 129, 151, 169, 175, 179-180, 182, 187, 194, 212-213, 234, 237, 263, 289, 295, 299
Untied States Air Force, 255
University of Michigainia (Michigan), 143, 146

INDEX

Upper Canada, 14, 17-21, 23, 26-28, 30, 33, 35, 46, 260, 263, 272
Upper Sandusky, OH, 97, 286
Urbana, OH, 272
Valley Forge, PA, 60, 194
Van Beckel, Peter Johan, 182
Vanfleet, Colonel, 143-145
Vermont, 14
Vincennes, IN, 55, 68, 168, 209, 265, 267-272
Virginia, 54, 70-72, 75, 79, 97, 103-104, 106, 183-184, 186, 202-204, 206, 210-211, 287
Virginia Company, 4
Vistula, 141
Waashaa Monetoo (Great Spirit), 149-151, 154, 157, 159, 164, 169-171, 174, 270, 297
Wabash River, 55, 155-156, 168, 196, 267-268, 270, 291
Wapokeneta, OH, 132-133, 139
War of 1812, 45, 96, 111, 175, 212, 231, 241, 258-259, 264, 295
Warren County, OH, 81
Warren, OH, 234, 247
Washington City, 98, 112, 117
Washington County, PA, 54, 80
Washington, George, 16, 85, 179, 184, 194, 195, 197-198, 221, 299
Washington's Indian War, 257
Washington, KY, 53-54
Wau-Bun, 253, 285
Wau-bau-see, 291
Way, Willard, 143
Wayne, General Anthony, 63-66, 81,` 129, 148, 152, 273, 285
Waynesburg, PA, 52
Wea Towns (Ouiatanon), 209
Wells, Captain Saul, 132
Wells, Mr., 215
Wells, William, 290-291
West (the), 1, 7, 54, 86, 194, 201, 213, 218, 223, 257, 280, 299

Western Reserve, 223, 230, 234, 246-248, 252
Western Spy, 68
West VA, 125
Whiplash, Snidely, 30
Whipple, Sergeant, 38
White, Hugh, 233
White River, 156, 159, 161, 163, 166
Whitestown, NY, 233
Wickliffe, KY, 202
Wilkinson, General, 38
Williams, Ezechial, 234-237
Windsor, OH, 247
Winnemac, 134, 136, 164
Winning of the West, 69
Wisconsin, 10, 218
Wisconsin Historical Society, 103
Wisconsin Territory, 213, 218, 288
Witlock, Mrs., 269
Woodford, KY, 89
Woodward, Augustus, 142
Worthington, OH, 39
Worthington, Thomas, 132-133
Wright, Rev. Abraham, 34
Wyandot, 97, 158
Yellow Jackets, 165
Xenia, OH, 54
Yohogania County, VA, 74
Yorktown, 13, 102
Young, John, 233, 235
Young, Mary, 233
Youngstown, OH, 233
Ziesberger, David, 300

www.ingramcontent.com/pod-product-compliance
Lightning Source LLC
Chambersburg PA
CBHW021353290426
44108CB00010B/221